Translation Strategies
Estrategias para Traducción

by E. Brinton, E. Cruz, R. Ortiz y Ortiz, C. White

MACMILLAN
PUBLISHERS

First published 1981
Reprinted 1985 (twice), 1987, 1989, 1990, 1991, 1994

Published by MACMILLAN PUBLISHERS LTD
London and Basingstoke

ISBN 0 – 333 – 32893 – 0

Printed in Hong Kong

The authors and publishers have made every effort to trace
the copyright holders of extracts in the book. If any have
been inadvertently overlooked, the publishers will be pleased
to make the necessary arrangement at the first opportunity.

UWLP

Table of Contents

Introduction   3
PART I — Short Passages for Translation   5
PART II — Longer Passages for Translation   69
PART III — Literary Translation   107
PART IV — Technical Translation   161
APPENDIX A — Points of Grammar   176
APPENDIX B — Hints on Handling, Some Useful Techniques   186
SOME USEFUL AIDS TO TRANSLATION   192

Introduction

Purpose and nature of the book

The aim of this introductory course is threefold:
(i) to provide a selection of passages covering a wide range of material for translation from Spanish into English and from English into Spanish,
(ii) to help create a greater awareness of the many problems confronting the translator and suggest some ways of dealing with them,
(iii) to help users to develop good translation habits.

It is assumed that users of this book will have a reasonable competence in both languages, i.e. that they will have reached at least somewhat beyond the level of English required for the Cambridge First Certificate Examination (FCE) or that required for O levels in Spanish in the General Certificate Examination.

An analysis of the mistakes made by translators would suggest that most of them, apart from those due to insufficient knowledge of the language or the subject matter, stem from three sources:
(i) a too hasty or superficial reading of the material to be translated,
(ii) failure to choose the right equivalent to translate a given word in its context,

(iii) unnatural or confused constructions in the language of the translation. The exercises here are intended to help the students to overcome these faults.

The questions on the passages are designed to focus students' attention on the meaning of the text as a whole, and vary in difficulty and depth as the book progresses. The questions following the Spanish passages are in English, and the questions following the English passages in Spanish. The purpose of this is to start the student thinking about the subject matter of the text in the language he is going to use to translate it. After some texts students are given a number of alternative translations for words or phrases and asked to number them in order of their preference in the context. This is not intended as a multiple choice exercise where there is *one* correct answer, but as a starting point for consideration and discussion. There may be several acceptable possibilities. The questions raised by these alternatives include determination of the exact meaning and the best equivalent in the language of the translation, problems of grammatical construction, collocation, register, style and so forth.

The Grammatical Appendix is in no wise an attempt at a formal grammar, but a selection of the grammatical difficulties found in translating the texts, grouped under grammatical headings for convenience so that students may relate their experience of handling individual difficulties with other similar examples.

Again, Appendix B, on Handling Techniques, is not intended to be in any way exhaustive; it is merely hoped to direct students' attention to some useful procedures when faced with different types of problems in the texts. All examples are from the texts in the book so that the students may refer to the exact context. The suggested translations are only *one* way of handling the problem; they are by no means the only possibility.

Although, because of the wide range of material, the Spanish taken from both Spanish and Latin American sources and the English from both sides of the Atlantic, it is difficult to state categorically that each passage is easier than the one following it, an effort has been made to preserve some measure of grading in each part. The beginning texts in each part may be easier than the final selections in the part before, but basically Part I is easier than Part II or Part III. Part IV introduces a different type of technique.

Suggestions for the use of this book

The book is designed for either class or individual use. While it is possible, of course, to work through the passages in order, the book also lends itself to more flexible treatment. If the students are beginners in translation it might be wise to do at least 30 or 35 selections from Part I before moving on to material in Parts II, III or IV. If more variety is then desired, some of the easier passages in Parts II, III and IV may be tried.

For students who want an introduction to technical translation a course might include, for example, 30 passages from Part I, 3 or 4 from Part II and all of Part IV.

For students, on the other hand, whose main interest is literary translation, the course would consist of 30 or so passages from Part I, some 15 or 20 passages from Part II and all of Part III.

PART I Short Passages for Translation

This section contains a wide variety of short passages taken from different areas of general communication: news items, accidents, people, places, sport, instructions, recipes, problems of modern society, reviews of plays, films, books.

It should serve as an introduction to the basic elements of the translation process and direct students' attention to both lexical and grammatical difficulties, particularly in those areas where the contrasts between English and Spanish most often lead to misunderstandings and mistakes. The exercises are designed to help students to develop the translation skills, the main emphasis being on determining the meaning of the original and the purpose of the writer, and to practise conveying this effectively in the second (or target) language. A section of further exercises follows some units, where the student is given the chance to go over certain items of grammar and vocabulary encountered within the unit.

Students are advised to read the passages in English and Spanish in each unit before starting to translate, as familiarity in both languages with the material to be translated is an important part of the preparation of a translator.

Notes on each passage, with references to the Appendices where appropriate, appear at the end of each unit.

Contents of Part I

UNIT I   News Items   8
  1   Chocan estudiantes . . .
  2   Tear gas for anti-government demonstrators . . .
  3   Paro obrero en la mina La Caridad
  4   Black journalists arrested

UNIT II   News Items — Commentary   14
  5   'El trabajo de prensa en Moscú . . .'
  6   'The appearance of a new type of newspaper . . .'
  7   'Como le estaba diciendo . . .'
  8   'On stage or screen the need . . .'

UNIT III   Accidents and Crime   17
  9   Acabó el fuego en Monterrey con una 'ciudad perdida'
 10   Death Toll put at 50 in Moscow hotel fire
 11   Cinco enanos asaltan a una cooperativa en Lima, Perú
 12   Armed bank raider slips away

UNIT IV   More News Items   22
 13   Drogas en estampas para albumes de escolares en Perú
 14   Pupils 'given drugs to keep them quiet'
 15   Ni Poe lo pensó
 16   'Cheap trick' at the Louvre

UNIT V   Recipes and Instructions   27
 17   Recetas
 18   Recipes
 19   Instrucciones para voltear o cambiar el empaque de una
      olla a presión
 20   Operating instructions for steam iron

UNIT VI   Incidents and Conversations   34
 21   'Martín esperó, pasó el tiempo . . .'
 22   'Suddenly, without any warning . . .'
 23   'Conforme me alejaba . . .'
 24   'This is the first I heard . . .'

UNIT VII   Anecdotes   37
 25A   'Cuando don Ulises . . .'
 25B   'Afortunadamente don Nicéforo . . .'
 26   'It was not till the man turned round . . .'
 27A   'Llegó mi turno de relatarle a don Melitón . . .'
 27B   'En los casi veintitrés años que llevaba . . .'
 28A   London revisited
 28B   Speed

UNIT VIII   Description   41
 29A   'Los dos hombres abandonaron . . .'
 29B   'De Londres a Edimburgo . . .'
 30A   'The hill was long, shaped like . . .'
 30B   'Chewlips was ignorant . . .'
 31   Tepotzotlán, México
 32A   Coimbra, Portugal
 32B   Canterbury, England

UNIT IX   Sport and Adventure   46
 33   'Para las masas, el acontecimiento . . .'
 34   Epsom and the Derby
 35   Requiem por un inglés
 36   'At eight minutes to eight . . .'

UNIT X   Present Day Problems 1   51
 37   Enfermedades cardiovasculares . . .
 38   Airport hazards

39   Menos pluriempleo
40   Unemployment in the industrialized countries

UNIT XI   Present Day Problems 2   **55**
41   Medida para paliar la concentración urbana
42   'The cheap-and-nasty housing . . .'
43   El mundo en crisis
44   Material and industrial changes
45   Me voy pa'l pueblo
46   Country diary

UNIT XII   Reviews   **63**
47   *Un crimen impune*
48   *'Tarka the Otter* is a very worthy . . .'
49   *'La comedia sin título* es un intento . . .'
50   *'Bitter Apples* is a musical . . .'
51   'En *Las amables veladas con Cecilia* la serie de . . .'
52   'Not only was Mariano Azuela the first . . .'

Unit I News Items

These are brief news items. Do not translate word for word or even phrase by phrase. Consider the information to be conveyed, then write each sentence of your translation so as to communicate the meaning most clearly in the language you are translating into. This will often mean rephrasing the original sentence.

When you have finished your translation, read it through as an original news item without referring to the first language. Is the meaning clear? Finally, re-read the original and make sure all the information is clearly conveyed in your version.

1   Chocan estudiantes con la Guardia Nacional panameña en Colón[1,2]

Automóviles particulares quemados,[3] patrulleros apedreados y ventanas de edificios públicos rotas, fue el <u>saldo</u> de un enfrentamiento ocurrido[4] hoy entre estudiantes y efectivos de la Guardia Nacional en la ciudad de Colón, se informó aquí.[5]

Efectivos[6] del ejército <u>lanzaron gases lacrimógenos</u> para dispersar a unos cincuenta jóvenes.

Fuentes gubernamentales señalaron después que 'elementos ajenos al movimiento estudiantil' originaron las desórdenes en la ciudad. Según el ministerio de Educación, los plantamientos estudiantiles <u>se centran en dos aspectos</u>: la situación socio-económica de Colón y <u>reivindicaciones educativas.</u>
Excelsior (adapted)

I   Read the passage carefully, then answer the following questions in English:
What was the outcome of the clash between students and police?
Who was officially blamed for the outbreak?
What is meant by *reivindicaciones* in this context?

II   Mark the following translations 1, 2, 3, in order of your preference in the context. Mark X any you consider unacceptable. Give a better version if one occurs to you.
a   saldo
  ☐ aftermath   ☐ outcome
  ☐ result   ☐ balance

b lanzaron gases lacrimógenos
- ☐ threw tear gases
- ☐ used tear gas
- ☐ hurled tear gas

c elementos ajenos
- ☐ foreign elements
- ☐ strange individuals
- ☐ persons outside

d se centran en dos aspectos
- ☐ concentrate on two main aspects
- ☐ are centred round
- ☐ focus on

e reivindicaciones educativas
- ☐ educational claims
- ☐ educational vindications
- ☐ educational reforms

III   Translate the passage into English.

2   Tear gas for anti-government demonstrators in Iran[7]

Police used tear gas on[8] thousands of anti-government demonstrators who rampaged through[9] two southern Iranian towns in the first outbreak of violence in a month, newspapers reported on Saturday.

The demonstrators were intercepted by the police who wanted to disperse them.

At first they tried to control the mobs with water hoses but the demonstrators began stoning the police and continued their demonstration, so[10] the police had to use tear gas to subdue them.

The paper said two policemen and several demonstrators were injured in the clash.

The News, Mexico City (adapted)

I   Read the passage carefully, then answer the following questions in Spanish:

¿ Qué hicieron los manifestantes?

¿ Cuánto había durado el período de calma?

¿ Por qué lanzó la policía gases lacrimógenos sobre las turbas de manifestantes?

II   Mark the following translations 1, 2, 3, in order of your preference in this context. Mark X any you consider definitely unacceptable. Give a better translation if one occurs to you.

a two southern Iranian towns
- ☐ dos poblaciones sureñas iranias (iraníes)
- ☐ dos pueblos iranios (iraníes) sureños
- ☐ dos poblaciones en el sur de Irán

b began stoning
- ☐ empezaron apedreando
- ☐ empezaron a apedrear
- ☐ empezaron a lapidar

c were injured
- ☐ resultaron heridos
- ☐ fueron heridos
- ☐ estaban heridos

III   Give two alternative translations for the following:
rampaged through two towns

IV   Translate the passage into Spanish.

3   Paro obrero en la mina 'La Caridad'

En un clima de <u>tensión que se agrava cada minuto</u>,[11] viven los 18,000 habitantes de la población de Nacozari, Sonora, <u>al cumplirse</u>[12] hoy <u>ocho días de paro</u> en la mina de cobre La Caridad, segunda[13] de Latinoamérica. Un incidente provocado por <u>el nerviosismo</u> estuvo a un paso de originar un estallido violento de graves proporciones entre obreros y vigilantes — policía y tropa — cuando se pagaban[14,15] salarios atrasados en las oficinas.

La cosa <u>no pasó a mayores</u>[16]; mientras tanto en la capital del estado los empresarios sonorenses condenaron el paro y acordaron reunirse[12] la próxima semana para comentar la situación. Se informó[14] también que se trató hoy el problema con el Presidente de la República que comisionó a <u>dos personas de su confianza</u> para ir a Nacozari a negociar una solución con los paristas.

Excelsior (adapted)

I   Read the text carefully, then answer the following questions in English.
Do not translate the text but try to use your own words.
How long had the miners been on strike?
What nearly caused a violent clash between miners and guards?
What action has the President taken?

II   Mark the following translations 1, 2, 3, in order of your preference in the context. Put an X beside any you consider unacceptable. Give a better version if one occurs to you.

a   ... tensión que se agrava cada minuto
   ☐ ... tension which is steadily worsening
   ☐ ... steadily mounting tension
   ☐ ... tension getting worse every minute
b   al cumplirse hoy ocho días de paro
   ☐ on ending today an eight days' strike
   ☐ as the strike ends eight days today
   ☐ as the strike ends its eighth day

c   el nerviosismo
   ☐ nervousness
   ☐ nerves
   ☐ the state of tension
d   no pasó a mayores
   ☐ didn't get out of control
   ☐ got no worse
   ☐ didn't go beyond that
e   dos personas de su confianza
   ☐ two people in his confidence
   ☐ two reliable men
   ☐ two men he trusts

III   Translate the passage into English

4 30 black journalists arrested

South Africa security police yesterday arrested thirty black journalists <u>who were demonstrating in central Johannesburg over</u> the detention of eleven of their colleagues.

The journalists were arrested <u>for holding demonstrations as they marched</u> towards John Vorster Square, where the police headquarters <u>is situated.</u> A white photographer was also detained. Six of the eleven journalists in detention work for the *World*, the leading black newspaper, <u>which was banned in the October security operation against anti-apartheid groups.</u>

The Daily Telegraph

I   Read the text carefully, then answer the following questions in Spanish:
¿ Por qué realizaban los periodistas una manifestación en el centro de Johannes-burgo?
¿ Hacia dónde se dirigía la manifestación?
¿ Cuándo y en qué circunstancias fue clausurado el *World*?

II   Mark X beside the best translation of the following expressions. Give a better alternative if you can think of one.
a   who were demonstrating in central Johannesburg over . . .
   ☐ que estaban manifestándose en el centro de Johannesburgo por . . .
   ☐ que realizaban una manifestación en el centro de Johannesburgo para protestar por . . .
   ☐ quienes hacían una demostración en el centro de Johannesburgo contra . . .
b   . . . for holding demonstrations as they marched . . .
   ☐ . . . por hacer manifestaciones mientras marchaban . . .
   ☐ . . . por hacer manifestaciones cuando se dirigían a . . .
   ☐ . . . por participar en una manifestación que se dirigía a . . .
c   . . . is situated
   ☐ . . . se sitúa
   ☐ . . . se encuentra
   ☐ . . . está localizada
d   which was banned in the October security operation against . . .
   ☐ que fue clausurado en octubre durante la operación de seguridad efectuada en contra de . . .
   ☐ que fue clausurado en la operación de seguridad en octubre contra . . .
   ☐ que fue clausurado durante la operación de seguridad de octubre contra . . .
e   anti-apartheid groups
   ☐ grupos anti-apartheid
   ☐ grupos que se oponen al apartheid
   ☐ grupos contra el apartheid

III   Translate the passage into Spanish.

Further Exercises

1 Translate into English:
a Se aplazó la construcción del hospital para el año siguiente.
b No llegan los cosmonautas hasta mañana, se informó por radio.
c Cerca de los dos coches se reunía un grupo de curiosos que aumentaba a cada momento.
d Al terminar el discurso tan provocador el orador dejó la tribuna.
e No era una escena que se pudiera describir fácilmente.

2 The words and expressions below all signify some kind of violent movement, either literally or figuratively. Choose the most appropriate word for each space. (*Note* If you are not sure of the meaning of any of them consult a good English-English dictionary.)

> rampaged through   surged forward   ran riot   erupted
> charged into

a The victorious soldiers . . . . the captured city, looting and plundering.
b The elephants, maddened by the noise, ... the crowd and many people were injured.
c The crowd . . . . towards the barriers and, for a moment, it looked as if they might break through.
d The volcano suddenly . . . . and destroyed the two nearest villages.
e Nobody could get any definite news about what had actually happened; rumours . . . . and confusion reigned.

3 Translate into Spanish:
a Yesterday a clash occurred between students and police; several students were injured but no one was killed.
b Two students were arrested for starting the trouble.
c Nobody could discover the truth; speculations ran riot.

Notes

1 See **Handling of Titles**, Appendix B1.
2 See **Translation of Proper Names**, Appendix B2.
3 See **Adjectives — Word Order**, Appendix A1.
4 See **Omissions and Insertions**, Appendix B4.
5 See **Stock Phrases**, Appendix B8.
6 *Efectivos* is often used to refer to police or soldiers in Mexico.
7 See **Handling of Titles**, Appendix B1, and **Omissions and Insertions**, Appendix B4.
8 *sobre*
9 There is often no word-for-word equivalent. Think about the exact meaning of *rampaged through*, using an English dictionary if necessary, and then express the idea in Spanish.
10 See **Connectives**, Appendix A2.
11 See **Rephrasing**, Appendix B3.

12   See **The Verb — Spanish Reflexive**, Appendix A7d.
13   Supply the definite article.
14   See **The Verb — Voice**, Appendix A7c.
15   See **The Verb — Tense**, Appendix A7a.
16   See **Transposition**, Appendix B5.

Unit II News Items—Commentary

In this unit it is the facts and the ideas expressed which are the most important. Make sure that you convey the meaning <u>clearly</u> in your translation.

5 El trabajo de prensa en Moscú <u>no parece fácil</u>. Un periódico extranjero no puede comprarse en la calle, salvo que sea el órgano de un partido comunista. Los diarios que se envían desde el exterior a los corresponsales <u>no tardan menos de cinco días</u> en llegar.[1] En tales condiciones, se hace[2] indispensable la escucha de radio de onda corta para enterarse de lo que sucede en el mundo. El mecanismo de censura es muy concreto: un hombre está encargado de controlar todo lo que se va a publicar sobre el país[1] que se le asigne, y nada sale en la prensa de toda la Unión Soviética <u>sin que él lo lea</u>.

F.C.E. June 1978

1 Read the above passage carefully, then answer the questions in English.
What are the difficulties of the foreign journalist in Moscow according to this writer?
What is the meaning of *concreto* here?

II Mark the following translations 1, 2, 3, in order of your preference in the context. Mark X any you consider unacceptable. Give a better version if one occurs to you.

a no parece fácil
  ☐ does not look easy
  ☐ seems difficult
  ☐ is apparently not easy

b no tardan menos de cinco días
  ☐ take no less than 5 days
  ☐ take at least 5 days
  ☐ don't . . . for at least 5 days

c sin que él lo lea
  ☐ without his reading it
  ☐ unless he has read it first
  ☐ unless he reads it

III Translate the passage into English.

6 The <u>appearance</u> of a new type of newspaper at the end of the nineteenth century <u>led to</u> developments which have transformed newspaper production into a major industry and largely replaced the family business by the great commercial corporation. The eighteen-nineties saw the introduction of newspapers sold at a halfpenny and <u>addressed</u>, not <u>to</u> the highly educated and <u>politically minded</u> minority, but <u>to</u> the millions whom the Education Act of 1870 had equipped with the ability to read but not with the capacity or the desire to absorb the material offered by the existing dailies.

F.C.E. June 1978

I   Read the passage carefully and answer the following questions in Spanish.
Qué fueron los cambios en los periódicos a fines del siglo XIX?
Cuál fue el efecto de esos cambios en la industria periodística?
Qué significa la palabra *developments* en este contexto?

II   Mark the following translations 1, 2, 3, in order of your preference in the context. Mark X any you consider unacceptable. Give a better version if one occurs to you.

a   appearance
  ☐ apariencia
  ☐ aparición
  ☐ aspecto

b   led to
  ☐ conducía a
  ☐ resultaba en
  ☐ dió lugar a

c   addressed to
  ☐ dirigidos a
  ☐ destinados a
  ☐ consignados a

d   politically minded
  ☐ de mente política
  ☐ de intereses políticos
  ☐ interesada en la política

III   Translate the passage into Spanish.

7 Como le estaba diciendo yo también en mis tiempos fui socialista y hasta anarquista — tanto él como el recién llegado[3] sonrieron ampliamente, como si estuvieran recordando algo chistoso — y aquí el amigo Pérez Moretti no me dejará mentir, porque juntos hemos pasado muchas cosas. Por otra parte, tampoco vaya a creer que nos avergonzamos. Soy de los que piensan que[4] no es malo que la juventud tenga en su momento ideales tan puros.[4] Ya hay tiempo de perder luego esas ilusiones . . . el hombre es por naturaleza desigual y es inútil pretender fundar sociedades donde los hombres sean[5] iguales.

F.C.E. June 1977, Ernesto Sábato (adapted)

I   Read the passage carefully and answer the following question in English.
What kind of an audience is the speaker probably addressing? Describe briefly his political attitude.

II   Translate the passage into English.

8 On stage or screen the need to use an actor as a being from Mars has certain disadvantages.[6] The Martian has to have two legs, like earthmen —

although we have seen a few Martians on wheels. He (she-Martians are rare) usually has two arms, two eyes, and so on, and a head fitted with electrical equipment. The main trouble is the need to communicate. In stories or on radio, Martians speak the language of the listeners. Film and television Mars-men in non-English-speaking countries often speak the local language but with the mouth movements of the same remarks in English.

F.C.E. June 1977, Richard Lewis (adapted)

I   Read the passage carefully and answer the questions in Spanish.
¿ Cuál es el problema que preocupa al autor aquí?
¿ Cómo se soluciona el problema de la comunicación entre los marcianos y los habitantes de nuestra tierra?
¿ Qué desventaja hay en esta solución?

II   Translate the passage into Spanish.

Further Exercises

1   Translate into Spanish:
a   It will take us at least six weeks to get the book.
b   The job seems to be quite specific; you should be able to do it easily.
c   Just study the section assigned to you each week; don't worry about the rest.

2   Translate into English:
a   En estos tiempos de crisis se hace indispensable la lectura de los periódicos.
b   A pesar de la actitud intransigente de ambos grupos la cosa no pasó a mayores.
c   Es inútil pretender vender artículos de lujo en lugares donde la gente no tenga dinero ni para satisfacer sus primeras necesidades.

Notes

1   See **The Verb — Use of Infinitive or Gerund**, Appendix A7e.
2   See **The Verb — Spanish Reflexive**, Appendix A7d.
3   Use a noun.
4   Be careful with the English construction.
5   How can you bring out in English the force of the Spanish *sean*?
6   Watch Spanish construction here. Rephrase.

Unit III Accidents and Crime

The following passages describe incidents in the news, disasters or crime. The translator's priority here is to convey clearly exactly what happened.

9 Acabó el fuego en Monterrey con una 'ciudad perdida'[1]

Una **'ciudad perdida'** en el barrio de Topochico, donde vivían más de doscientas familias <u>humildes</u>, fue arrasada esta mañana por el fuego, que en menos de cuatro horas redujo a cenizas casas de cartón, madera y lámina.

    Bomberos de Monterrey y socorristas de la Cruz Roja y Verde, informaron que[2] no se registraron[3] <u>desgracias personales,</u> <u>a pesar de que</u> el fuego consumió totalmente[4] las viviendas y muchos de los habitantes fueron sorprendidos por el <u>siniestro</u> cuando dormían.

    El gobierno del estado proporcionó ayuda a <u>los damnificados</u> entregándoles despensas, materiales para construcción, cobertores, láminas y otros enseres.

Excelsior (adapted)

I Read the text carefully, then answer the following questions in English:
What is the meaning of *ciudad perdida* here? How will you translate it?
What happened to it?
Was anybody injured?
What did the government do?

II Mark the following translations 1, 2, 3, in order of your preference in the context. Mark X beside any that you consider unacceptable.

a humildes
   ☐ humble
   ☐ poor
   ☐ modest

b desgracias personales
   ☐ personal misfortunes
   ☐ personal disgrace
   ☐ casualties

c a pesar de que
   ☐ in spite of
   ☐ although
   ☐ in spite of the fact that

d siniestro
   ☐ catastrophe
   ☐ disaster
   ☐ accident

e   los damnificados
    ☐ the victims
    ☐ the injured
    ☐ those who had suffered loss

III   Translate the passage into English.

10   Death toll put at 50 in Moscow hotel fire

Foreign correspondents <u>confirmed at least 18 deaths</u> Saturday in a fire that swept through[5] Moscow's showpiece[6] Hotel Rossiya, billed[6] as the world's largest. A Soviet doctor feared the final toll might reach between 50 and 60.

An official said the U.S. Embassy had tracked down all of about 200 U.S. citizens <u>who had been staying</u> at the Rossiya, a large modern building overlooking the Kremlin and Red Square.

The official Soviet tourist agency Intourist and the hotel management were preparing a list of foreign casualties for release today.

There were no official casualty figures from the Soviet government. The Tass news agency reported in a brief dispatch that the fire had taken place and that, according to the Moscow fire chief, the blaze had broken out in an elevator shaft.

The News, Mexico City

I   Read the passage carefully, then answer the following questions in Spanish.
¿ Qué sucedió el sábado en el Hotel Rossiya?
¿ Qué hizo la Embajada Norteamericana?
¿ Qué información dió la agencia Tass?

II   Mark the following translations 1, 2, 3, in order of your preference in the context. Mark X any you consider unacceptable. Give a better version if one occurs to you.
a   confirmed at least 18 deaths
    ☐ confirmaron que hubo por lo menos 18 muertos
    ☐ confirmaron por lo menos 18 muertos
    ☐ confirmaron por lo menos 18 muertes
b   who had been staying
    ☐ que habían estado quedando
    ☐ que estaban hospedados
    ☐ que habían estado hospedados

III   Give two more natural alternatives to the literal translation given below. Why do you think the literal translation is unacceptable?
a   A Soviet doctor feared the final toll might reach between 50 and 60.
    Un doctor soviético temía que el número de víctimas final llegara entre 50 y 60.
b   There were no official casualty figures from the Soviet government.
    No hubo un número oficial de víctimas del gobierno soviético.

IV   Translate the passage into Spanish.

11   Cinco enanos asaltan a una cooperativa en Lima, Perú

Lima, 14 de enero. Cinco enanos con la[7] cabeza[8] cubierta por[9] toallas, asaltaron una agencia de la Cooperativa de Crédito Santa Elena, del distrito limeño de Miraflores, de donde se llevaron 1,815 dólares, confirmó hoy aquí la policía.

El singular hecho ocurrió ayer al mediodía, cuando los pequeños delincuentes, provistos de pistolas, amedrentaron con fuerte voz a quienes estaban en el interior de la agencia.

El administrador de la cooperativa, Jorge Villanueva, denunció que los delincuentes se movilizaron velozmente para reunir el dinero hurtado. El botín fue de 200,000 soles (1,815 dólares).

Posteriormente, explicó el funcionario, los enanos emprendieron la fuga en un automóvil que les esperaba.[10]

La policía se ha lanzado[11] a la búsqueda de los delincuentes y citará a todos los enanos limeños para iniciar las investigaciones.

Excelsior

I   Read the passage carefully, then answer the following questions in English.
What was unusual about the raid?
In what city was the Credit Union situated?
Why didn't the people present stop the robbery?
How much was stolen?
How did the dwarfs get away?
What will be the first step in the police investigation?

II   Mark the following translations 1, 2, 3 etc. in order of your preference in the context. Put an X beside any you consider unacceptable. Give a better version if one occurs to you.

a   asaltaron
☐ assaulted
☐ made a raid on
☐ attacked
☐ held up

b   hecho
☐ deed
☐ event
☐ fact

c   amedrentaron con fuerte voz a . . .
☐ shouted threats at. . . . .
☐ frightened . . . with their shouts
☐ intimidated . . . . with loud threats

d   denunció
☐ reported
☐ denounced
☐ accused

III   Translate the passage into English.

12   Armed bank raider slips away

An armed raider yesterday smashed his way into[12] a Kent bank through the roof, lay in wait for the staff, then fled without a penny.

The would-be robbery at Lloyds Bank, St. Dunstans, near Canterbury, was discovered when Mr Terry Wilson, 22, a cashier, opened up.

He was confronted by the masked intruder and ordered to open the safes. When he said he had no keys, *he was bundled at gunpoint* into a cupboard. Another employee entered the building about 15 minutes later and freed Mr Wilson.

But when police slipped into the bank by the hole in the tiled roof, the raider had disappeared.

Mr Wilson said later: "While *he held the gun at me*, I felt surprisingly calm, but afterwards I was shaky."

The Daily Telegraph

I   **Read the passage carefully, then answer the following questions in Spanish:**
¿ Cómo logró el ladrón penetrar en el banco?
¿ Por qué huyó sin un centavo?
¿ Qué le hizo al señor Wilson?

II   **Compare the following expressions and find Spanish equivalents for each:**

a   smash one's way into
b   force one's way into
c   talk one's way into
d   bribe one's way into

III   **Give two Spanish equivalents for each of the italicized expressions.**

IV   **Translate the passage into Spanish.**

Further Exercises

Vocabulary Building Exercise. Here are some verbs describing different ways of speaking:

whisper	cry	shout	say	tell	utter	mumble
groan	scream	moan		mention	declare	grunt

Choose the correct form of one of the above verbs to fill each of the spaces below.

1   I wish you wouldn't . . . . I can't hear half you say. Why can't you pronounce your words distinctly?
2   There's no need to . . . . I'm not deaf. I should think anyone could hear you a mile away.
3   "That will do," he . . . . "I don't want to hear any more complaints.
4   She . . . . something in my ear but I couldn't hear what it was.
5   "Don't come any nearer," she . . . . , her voice rising hysterically.
6   I promise I won't . . . . anybody. I won't . . . . a single word.
7   He . . . . that he would never forget us if he lived to be a hundred.

8 What are you . . . . about? I can't pay you what I haven't got.

9 I am . . . . you this in confidence. I should prefer you not to

. . . . it.

10 "Oh dear," she . . . . , "I was afraid of getting my feet wet, and now, look at my shoes. I'll never be able to wear them again."

Notes

1   See **Handling of Titles**, Appendix B1 and **Adaptation**, Appendix B7.
2   See **Stock Phrases**, Appendix B8.
3   See **The Verb — Voice**, Appendix A7c.
4   Be careful with the word order here.
5   See above, Unit I, note 9.
6   What is the exact meaning of this word in the context?
7   See **Determiners**, Appendix A3.
8   See **Nouns**, Appendix A4.
9   See **Prepositions**, Appendix A6.
10 See **Transposition**, Appendix B5.
11 See **The Verb — Spanish Reflexive**, Appendix A7d.
12 Note that expressions like *smash one's way into* cannot be translated literally. They will need to be analyzed and the idea expressed differently in Spanish.

Unit IV   More News Items

Note use of present and past tenses.

13   Drogas en estampas para albumes de escolares en Perú

Los cromos y estampillas para pegar en albumes que los narcotraficantes están ofreciendo ahora a los escolares en Perú tienen pasta de cocaína mezclada con la goma.

Regalan primero el álbum y luego venden cromos o estampillas de correo engomados, con lo que[1] el niño pasa la lengua[2] por la goma e ingiere la cocaína, haciéndose rápidamente un adicto.

Los narcotraficantes actúan en las mismas puertas de los colegios, según denuncia del inspector superior de la Policía de Investigaciones de Perú, en declaraciones que hoy recoge la prensa local.

El inspector añadió que el año pasado, la policía detuvo a 1,016 traficantes de cocaína y a 1,406 consumidores.

En ambos casos, la mayor parte de los detenidos tienen entre 18 y 31 años de edad.[3]

Excelsior (adapted)

I   **Read the passage carefully, then answer the following questions in English:**
What are the drug pedlars selling in Peru?
Where do they sell their wares?
How did the local press get hold of the story?
How does the number of pedlars compare with the number of addicts arrested last year?
What observation does the writer make about those arrested?

II   **Translate the passage into English.**

14   Pupils 'given drugs to keep them quiet'[4]

Dr. Steven Box, of the University of Kent, claimed[5] that <u>naughty children were being labelled</u>[6] <u>'hyperactive' by their teachers</u> so that they could be given medical treatment to keep them quiet.

He said: "When most of us were at school, children who behaved in these ways were called[6] disruptive, disobedient, rebellious, anti-social, a bloody nuisance and naughty.[7]

"They were clipped around the ear, caned on the hand or slippered on the backside.

"Apparently there has been much medical progress from those uncivilised times. Children are no longer naughty, they are medical cases.[8]"

Writing in *New Society*, he said: "<u>Schoolchildren by the millions</u> in America and the tens of thousands in Britain <u>are being put on long-term programmes of drug therapy</u> simply because their behaviour does not fit in with the requirements of school.

The Daily Telegraph (adapted)

I   Read the passage carefully, then answer the following questions in Spanish:
¿ Cómo llaman ahora los maestros a los niños traviesos o desobedientes?
¿ Cómo se corregía antes a estos niños?
¿ Qué es lo que critica este artículo?

II   Mark the following translations 1, 2, 3, in order of your preference in this context. Mark X beside any you consider unacceptable. Give a better translation if one occurs to you.
a   Pupils given drugs to keep them quiet
  ☐ Se dan drogas a alumnos para que se callen
  ☐ Se dan drogas a escolares para tenerlos callados
  ☐ Drogas a escolares para mantenerlos quietos
b   naughty children were being labelled 'hyperactive' by their teachers
  ☐ los maestros estaban clasificando a los niños traviesos como 'hiperactivos'
  ☐ los niños traviesos estaban siendo clasificados como 'hiperactivos' por sus maestros
  ☐ Los maestros estaban llamando 'hiperactivos' a los niños traviesos
c   Schoolchildren by the millions . . . . . are being put on long-term programmes of drug therapy
  ☐ Millones de escolares están siendo sometidos a programas a largo plazo de terapia con drogas
  ☐ Millones de escolares están siendo sometidos a largos tratamientos de terapia con drogas
  ☐ A millones de escolares se les está sometiendo a tratamientos terapéuticos a largo plazo a base de drogas

III   Translate the passage into Spanish.

15 Ni Poe lo pensó

Antes de morir le tomó una foto a su victimario

Rawson, Argentina. Un fotógrafo profesional asesinado[9] alcanzó a fotografiar a su asesino antes de morir y la foto perdió al homicida.

Se trata de[10] un caso policial que *hubiesen aprovechado*[11] para sus argumentos la desaparecida Agatha Christie y el mismo Edgar Allan Poe.

La víctima tenía un estudio fotográfico y ejercía paralelamente las funciones de agente de cambio de moneda chilena.

Un día fue encontrado muerto en su estudio, *con el cráneo destrozado*. La falta de indicios hizo presumir que nunca podría aclararse[11] los motivos de su muerte.

Pero en una de sus cámaras fotográficas fue encontrada una placa sin revelar.[12] Como rutina, los investigadores la revelaron y en ella apareció la figura de uno de sus asesinos.

El crimen fue reconstruido paso a paso. Dos sujetos, con el pretexto de *sacarse una fotografía*, entraron en el estudio de Ostoich porque sabían que guardaba fuertes sumas de dinero.

Mientras el fotógrafo realizaba los preparativos para la fotografía, fue golpeado con una barra de hierro hasta caerse muerto.[13]

Los asesinos se apoderaron del dinero y huyeron, logrando atravesar la frontera con Chile.[12] Allí fueron detenidos por haber cometido[14] otros delitos y condenados a *purgar distintas penas*.

Uno de ellos murió en prisión y el otro, Gallardo, quien aparecía en la fotografía aludida, fue trasladado a Argentina y comparecerá ante la justicia argentina por un crimen cometido hace trece años y la mejor *prueba en su contra* es una fotografía tomada por su víctima cuando caía exánime a causa de los golpes recibidos.

Novedades (adapted)

I   Read the passage carefully, then answer the questions in English:
What is unusual about this case?
What did the murdered man do for his living?
Why did he have a lot of money on his premises?
What happened to the murderer in Chile?
What was chiefly responsible for bringing the man to justice?

II   Give several alternative translations for the italicized expressions. State which one you prefer and why.

III   Translate the passage into English.

16   'Cheap[15] trick' at the Louvre

On the night of December 15-16, the gem-encrusted[16] sword of Charles X was stolen from the Louvre's Galerie d'Apollon. The three thieves took flight after attacking and wounding[17] two guards. A week later, television producer[18] Jacques Rouland, commissioned by the weekly picture magazine Paris-Match, took a stroll[19] through the museum with a facsimile of the ceremonial sword. Photographs published later in Match implied that the imperturbable guards paid no attention whatsoever to the unusual sight[20] and allowed Rouland to carry out his 'joke' to the end.[21]

CGT[22] trade-union representatives for the Louvre guards complained early this month about a 'tactic which tends to put French museums' worst-paid employees in the wrong[21] by means of a cheap trick'. They noted that Rouland was told to stay out of the museum when he emerged from his car in the parking lot. The day after the theft, the CGT[22] representatives had already condemned inadequate staffing and training — a result of the lack of any official classification for trained watchmen. They stressed that sophisticated security measures are no substitutes for guards.

The Guardian

I   Read the passage carefully, then answer the following questions in Spanish.
¿ Qué robaron los ladrones?
¿ Qué pasó una semana más tarde?
¿ Por qué protestó esta acción la CGT?

II   Translate the passage into Spanish.

Further Exercises

1   Translate into Spanish:
a   He had no money whatsoever.
b   Whoever said that this was easy, was mistaken; it is by no means easy.
c   I'll come whenever you like.
d   I know nothing about it.
e   He takes his dog with him wherever he goes.

2   Choose the correct prepositions for the spaces below.
a   As they were walking . . . . the gallery they noticed that there was a wide space . . . . two paintings where another had obviously been removed.
b   What are the qualifications . . . . entry . . . . the Airforce?
c   Well, those are the general principles; you'll have to work . . . . the details . . . . yourselves.
d   You know Charles was . . . . the right when he protested . . . . that regulation.
e   There are no substitutes . . . . intelligence and hard work. Those who rely . . . . any substitutes whatsoever are making a big mistake.

3   Vocabulary Building Exercise. Here are some verbs describing different forms of moving:

stroll	saunter	stride	creep	hurry	glide
linger	loiter	amble	run	stagger	stumble

Choose the correct form of one of the above verbs to fill each of the spaces below.

a   The children . . . . quietly down the stairs and out into the garden; no one made a sound.

b   It's no use . . . . about, boys; the meeting won't be over for another four hours at least.

c   Although he was very week from loss of blood, he managed to . . . . into the room.

d   The two men . . . . briskly down the street; they looked imposing in their new uniforms.

e   The lecture was over at 9 o'clock but some people . . . . till 9.30, asking the lecturer questions.

f   The two girls . . . . down the street, hand in hand, looking in all the shop windows.

g   Finally an old man . . . . vaguely into the room and asked them if they had seen Mr Brown.

h   The toddler got almost halfway across the room before he . . . . and fell.

i   When I saw them they were . . . . down the street without a care in the world.

j   There's no need to . . . . , there's plenty of time.

Notes

1   See **Connectives**, Appendix A2.
2   Find one word in English for this phrase.
3   Unnecessary in English.
4   What is being given to the pupils? Can you find one Spanish word to describe the pupils referred to?
5   What is the meaning of *claim* here?
6   See **The Verb — Spanish Reflexive**, Appendix A7d.
7   Watch punctuation.
8   *casos clínicos*
9   Use a clause in English to translate *asesinado*.
10   See **Stock Phrases**, Appendix B8.
11   See **The Verb — Mood and Modals**, Appendix A7b.
12   See **Transposition**, Appendix B5.
13   *He was beaten to death . . .*
14   See **The Verb — Use of Infinitive or Gerund**, Appendix A7e.
15   What is the exact meaning of *cheap* here?
16   *con incrustaciones de piedras preciosas*
17   See **The Verb — Use of Infinitive or Gerund**, Appendix A7e.
18   See **Determiners**, Appendix A3.
19   What does *stroll* mean? Express the idea in Spanish.
20   Find an equivalent phrase, for example *extraño suceso*.
21   Rephrase.
22   *Confédération Générale du Travail*. Keep same letters.

Unit V   Recipes and Instructions

Recipes

Compare the English and Spanish recipes. Notice the way they are set out in English and Spanish, and the vocabulary. Note the Spanish use of the reflexive where English uses the imperative form of the verb. Note use of lbs (pounds) and oz (ounces) in English and grams in Spanish. See conversion tables for equivalents. (*Note* Since some English-speaking countries are now changing over to the metric system, weights may be given in grams in English.)

17 Recetas

A   Sopa de cebollas

2 tazas de cebollas cortadas en ruedas muy finitas
50 gramos de mantequilla
2 tazas de caldo de res o pollo

1/2 taza de agua
1/2 cucharadita de salsa inglesa
4 rebanadas de pan tostada
1/4 taza de queso parmesano rallado

Se sofríe[1] la cebolla en mantequilla, cuando esté blandita y ligeramente dorada, se le añade el caldo,[1] agua y salsa inglesa, se deja a fuego lento durante 25 minutos aproximadamente, se sirve sobre el pan tostado, cortado en cuadritos, se polvorea de queso y si se desea se pone unos minutos más al horno.

B   Sopa de ajos[2]

2 cucharadas de aceite de oliva
2 dientes de ajo
2 tazas de agua o caldo

Sal y pimienta al gusto
1 huevo
2 o 3 rebanadas de pan

En el aceite caliente se sofríen los ajos hasta que estén dorados. Se sacan los ajos y se le añade el huevo entero o batido, las migas de pan y se sazona al gusto de sal y pimienta. Se sirve inmediatamente.[1]

Cocina al minuto, Nitza Villapol y Martha Martínez

C Sopa sustanciosa

Cantidades:

4 cucharadas de aceite	1 cebolla
6 huevos cocidos	1 1/2 litros de caldo
300 gms de jitomate	1/16 de litro de vino jerez
8 higados de pollo	125 gms de jamón cocido

Manera de prepararse:

Se asa el jitomate, se pela y se fríe en el aceite, ya molido con la cebolla y colado, se le agrega el vino, las claras de huevo picadas, el jamón cortado en cuadritos y los higaditos también cocidos y picados.

*Las mejores recetas de las cocinas: mexicana,
española y francesa,* Alma Lobo Aragón

D Chiles rellenos

Ingredientes:

12 chiles poblanos	4 huevos
280 gramos de lomo de cerdo picado	1 raja de canela
	2 cebollas
280 gramos de jitomate	3 acitrones
280 gramos de ternera	2 cucharadas de vinagre
675 gramos de jitomate para el caldillo	1 taza de caldo
	1 rama de perejil
225 gramos de manteca	1/2 cucharadita de canela
60 gramos de almendras	Sal y pimienta
60 gramos de piñones	
60 gramos de harina	

Modo de hacerlos:

En dos cucharadas de manteca se fríe la cebolla finamente picada y las carnes, se agrega el jitomate asado, molido y colado, las almendras peladas y cortadas en tiritas, el acitrón picado y los piñones; se sazona con el vinagre, el polvo de canela, sal, pimienta y una pulgarada de azúcar, y se deja en el fuego hasta que se espesa.

Los chiles se asan, se envuelven en una servilleta dejándolos así media hora; entonces se les quita la piel, se abren verticalmente, se desvenan, se les quitan las semillas, se rellenan con el picadillo, se revuelven en la harina y en los huevos que estarán batidos, se fríen en la manteca y se ponen en el caldillo a que hiervan un poco; se vacían en un platón y se espolvorean con perejil picado.

El picadillo se hace como sigue: En una cucharada de manteca se fríe el jitomate asado, molido con la cebolla y la canela y colado, y el caldo se sazona con sal y pimienta; cuando espesa se agregan los chiles a que den un hervor.

Cocina mexicana, Concepción Gandía de Fernández

18   Recipes

A   Hearty Vegetable-Bean Soup

1/2 lb dried white kidney beans
1/2 lb zucchini
3 medium white turnips (1 lb)
1 large potato
6 medium carrots (1 lb)
2 celery stalks with leaves
2 onions
1 onion, studded with whole cloves

1 whole bay leaf
1 can (1 lb 1 oz) whole tomatoes, undrained
1 tablespoon dried basil leaves
1/8 teaspoon dried hot red pepper
1 1/2 tablespoons salt
2 tablespoons olive or salad oil
2 tablespoons chopped parsley

1.   Day before, soak beans overnight in cold water to cover.
2.   Next day, drain beans in colander; rinse under cold water.
3.   Prepare vegetables. Dice zucchini; pare and dice turnips and potato; Pare carrots, slice thinly; slice celery. Coarsely chop 2 onions.
4.   Turn beans into a 6-quart Dutch oven with 6 1/2 cups water; bring to boil[3] over medium heat.
5.   Add prepared vegetables and remaining ingredients, except oil and parsley. Bring back to boiling,[3] reduce heat and simmer, covered, 2 1/2 hours, or until beans are tender. Add about half cup water during cooking, if necessary.
6.   To serve, remove and discard onion with cloves and the bay leaf. Stir in oil. Taste for seasoning. Sprinkle with parsley.
Makes 4 1/2 quarts.

McCall's Budget Cooking (adapted)

B   Onion Soup

Onion soup, with vegetable substituted for meat stock, is used for meals 'au maigre'.
Sauté until well browned,[4] but not burned:
    1 1/2 cups thinly sliced onions
in:
    3 tablespoons butter
Add:
    6 cups beef or chicken stock
    1/4 teaspoon freshly ground black pepper
Cover and cook over low heat or in a 275° oven for 30 minutes. Either way, the soup is now put into a casserole, covered with:
    6 slices toasted French bread
Sprinkle over the toast:
    1 cup grated Parmesan cheese
Heat in the oven for about 10 minutes or until the cheese is melted. Add:
    (A dash of cognac or dry sherry)

The Joy of Cooking,
Irma S. Rombauer and Marion Rombauer Becker

C Ham-cheese Sandwich Soufflé

Margarine, softened
12 slices day-old or firm-type white bread, trimmed
6 slices baked or boiled ham
1 package (8 oz) sharp Cheddar or process American cheese slices (8 slices)
3 eggs
2 cups milk
1 teaspoon dry mustard
1/2 teaspoon salt
Dash of white pepper
Paprika to taste

Lightly spread margarine on each slice bread. Make 6 sandwiches with 6 slices each ham and cheese. Dice remaining two slices cheese; set aside. Cut sandwiches in diagonal halves and arrange, slightly overlapping with points up, in two rows in 12x8x2-inch baking dish. Beat eggs, milk, mustard, salt and pepper until frothy.[4] Pour slowly over sandwiches to moisten. Sprinkle with reserved diced cheese and paprika. Cover with plastic and refrigerate at least 1 hour or overnight. Bake uncovered in preheated 350° oven about forty-five minutes or until custard is set. Serve at once. Makes 4 to 6 servings.;

Woman's Day

I   Translate the recipes, making sure that the ingredients and instructions are clearly set out in each language.

II   Write one of your own recipes in English and in Spanish.

Instructions

The most important things to be borne in mind when translating instructions are clarity and accuracy.

19   Instrucciones para voltear o cambiar el empaque de una olla a presión

Después de un tiempo de uso, el empaque de la olla por la acción del calor tiende a voltearse un tanto hacia arriba. Esto ocasiona escapes de vapor con detrimento a la cocción a presión. Entonces hay que voltear el empaque siguiendo este procedimiento.

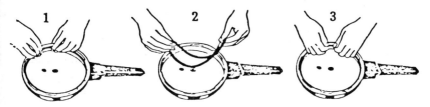

El procedimiento es simple: (1) Quite el empaque con cuidado.
    (2) Voltéelo.
    (3) Colóquelo en la ranura de la tapa dejando hacia afuera la parte que antes estaba hacia adentro.

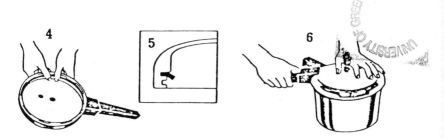

(4) Ajústelo con los dedos.
(5) Corte transversal de la tapa mostrando el empaque volteado.
(6) La primera vez que se tapa la olla después de haber volteado el empaque es necesario hacer presión con la mano sobre la tapa para que cierre.

VALVULA DE SEGURIDAD

La válvula de seguridad permite la salida del vapor cuando hay exceso de presión o cuando la válvula de escape se halla obstruída. Además de su función protectora, la válvula de seguridad actúa como válvula contra vacio evitando la evaporación de los jugos y sabores y consecuentemente la resequedad de los alimentos.

Book of Instructions for Olla a presión Superchef

I   Study the sketches carefully and make quite sure you can follow the instructions. If you have a similar pressure cooker, practise with it.

II   Translate the instructions into English.

20 Operating instructions for steam iron

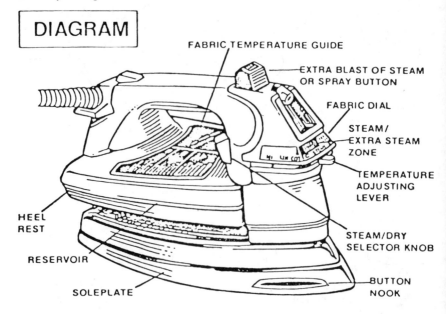

DIAGRAM

FABRIC TEMPERATURE GUIDE

EXTRA BLAST OF STEAM OR SPRAY BUTTON

FABRIC DIAL

STEAM/EXTRA STEAM ZONE

TEMPERATURE ADJUSTING LEVER

HEEL REST

STEAM/DRY SELECTOR KNOB

RESERVOIR

BUTTON NOOK

SOLEPLATE

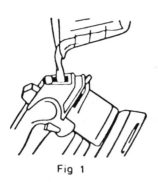

Fig 1

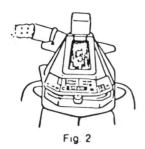

Fig. 2

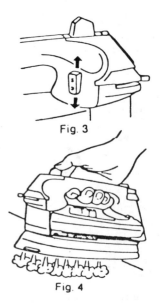

Fig. 3

Fig. 4

NOTE:
A pressing cloth is recommended on fabrics that have a tendency to shine or water-spot.

TO STEAM IRON

NOTE: Some material may water-spot or stain with moisture. Check garment label for ironing instructions.

1. TO FILL — Press Steam/Dry Selector Knob on side of handle down and put to Dry position. Tilt iron as illustrated in Fig. 1 — and direct steam of water from the tap of filling container into the opening of the fabric plate. Fill iron to "FULL" line on the top of the reservoir. Avoid overfilling and never fill any iron while it is plugged into the electrical outlet.

2. Plug iron into any 120 volt AC outlet — with Steam/Dry Selector Knob still at dry position.

3. SET TEMPERATURE ADJUSTING LEVER ON STEAM ZONE. ALL STEAM IRONING must be done in the STEAM ZONE on fabric dial (Fig. 2), adjusted to the proper position within the zone as indicated on fabric chart located on back cover, depending upon the fabric being ironed. Heat iron on heel rest for approx. 1 minute or more.

4. START STEAM FLOW — Flip Steam/Dry Selector Knob upward to STEAM position. Periodically, move Steam/Dry Selector Knob up and down a few times. This cleans out the water passage to maintain steam volume. (Fig. 3)

5. STEAM STOPS AUTOMATICALLY whenever iron is placed in the heel rest position. Steam can also be stopped by moving Steam/Dry Selector Knob down to Dry position.

6. TO REFILL HOT IRON — When clearly visible water level in reservoir becomes low, iron should be refilled as per instructions under item 1. TO FILL

I   Study the diagrams carefully and make quite sure you understand the instructions. If you have a similar steam iron, practise with it.

II   Translate the instructions into Spanish.

Notes

1   See **The Verb — Spanish Reflexive**, Appendix A7d.
2   *Garlic*, uncountable in English.
3   *Ponga a hervir*
4   See **Omissions and Insertions**, Appendix B4.

Unit VI Incidents and Conversations

21 Martín esperó, pasó el tiempo y el viejo no despertó. Pensó que ahora se había dormido de verdad y entonces, poco a poco, tratando de no hacer ruido, se levantó y empezó a caminar hacia la puerta por la que había entrado Alejandra. *Su temor era grande* porque las luces del alba ya iluminaban la pieza de don Pancho. Pensó que podía tropezar[1] con el tío Bebe, o que la mujer de servicio *podría estar levantada*[1] — Y entonces ¿qué les diría?

Sintió, o le pareció sentir unos pasos en el corredor. *Puso su oído contra la puerta* y escuchó con ansiedad . . .

F.C.E. December 1978

I   Think carefully about the meaning of the italicized expressions. Think of several ways of conveying the same meaning in Spanish. This should help you to find English equivalents.

II   Translate the passage into English.

22 Suddenly, without any warning, a boat appeared coming towards her at speed. For a moment she thought it was their own boat; then saw it was one she had never seen before.

"*Look out!*" cried Vicki. "You'll *run me down*!"

The occupants of the boat — two men — evidently couldn't hear, or didn't see her. The craft came nearer, *throwing up a double wall of foam on either side.* Then came a shout from the other direction.

"Jump for it! Jump!"

The voice was so urgent, so compelling, that Vicki jumped. And not a second too soon. The strange boat *ran right over her skis*, as they floated about on the water, *smashing them to matchwood.*

F.C.E. June 1978

What impression is created by the writer of this passage? How can this be conveyed in Spanish?

I Think carefully about the meaning of the italicized expressions. Think of several ways of conveying the same meaning in English. This should help you to find Spanish equivalents.

II Translate the passage into Spanish.

The next two passages consist mainly of conversation. Try to 'listen' to the conversation in the original language and also in the target language. Does your translation 'sound natural'?

23   Conforme me alejaba de las últimas calles del pueblo y entraba en las más concurridas, que conducían a la plaza, me sentía ligero y alegre. Al entrar en un bar, sobre el ruido de las conversaciones y del vapor de la cafetera, oí, clara y seca, la voz de Elena.
  — Bueno ¿ es que no quieres saludarme? — sonrió, desde la mesa junto a la cristalera.
  — No te había visto. ¿Estás sola?
  — ¿ Y tú? ¿No te espera tu gran amor? Y la pobre Dora tan tranquila suponiendo que estás de negocios por Barcelona. Te encuentro muy bien, ¿sabes? Como más moreno.
  — ¿ Qué haces aquí?
  — Bebo mi jugo de tomate.
  — ¿También tú tienes un gran amor en este pueblo?
  Dejó de sonreír.

F.C.E. June 1979

I Translate the passage into English.

24   "This is the first I heard that there was a young man on the aeroplane," Mr Carteret said.
  "You saw him," Mrs Carteret said. "He was there when we met her. You saw him come with her through the customs."
  "I can't remember seeing her with anybody."
  "I know very well you do because you remarked his hat. You said what a nice colour it was. It was a sort of leaf-green one with a turn-down brim — "
  "Good God," Mr Carteret said. "That fellow? He looked forty or more. He was as old as I am."
  "He's twenty-eight. That's all. Have you made up your mind which side you're going to sleep?"

F.C.E. December 1978

I Translate the passage into Spanish.

Further Exercises

Aunque la moto del médico no había vuelto a sonar por las calles del pueblo, todos sabían que el doctor Marco había regresado.

Diego Ribalta intentó visitarlo dos veces. Llegó hasta su casa, *anduvo llamando con insistencia el timbre de la entrada*, pero nadie salió a abrirle.

Cuando menos lo esperaba, lo encontró en la cocina, demacrado la barba descuidada y en los ojos una solemnidad de cadáver.

Había venido andando, probablemente, para no ser descubierto.

— Bien, aquí me tiene.

— *Llevo[2] tres días intentando hablarle* — dijo Diego Ribalta —

— ¿Dónde se ha metido usted?

— Estaba escondido.

F.C.E. December 1977, Mercedes Salisachs (adapted)

1   Read the above passage carefully, then answer the following questions in English:
Why hadn't the doctor come back on his motor-cycle?
Where did Diego Ribalta eventually find him?
What did he look like?
Where had he been?
2   Give at least two ways of translating each of the italicized expressions and put a tick beside the one you prefer.
3   Translate the passage into English.

Notes

1   Watch the use of auxiliaries here See **The Verb — Mood and Modals**, Appendix A7b
2   See **The Verb — Tense**, Appendix A7a

Unit VII   Anecdotes

This unit contains several anecdotes. The priority of the translator here will be to *tell the story*, keeping as close as possible to the manner and tone of the writer. Try to convey the total impression.

25A   Cuando don Ulises quiso[1] reaccionar, ya era tarde, El mismo día que ordenó encarcelar a los estudiantes, acusándolos de comunistas, una columna rebelde de mil hombres salía a la ciudad de Morelia. Yo tuve la oportunidad de verlos. Desfilaban en autobuses, en autos particulares y de alquiler, llevando banderas y cartelones. Las mujeres salían de sus casas a despedirlos y los muchachos gritaban:
— Tengan confianza. Pronto seremos libres.
Un hombre lloraba en la acera.
— Ah señor cura — me dijo — lo que no hicimos los viejos en treinta años lo han hecho los jóvenes en dos semanas. Es un milagro de la Virgen.

F.C.E. June 1978

I   Read the story carefully. Summarize in English what happened. What impression does the incident make on you?

II   Mark the following translations 1, 2, 3, in order of your preference in this context. Mark X beside any you consider unacceptable. Give a better version if one occurs to you.

a   reaccionar
  ☐ to react
  ☐ to take action
  ☐ to change
b   ordenó encarcelar a los estudiantes
  ☐ had the students put in gaol
  ☐ ordered the students to be imprisoned
  ☐ ordered the arrest of the students

c   desfilaban
  ☐ they paraded past
  ☐ they filed past
  ☐ they drove past

III   Translate the passage into English.

25B Afortunadamente don Nicéforo, *alarmado por nuestra ausencia de toda una noche,*[2] a la mañana siguiente se echó a buscarnos y no tardó en enterarse de que estábamos *detenidos* en la comisaría. Valiéndose de sus influencias[3] con el general[4] Aguirre, y mediante la *intervención un tanto desganada* del señor consul de España, logró que nos pusieran[5] en libertad antes de que el Capitán pudiera sacrificarnos según los cánones del rito azteca. La multa o la mordida — no lo sé[6] — ascendió a cien pesos, que *difícilmente pudimos* pagar entre los tres. Don Nicéforo nos prestó algún dinerillo, el cual devolvimos más tarde desde México, con un módico interés del veinte por ciento.

Marco A. Almazán

I   Read the passage carefully and answer the following questions in English.
Why had don Nicéforo become alarmed?
What had happened to the three young Spaniards?
How did don Nicéforo manage to get them out?
How did they manage to pay the fine?

II   Consider the italicized expressions carefully and decide the best way to convey the impression in English.

III   Translate the passage into English.

26 It was not till the man turned round, and I met his eye, that I fully awoke — awoke to danger. I had never seen a murderer, but I knew that the man who was so steadfastly peering at me now . . . I shut my eyes. I tried to think. Could I be dreaming? In books I had read of people pinching themselves to see whether they were really awake. But in actual life there never was any doubt on that score. The great thing was that I should keep all my wits about me. Everything might depend on presence of mind. Perhaps this murderer was mad. If you fix a lunatic with your eye . . .

Screwing up my courage, I fixed the man with my eye. I had never seen such a horrible little eye as his. It was a sane eye, too. It radiated a cold and ruthless sanity. It belonged not to a man who would kill you wantonly, but to one who would not scruple to kill you for a purpose, and would do the job quickly and neatly, and not be found out.

Max Beerbohm

I   This passage contains a number of short English sentences. Consider how to combine the ideas in Spanish.

II   Think of one or more alternative ways of expressing the meaning of the following idiomatic expressions, then translate them.
a   I met his eye
b   on that score
c   keep all my wits about me
d   screwing up my courage
e   to be found out

III   Translate the passage into Spanish.

27A Llegó mi turno de relatarle a don Melitón mis andanzas de los últimos años. Siempre *de agente viajero*, vendiendo libros por toda la República, visitaba[7] Puebla con bastante frecuencia ya que en dicha ciudad contaba con buena clientela, principalmente entre la numerosa colonia española. Para mí, Puebla es la más española de las ciudades mexicanas, no sólo por su arquitectura, sino por el carácter tradicionalista de sus habitantes y el ambiente en general. Es cierto que le falta *el bullicio*[8] *y la alegría* de las poblaciones de mi tierra, pero *eso lo suple*[9] con su misticismo y cierta renuencia al cambio, cierto apego a las viejas costumbres y a vivir en el pasado.

Marco A. Almazán

I Read the passage carefully and then describe the writer's opinion of Puebla.

II Consider the italicized expressions and decide the best way to convey the meaning in English.

III Translate the passage into English.

27B En los casi veintitrés años que llevaba[10] de vivir en México sólo había visto la nieve de lejos en las cimas de los volcanes. En Chihuahua y en Sonora me *tocaron dos o tres nevadas*, pero de poca monta: apenas unos cuantos centímetros que al día siguiente se derretían *transformándose en lodazales*. Con el correr de los años, la nieve se convirtió en una obsesión para mí: *de noche*[11] soñaba[10] que era nuevamente zagal y que me revolcaba en ella hasta casi ahogarme. Y *de día*[11] cuando *por cualquier circunstancia* recordaba mi tierra o mis mocedades, invariablemente eran imágenes nevadas las que se agolpaban en mi mente con singular insistencia.

Marco A. Almazán

I Consider the italicized expressions and decide the best way to convey the meaning in English.

II Translate the passage into English.

28A London Revisited[12]

One of the greatest Englishmen said that the man who is tired of London is tired of life.[13]

Well, Dr. Johnson had a way of[14] being right[15]. But he had a way of being wrong too — otherwise we shouldn't love him so much. And I think that a man who is tired of London may merely be tired of life *in London*. He won't, certainly, feel any such fatigue if he was born and bred in a distant country, and came to London and beheld London only when he had reached maturity. Almost all the impassioned lovers of London have spent, like Dr. Johnson, their childhood and adolescence in the country. Such was not my own fate.

Max Beerbohm

I Read the passage carefully, then express briefly in Spanish the author's answer to Dr. Johnson.

II Consider the three translations of the following sentence and mark X the one you prefer. Give your reasons.
Such was not my own fate
☐ Eso no fue mi propio destino
☐ Eso no fue el caso mío
☐ Eso no me pasó a mí

III Translate the passage into Spanish.

28B Speed

The other day a motorist friend of mine was complaining to me bitterly, even violently, about the behaviour of pedestrians. They were abominably careless and stupid, he insisted. I hate to see anyone agitated by a grievance, and I tried to soothe my friend by an appeal to reason. I said, "No doubt we pedestrians are very trying.[16] But you must remember that, after all, we were on the roads for many, many centuries before you came along in your splendid car. And remember, it isn't we that are threatening to kill <u>you</u>. It is you who are threatening to kill <u>us</u>. And if we are rather flustered, and occasionally do the wrong thing, you should make allowances — and, if the worst comes to the worst, lay some flowers on our graves."[17]

Max Beerbohm

I Translate the passage into Spanish.

Notes

1 See **The Verb — Tense**, Appendix A7a.
2 See **Transposition**, Appendix B5.
3 See **Nouns**, Appendix A4.
4 See **Determiners**, Appendix A3.
5 See **The Verb — Mood and Modals**, Appendix A7b.
6 Insert *which*
7 See **The Verb — Tense**, Appendix A7a.
8 *bustle*
9 See **Pronouns**, Appendix A5.
10 See **The Verb — Tense**, Appendix A7a.
11 See **Prepositions**, Appendix A6.
12 *Retorno a Londres*
13 What is the meaning of *greatest* here?
14 Can you think of another way of saying *had a way of* in English?
15 Try to reproduce the proverbial tone of this statement.
16 What is the meaning of *trying* here?
17 There are a number of short sentences in this passage. You may need to combine some of them in Spanish.

Unit VIII   Description

29A   Los dos hombres abandonaron la cuadra y atravesaron el portal sin detenerse, a pesar de que ya no se rezaba en la cocina y las mujeres habían empezado a comentar las virtudes de la enferma. Salieron a la calle y, sin cruzar una sola palabra, descendieron la cuesta, llegando a la plaza a través de <u>un silencio apretado</u>. <u>La noche se aplastaba contra el humilde caserío</u>, del que sólo se destacaba la cuadrangular y <u>achatada</u> torre de la iglesia. El blando rumor de las pisadas quedaba ahogado por el <u>acompasado chasquido</u> de los pantalones de pana. Hasta que cruzaron el puente no se despertaron los ladridos de los perros.

C.P.E. December 1977, A.M. de Lera (Adapted)

Here, although there is some narrative, the author is using mainly description to achieve a certain effect. The general atmosphere created is one of stillness and quiet. There is economy of words and movement. The translator will try to convey the simplicity of the scene. This will affect the choice of words used and the construction of the sentences.

I   Read the passage carefully and try to picture to yourself the scene. What exactly do the words and expressions underlined suggest to you?

II   Mark the following translations 1, 2, 3, in order of your preference in the context. Mark X beside any you consider unacceptable. Give a better version if one occurs to you.

a   un silencio apretado
  ☐ a tight silence
  ☐ an oppressive silence
  ☐ a heavy silence

b   La noche se aplastaba contra el humilde caserío
  ☐ Night fell on the poor village
  ☐ Night overwhelmed the humble settlement
  ☐ Night descended upon the lowly settlement

c   achatada
  ☐ squat
  ☐ stubby
  ☐ flattened

d   acompasado chasquido
  ☐ measured rubbing
  ☐ rhythmical rustle
  ☐ rhythmical sound

III   Translate the passage into English.

29B   De Londres a Edimburgo hay seis horas de tren.[1] A un lado y otro de las vías los campos son fértiles, el ganado abundante y las casas muy iguales. La verdad, pensaba yo mirando por la ventanilla es que a este país sólo le falta dinero — lo demás lo tiene. Tiene paz, unas instituciones democráticas y una seguridad social comprensiva y generosa.[2] Viven[3] bien: el 78 por 100 de las casas tienen jardín propio. Todos los niños están asistidos por el Estado en la educación. Quien[4] pierde el empleo recibe subsidio de acuerdo con sus necesidades y 'status' (si tenía televisión en color comprada a plazos, el subsidio no lo ignora). En fin, el montaje es grandioso. Pero la financiación, por[5] fuertes que sean los impuestos, resulta agobiante.

C.P.E. December 1979

What is the purpose of the writer here? The translator's task will be to convey clearly in normal English the picture presented and the comments upon it.

I   Translate the passage into English.

30A   The hill was long, shaped like a pig's back and rounded with the rubbish of three and a half thousand years. An open hole showed how this went down to a depth of ten metres or so. At the bottom of the hole, a pattern of worked stones showed the crude outlines of the ancient settlement, built on the same hard rock as the rest of the area.

Because of its length, the hill had been divided into three sections, and because of Teitleman the archeologists had dealt with the two westerly ones first. Both of these had been opened up the previous season, and now the whole expedition was engaged on the third.

F.C.E. December 1977, Lionel Davidson (adapted)

The translator's task is to convey the picture. Try to see the hill and imagine what you would see if you looked through the hole. In trying to convey this in Spanish you will need to rephrase.

I   Read the passage carefully, then answer the following questions in Spanish:
¿Qué había dado su forma redonda al cerro?
¿Qué se veía a través del hoyo?
¿Qué quiere decir *worked stones*?

II   Translate the passage into Spanish.

30B   Chewlips[6] was ignorant about everything except money, and he was the only ignorant person I ever met that was interesting to speak to.[7] He was a fairly big lad of eighteen, and he had dark hair, well oiled with *margarine off his bread*, and a gold filling in one of his teeth. He had a serious <u>face</u> and listened with great attention. When one dinner time <u>a bloke</u> was saying that the sun was made of burning gas, something from a book he'd been reading, Chewlips went over to look through the window and *up at the sun*, as if he'd never seen it before.

F.C.E. December 1977, Brendan Behan (adapted)

Here the writer is creating an impression of the lad Chewlips. He does this by describing his physical appearance and then giving an example of his behaviour to illustrate his remarks about his personality. The task of the translator is to convey the same impression in *natural* Spanish. Why do you think Chewlips was *interesting to speak to?*

I   **Choose the best translation for:**

a   face
- ☐ cara
- ☐ rostro
- ☐ semblante

b   a bloke
- ☐ cierto tipo
- ☐ un sujeto
- ☐ alguien

II   **Translate the passage into Spanish. The italicized expressions will need particular care. How will the Spanish constructions differ from the English?**

31   Tepotzotlán, México

<u>Destaca en el pueblo</u> la incomparable iglesia y Convento de San Francisco Javier, construídos hace cuatrocientos años, de fachada y torre barrocas e interiores churriguerescos.[8] Es una de las mas espléndidas construcciones del Continente Americano. <u>Fue transformado en el Museo Nacional de Arte Virreinal</u>, el 19 de septiembre de 1964.

El templo es imponente. Los altares enchapados en oro, las maderas finamente talladas y los ricos ornamentos, le confieren al conjunto un carácter de imponderable belleza. Entre los muchos objetos importantes que contiene el museo, se encuentran delicadas obras de incalculable valor: esculturas, un crucifijo de marfil con las características de que el Cristo tiene rasgos orientales;[9] una pétrea escultura de la Virgen y el Niño; y pinturas firmadas por artistas de renombre. El vertedero[10] de la fuente del patio está formado por <u>una pieza prehispánica</u> que representa una serpiente emplumada.

Guía AMA 1975-76

This passage is part of a description taken from a Guide Book. The translator's first priority will be to convey accurately to the reader the impression created by the writer.

I   What facts about the building and its contents are given in this passage?

II   **Mark the following translations 1, 2, 3, in order of your preference in the context. Mark X beside any you consider unacceptable. Give a better version if one occurs to you.**

a Destaca en el pueblo . . .
☐ The most outstanding feature of the village is . . .
☐ Outstanding in the village is . . .
☐ The most remarkable building in the village is . . .

b Fue transformado en el Museo Nacional de Arte Virreinal
☐ It was made the Museum of Viceregal Art
☐ It became the Museum of Colonial Art
☐ It was transformed into the Museum of Colonial Art

c una pieza prehispánica
☐ a prehispanic piece
☐ a prehispanic statue
☐ a prehispanic stone

III   Translate the passage into English.

32A   Coimbra, Portugal

However, the University possesses one unique jewel in the great secular baroque Library, built by D. Joao V between 1717 and 1728. It consists of three lofty rooms, so elegantly proportioned that their size is almost unnoticed,[11] with painted ceilings, and galleries running round the book-lined walls. These galleries, their exquisite balustrades and slender graceful supporting columns are richly painted and gilt, each room in[12] a different colour — a matchless green, a deeper green, and the third in an astonishing shade between lacquer-red and tango. The whole thing is uniquely original and indescribably beautiful. Happy the students who, like Dr. Salazar, have pursued their studies here!

The Selective Traveller in Portugal, Ann Bridge and Susan Lowndes

I   Read the description carefully, then answer the questions in Spanish.
¿ Qué quiere decir *one unique jewel*?
¿ Cuál es la joya?
Describa la biblioteca según la impresión que Vd. tiene.

II   Translate the passage into Spanish.

32B   Canterbury, England

Canterbury in the 1970's owns its share of supermarkets and department stores, as well as a noisy bus station and a main street ever full of traffic, but its cathedral, a dream of Gothic towers, continues to give out the idea that there is 'no such thing as change on earth'. So do the jackdaws,[13] the rooks[14] and the ivied gabled ends,[15] the ruined walls, the ancient houses and — away from that main street — the pastoral landscape, the serene air of which Dickens also spoke.

National Geographic

Read carefully. Try to get the impression of Canterbury conveyed in this passage. What does *give out* mean here?

I Translate the passage into Spanish.

Notes

1 What is the most natural way of saying this in English? See **Modulation**, Appendix B6.
2 Watch use and omission of the article.
3 Supply the subject here.
4 See **Pronouns**, Appendix A5.
5 See **Prepositions**, Appendix A6.
6 This is obviously a nickname. Try to find an equivalent in Spanish.
7 Watch preposition here.
8 See **Nouns**, Appendix A4.
9 What is the simplest way of describing the Crucifix?
10 *spout*
11 You will need to break your sentence here and begin a new sentence with a new subject.
12 See **Prepositions**, Appendix A6.
13 *grajillas*
14 *grajos*
15 *aguilones*

Unit IX Sport and Adventure

33 Para las masas, el acontecimineto máximo del deporte <u>hípico</u> lo[1] constituye el 'Derby'. Esta clásica carrera, celebrada por primera vez en 1780, es un espectáculo inigualado en el mundo, no sólo por[2] el marco y las circunstancias en que se celebra, sino por la diversidad de gente <u>que a[2] él concurre</u>, y los distintos atractivos <u>que en él intervienen</u>. El que en un día[3] de trabajo medio millón de personas de todas las clases[3] puedan dejar sus ocupaciones y oficios y trasladarse al[2] campo para contemplar un espectáculo que técnicamente dura unos pocos minutos, es algo difícil de explicar. Verdad es que pocas veces tiene uno[4] la oportunidad de[2] ver correr juntos a los mejores caballos del mundo <u>para disputarse un premio</u> de más de dos millones de pesetas, pero éste no es el único atractivo que persiguen[5] esas quinientas mil personas que llenan las ondulantes praderas de Epsom. La carrera ofrece el mejor pretexto para pasar el día al aire libre, y la pradera circundada por la pista, se convierte en un parque de atracciones lleno de contrastes y colorido. En las tribunas se hallan, invariablemente, la Familia Real y las figuras más importantes del país, y en las distintas secciones del recorrido se ven representados todos los sectores sociales en una mescolanza difícil de <u>discernir</u>.

L.C.E., Jorge Marin

I Which of the following is the writer trying to do in this passage:
☐ describe a scene?
☐ create an impression?
☐ tell a story?
How will this affect your translation?

II Mark the following translations 1, 2, 3, in the order of your preference in this context. Mark X any you consider unacceptable. Give a better version if one occurs to you.

a hípico
☐ horse
☐ equine
☐ horse racing

b que a él concurre
☐ who gather here
☐ who go to it
☐ who meet in it

c   que en él intervienen
    ☐ who take part in it
    ☐ who are part of it
    ☐ who intervene in it
d   para disputarse un premio
    ☐ to dispute a prize
    ☐ to compete for a prize
    ☐ to quarrel over a prize

e   discernir
    ☐ disentangle
    ☐ separate
    ☐ discern

III   Translate the passage into English.

34   Epsom and the Derby

Epsom should be seen as it is the most famous place in the racing world, and if you happen to stay in London[6] at the end of May or at the beginning of June <u>when the Derby is run</u>, you should go to Epsom Downs to witness the racing. The Victorian artist Frith made a celebrated painting of Derby Day, when all manner of sideshows, fairground rides, gypsies and tumblers <u>descended on the course</u>. It is still a boisterous and gay occasion, with the fairground fringe very evident, if slightly less picturesque than in Victorian days. Any illusions that the English are placid and undemonstrative will be totally shattered here.

Epsom became established as a fashionable watering place in the mid-eighteenth century, though mineral springs had been discovered there much earlier, in 1620. Horseracing was introduced here by James I as a courtly diversion, but assumed a permanent establishment in 1780 when the Derby and the Oaks were run. These races are named after the 12th Earl of Derby and his seat, The Oaks, which is nearby. The grandstand (in Frith's picture) was built in 1829 but rebuilt later.

The Face of Britain, Fodor

What 'racing world' is referred to here? (See **33**.) What is meant by *the course, assumed a permanent establishment*? It is important to think out clearly the meaning of the underlined expressions.

I   Mark the following translations 1, 2, 3, in order of your preference in the context. Mark X any you consider unacceptable. Give a better version if one occurs to you.

a   when the Derby is run
    ☐ a la fecha del Derby
    ☐ al tiempo del Derby
    ☐ cuando se corre el Derby

b   descended on the course
    ☐ se instalaron en el parque de atracciones
    ☐ invadieron los alrededores del hipódromo
    ☐ invadieron la pista

II   Translate the passage into Spanish.

35 Requiem por un inglés·

Quién no recuerda a aquel singular torero rubio que hablaba andaluz[7] con acento inglés[8] y que con un tesón y un valor <u>a toda prueba</u> se fue abriendo paso[9] en el difícil y a veces no muy sano camino del[10] toreo. Henry Higgins o Enrique Cañadas, retirado de los ruedos desde hace unos años, y que contaba treinta y tres, encontró hace unos días la muerte cuando volaba con una cometa delta.[11] Su compañera Isabel Durán vió con sus propios ojos cómo su Henry, al despegar de un montículo se enredaba en un torbellino y se estrellaba sin remisión contra las rocas de un cerro cercano. Pero para Isabel, como para los padres,[8] él inglés y ella irlandesa nacida en México, que tanto le ayudaron a lo largo de[10] su difícil carrera, como para sus amigos y seguidores, Henry no será olvidado.

En su libro *To be a matador*, Henry cuenta cómo para llegar a la fama <u>pasó de todo y más</u>. Amaba a España, al toreo y a los toros más que muchos nativos <u>que hacen patria</u>.

Con Isabel, intentaba ahora encontrar la serenidad después de una vida de penalidades. Pero el amor al[10] riesgo[8] le hizo aprender a volar, y a pesar de que[12] lo practicaba con disciplina y prudencia, lo inevitable es inevitable. <u>Lástima.</u>

Cambio 16

I   Read the passage carefully, then answer the questions in English.
How did Henry Higgins differ from other bullfighters?
What caused his death?
Had his life been peaceful or full of difficulties?

II   Think of three possible translations for *singular* **and** *tesón* **and decide which is the best in context.**

III   Mark the following translations 1, 2, 3, in order of your preference in the context. Mark X any you consider unacceptable. Give a better version if one occurs to you.

a   a toda prueba
   ☐ equal to anything
   ☐ undaunted
   ☐ indomitable
b   pasó de todo y más
   ☐ endured all kinds of difficulties
   ☐ underwent everything and more
   ☐ went through more than
      everything

c   que hacen patria
   ☐ who claim to love their
      country
   ☐ who pride themselves on their
      patriotism
   ☐ who boast of their patriotism
d   Lástima
   ☐ A pity
   ☐ Too bad
   ☐ Unfortunately

IV   Translate the passage into English.

36   At eight minutes to eight on 20 May 1927 Lindbergh *coaxed*[13] his machine into the air above New York airport. It was so heavily[14] loaded with extra petrol tanks that three times it *bumped down* again and when it did eventually rise it only just *cleared* a tractor standing in a field nearby. Lindbergh's friends who watched the little silver monoplane slowly disappear never expected to see its pilot again. Then this very brave man began his lonely flight of 33½ hours, over[15] Newfoundland, through fog and ice and on over Ireland and England to[15] Paris. His two greatest worries were that he would lose his way or fall asleep. Actually <u>he steered a very true course</u>, and when he landed at Le Bourget airport, Paris, he still had enough petrol to fly another thousand miles.

F.C.E. June 1979

I   Read the passage carefully, then answer the following questions in Spanish:
¿ Por qué tuvo Lindbergh dificultad en despegar?
¿ Cúales fueron sus más graves problemas?

II   Think out carefully the meaning of the italicized words in the passage, then find the best Spanish equivalents.

III   Consider the following translations and say which one you prefer in the context and why you prefer it.
he steered a very true course
☐ dirigió su vuelo con alta precisión
☐ condujo su vuelo con alta precisión
☐ encauzó su vuelo con alta precisión

IV   Translate the passage into Spanish.

Further Exercises

Here are some verbs of visual perception:

contemplate	gaze (at)	glare (at)	glimpse	look (at)
peep (at)	peer (at)	perceive	notice	scrutinize see
stare (at)	watch			

Discuss the meaning and use of each verb, then complete the following sentences with the correct form of the most appropriate verb.

1   The old man . . . . shortsightedly at the book they placed in his hands.
2   The two men stopped talking and . . . . angrily at the intruder.
3   The children . . . . at the funny old woman and her pig.
4   The lawyer . . . . the deed very carefully.
5   The artist finished the portrait and . . . . his handiwork with satisfaction.
6, 7   Peter . . . . the men taking the casks out of the boat, but he was so carefully hidden that they . . . . him.
8   The children . . . . spellbound at the scene before their eyes.

9   The servant shut the door quickly, but not before Max . . . . his cousin and another man standing in the hall.

10   Do let me see the baby; I won't wake her. Just let me . . . . at her for a moment from the doorway.

Notes

1   See **Pronouns**, Appendix A5.
2   See **Prepositions**, Appendix A6.
3   See **Determiners**, Appendix A3.
4   Be careful with word order.
5   See **Transposition**, Appendix B5.
6   See **Transposition**, Appendix B5.
7   See **Adaptation**, Appendix B7.
8   See **Determiners**, Appendix A3.
9   See **The Verb — Tense**, Appendix A7a.
10   See **Prepositions**, Appendix A6.
11   Watch constructions in this sentence and the two following ones, especially the order of words and phrases.
12   See **Connectives**, Appendix A2.
13   You will need several words to express this idea.
14   Omit
15   Supply a verb here.

Unit X Present Day Problems **1**

The next two Units, X and XI, deal with different aspects of present day problems. Here the translator must make sure he conveys clearly the facts reported and the comments upon them. It will often be necessary to *normalize* the English or the Spanish of the translation so that the communication may be easily understood by the reader.

37 Enfermedades cardiovasculares, las más mortales en ciudades industrializadas

Las[1] enfermedades cardiovasculares <u>son las que más muertes causan</u> en las naciones industrializadas donde representan 50 por ciento de las defunciones.[2] En el mundo causan 30 por ciento de los fallecimientos a los 40 años; 40 por ciento de los decesos a los 50 años; 50 por ciento a los 60 años y 60 por ciento de personas cerca a los 70 años.

<u>Un estudio del Consejo Mexicano contra la Hipertensión Arterial, señala lo anterior</u> y <u>subraya</u> su propósito de <u>fomentar</u> en el pueblo la[1] conciencia de la importancia que tiene la vigilancia permanente de la presión arterial, para[3] detectarla y controlarla cuando excede de los parámetros normales 110–70.

Manifiesta que estas enfermedades que eran raras a principios de siglo, en las últimas décadas se han hecho notables por el aumento de mortalidad por[3] cardiopatía coronaria en las sociedades urbanas y es practicamente desconocida en las poblaciones de escaso progreso industrial.

Añade que si bien en los países en desarrollo ese[1] mal tiene un posición intermedia entre las razones fundamentales de fallecimientos, en todas ellas la mortalidad por enfermedades cardiovasculares va en aumento.

Excelsior

I Read the passage carefully and then answer the following questions in English:
In which countries is heart disease the chief cause of death?

What precaution is recommended by the Mexican Anti-Arterial-Hypertension Association?
What is now happening in the developing countries?

II   Mark the following translations 1, 2, 3, in order of your preference in this context. Mark X beside any you consider unacceptable.

a   son las que más muertes causan
   ☐ cause most deaths
   ☐ are those which cause the largest number of deaths
   ☐ are the chief cause of death
b   Un estudio. . . . señala lo anterior
   ☐ the above facts are stated in a paper . . .
   ☐ the above is pointed out in a paper . . .
   ☐ the above facts are given in a study . . .

c   subraya
   ☐ announces
   ☐ stresses
   ☐ emphasizes
d   fomentar
   ☐ foster
   ☐ foment
   ☐ encourage

III   Translate the passage into English.

38   Airport hazards

Cracked windows, rattling crockery,[4] drowned-out conversations: people who live near airports constantly complain about such troubles. But these may be the least bothersome effects of jet noise.[5] Constant exposure[5] to the roar[6] and whine[6] of aircraft, report two acoustical experts,[2] may represent a serious hazard to health.

William Meecham and Neil Shaw of the University of California, Los Angeles, studied disease and death statistics[5] over[7] a two-year period in a community two to three miles from the main touchdown point at Los Angeles International Airport. The residents of the area were exposed[8] to noise levels of 90 to 115 decibels 560 times a day. Meecham and Shaw discovered that the mortality rate from all causes[5] was nearly 20% higher among this group than among residents of a similar neighbourhood eight to nine miles from the landing strip.

Most striking was the finding that cases of cirrhosis of the liver due to drinking were 140% higher among those who lived near L.A. International.[5] Less significant increases were also noted for[7] deaths from heart disease, strokes, lung cancer, suicide and auto accidents. Noise-induced stress, point out the Californian investigators, can lead to everything from[7] hypertension to quaffing too many Martinis.

Newsweek

I   Read the passage carefully, then answer the following questions in Spanish:
¿ Cuál es el peligro más grave que amenaza a los que viven cerca de un aeropuerto?
¿ Cuál fue la estadística más espectacular que el estudio de los señores Meecham y Shaw reveló?

II   Think out carefully the meaning of the title. Who is exposed to the hazards?

III   Translate the passage into Spanish.

39   Menos pluriempleo[9]

El problema más importante y, sin duda, de más urgente solución que tiene planteado el país es el del paro, sobre todo en regiones subdesarrolladas como Andalucía, Extremadura y Canarias, incidiendo esta verdadera calamidad nacional especialmente en <u>la juventud</u> y <u>personas maduras</u>, y constituyendo la desesperación de miles y miles de familias <u>modestas</u> que son las que verdaderamente — <u>vamos a dejarnos de historias</u> — sufren la crisis.[10]

En esta situación pienso que una de las medidas que se podrían tomar para dar una salida a la crisis sería eliminar en la medida de lo posible el pluriempleo, que como todos sabemos es <u>práctica mayoritaria</u> entre la población activa española. Claro está que dicha medida sólo podrá ser eficaz si se procura a todos los trabajadores unos salarios dignos, pues también es cierto que muchas veces el pluriempleo es consecuencia de una capacidad adquisitiva insuficiente para hacer frente a la inflación que se come nuestros sueldos.

Cambio 16

I   Read the passage carefully and answer the following questions in English:
What is the problem the writer mentions?
What are the various meanings of *paro*? Which is clearly indicated here?
What is his solution?

II   Mark the following translations 1, 2, 3, in order of your preference in this context. Mark X beside any you consider unacceptable. Give a better alternative if one occurs to you.

a   la juventud
☐ the young
☐ youth
☐ young people

b   personas maduras
☐ the old
☐ mature people
☐ older people

c   modestas
☐ poor
☐ modest
☐ humble

d   Vamos a dejarnos de historias
☐ Let's stop beating about the bush
☐ Let's not mince matters
☐ Let's come to the point

e   práctica mayoritaria
☐ majoritarian practice
☐ the practice more often than not
☐ practised by more than half

III   Translate the passage into English.

40 Unemployment in the industrialized countries

As unemployment in the industrialized countries rises gradually towards 16 million, *it is becoming clear* that Western economies face two quite distinct problems. One, as we realized *during the great inflationary scare* a couple of years ago, was getting economic growth without. The other, it now turns out, is getting economic growth at all.

The first is essentially a political problem of persuading people not to demand more in wages than the worth of what they produce. The prevailing cure is called monetarism, in which governments simply refuse *to make the extra money available to the economy*.

Monetarism has been applied *religiously* by most Western governments since 1974. As a result, *inflation rates have fallen back from the brink of catastrophe*. So far, voters' fears of inflation remain generally stronger than their greed, and they have not forced governments to abandon tight monetary controls.

The monetarist strategy, however, assumes that there will be enough real growth in national economies to *sop up* most unemployment — but since 1974 this growth hasn't occurred. The worst of the current recession was past in most Western countries by the end of 1975, but average real growth rates in the past two years have *hovered* below 4 per cent. They may fall again between now and 1980.

'The Third World's Role', *Toronto Star*, Gwynne Dyer (adapted)

I   Read the passage carefully and answer the following questions in Spanish:
¿ Cuáles son los dos problemas principales que plantea a los países industriali-zados el crecimiento del desempleo?
¿ En qué consiste la solución llamada *monetarismo*?
¿ Qué presupone esta solución?

II   Think out the exact meaning of the italicized expressions and give one or more alternative ways of conveying the same idea.

III   Translate the passage into Spanish.

Notes

1   See **Determiners**, Appendix A3.
2   See dictionaries for the use of the different words for expressing the death rate in English.
3   See **Prepositions**, Appendix A6.
4   *the rattle of crockery*
5   Rephrase.
6   Think of Spanish words which will describe these sounds.
7   Watch preposition here.
8   Watch tense here.
9   The translator has to choose here between using a coined word like *pluriemployment* of which the meaning is clear, or an explanatory phrase, e.g. *fewer holders of more than one job*.
10   The first sentence of the passage is rather long: make into two English sentences.

Unit XI   Present Day Problems **2**

41   Medida para paliar la concentración urbana

Es un <u>hecho</u> — cuyas[1] causas son complejas y múltiples — que el crecimiento de la capital de la República <u>no se debe tanto a</u> la dinámica interna de esta urbe, cuanto a la corriente migratoria que converge[2] en ella desde todos los puntos del país. Compatriotas de provincia aumentan, con[3] un caudal que no cesa, la cifra demográfica de la zona metropolitana, ocasionan problemas graves de prestación de servicios, <u>en lo personal y lo familiar</u>, se ven envueltos en dificultades de variada índole, pues no es la megalópolis el paraíso que habían creído vislumbrar desde lejos. El director de Asistencia Social de la Secretaría de Salubridad ha estructurado un plan para <u>evitar tales conflictos</u> a los nuevos capitalinos. Se pretenderá, de acuerdo con esta idea, dotarlos de ocupación remunerativa y útil de tal modo que[4] no caigan en los trasfondos de la subocupación y no desciendan — lo que es ahora frecuente — a la[5] vagancia, el vicio y la delincuencia. ....

Se calificará a estas personas — campesinos muchas de ellas — para que funjan como obreros calificados, y se les facilitará más tarde su aceso a las fuentes de empleo en que mayor rendimiento puedan tener. Es a no dudar una sana y benéfica iniciativa, que <u>habrá de paliar</u> uno de los grandes males de la gran concentración urbana en que vivimos.

Excelsior (adapted)

I   Read the above passage carefully and answer the following questions in English:

Why is the population of Mexico increasing so rapidly?

In what services particularly does this increasing population create problems?

What is the plan of the Director of Social Welfare?

II   Mark the following translations 1, 2, 3, in order of your preference in the context. Put an X beside any you consider unacceptable. Give a better translation if one occurs to you.

a   hecho
    ☐ deed
    ☐ fact
    ☐ event
b   no se debe tanto a . . .
    ☐ is due not so much to . . .
    ☐ is not so much due to . . .
    ☐ is not so much owing to . . .
c   en lo personal y lo familiar
    ☐ for individuals and families
    ☐ personally and familiarly
    ☐ in persons and families

d   evitar tales conflictos a . . .
    ☐ spare the . . . such conflicts
    ☐ avoid such conflicts for the . . .
    ☐ elude such conflicts for the . . .
e   habrá de paliar
    ☐ is bound to palliate . . .
    ☐ is bound to relieve . . .
    ☐ will have to ameliorate . . .

III   Translate the passage into English.

42   The *cheap-and-nasty*[6] *housing* originally provided for the workers in mills[7] and mines as near as possible to their work provided the pattern for nearly all working-class housing for almost the whole of the nineteenth century.

However heavy the sufferings of the poor, however alarming the death rate from tuberculosis, cholera, diphtheria and similar diseases of overcrowding, the Industrial Revolution brought material success and prosperity to England, and later *to other countries to which it spread*. And when a country prospers its population generally rises, especially when *there are no great wars to upset trade* and communications. <u>Children and old people might die</u> off at alarming rates but those who survived infancy during these periods of prosperity were tough, and they were prolific.

C.P.E. June 1977, P. Maguire (adapted)

I   Read the above passage carefully and answer the questions in Spanish.
¿ Cuáles fueron las ventajas y cuáles las desventajas que le trajo la Revolución Industrial a Inglaterra?
¿ En qué condiciones se aumenta la población de un país?

II   Consider carefully the meaning of the italicized expressions in the passage and suggest alternative Spanish translations.

III   Which of the translations of the following statement do you prefer? Give your reasons. Can you think of a better translation?
Children and old people might die
☐ Aunque los niños y los ancianos murieran
☐ No importaba que los niños y los ancianos murieran
☐ Tal vez los niños y los ancianos murieran

IV   Translate the passage into Spanish.

43   El[8] mundo en crisis — sombrío panorama

Periódicamente se filtran[10] noticias[11] alarmantes en relación con la[8] economía mundial. Aunque la[8] mayoría de ellas se relacionan con <u>los países llamados tercermundistas</u>, donde podría explicarse la aguda y perenne crisis en que viven por la carencia de recursos y <u>la desorganización secular que padecen</u>,[12,13] la cosa resulta más preocupante cuando nos enteramos que naciones muy adelantadas y prósperas como Alemania Occidental, Estados Unidos, Japón y Francia, <u>están dadas a la tarea de confeccionar</u> nuevos proyectos económicos que sirvan[13] para estimular la economía y <u>tonificar sus propios requerimientos</u> internos.

Las razones para este sombrío panorama, que bien puede catalogarse de internacional, son bastante conocidas y por su misma[14] reiteración <u>se han llegado a hacer populares</u>. Ellas son el crecimiento demográfico inusitado, la inflación generalizada, la insuficiente producción de alimentos, el desempleo multiplicado, <u>las restricciones monetarias</u> y, añadiéndose a estos factores <u>de suyo gravísimos</u>, una auténtica y colectiva crisis de confianza.

Excelsior, Eduardo Borrell Navarro

I   Read the passage carefully and summarize the ideas in English.

II   Mark the following translations 1, 2, 3, in order of your preference in the context. Mark X any you consider unacceptable. Give a better version if one occurs to you.

a   los paises llamados tercermundistas
  ☐ the countries called Third World
  ☐ the so-called Third World countries
  ☐ countries called Third World

b   la desorganización secular que padecen
  ☐ the disorganization they suffer
  ☐ their secular disorganization
  ☐ their traditional lack of organization

c   están dadas a la tarea de confeccionar . . .
  ☐ are given to the job of creating . . .
  ☐ are engaged in the task of drawing up . . .
  ☐ are engaged in the task to work out . . .

d   tonificar sus propios requerimientos internos
  ☐ boost their proper internal requirements
  ☐ tone up their own local needs
  ☐ stimulate their own domestic demands

e   se han llegado a hacer populares
  ☐ have succeeded in becoming generally accepted
  ☐ have made themselves popular
  ☐ have become generally accepted

f   las restricciones monetarias
  ☐ monetary control
  ☐ currency restrictions
  ☐ restrictions concerning money

g de suyo gravísimos
☐ very serious themselves
☐ their own very serious
☐ very serious in themselves

III   Translate the passage into English.

44   Material and industrial changes

The social developments[15] in the last decades of the eighteenth century ensured the emergence of Britain as the first nation-state of a new type, that form of industrialist-capitalist democracy which reached maturity about the end of the nineteenth century. The transition from our older economy of agriculture and domestic handicrafts[16] was quite spontaneous, not directed from above or regulated in any way except by the laws inherent in the new system of production. In no long time, the cumulative effect of the introduction of mechanical improvements provoked an upheaval affecting the community at all levels. From the eighties onwards,[17] the scale and tempo of change[18] were visibly increasing,[19] and in a single generation the mode and manner of living which had fostered the brief splendour of a native classicism had become[20] incompatible with social reality.

A sense of change had been in the air for some time. It was stimulated from many sources, from the writings of the French Enlightenment which circulated freely here, from the spread of[21] interest in[21] scientific discoveries and their possible applications, from the American example in setting up a constitution without hereditary legislators, from speculations as to the perfectibility of man.

The Pelican Guide to English Literature,
Edgell Rickword

I   Read the passage carefully and summarize the ideas in Spanish.

II   Mark the following translations 1, 2, 3, in order of your preference in the context. Mark X any you consider unacceptable. Give a better version if one occurs to you.

a   The social developments in the last decades of the eighteenth century ensured the emergence of Britain as the first nation-state . . .
☐ Los adelantos sociales en las últimas décadas del siglo XVIII aseguraron la emergencia de Inglaterra como el primer estado-nación . . .
☐ Los cambios sociales que se produjeron en las últimas décadas del siglo XVIII dieron como resultado el surgimiento de la Gran Bretaña como el primer estado-nación . . .
☐ Como resultado de los cambios sociales en las últimas décadas del siglo XVIII Gran Bretaña surgió como el primer estado-nación . . .

b   . . . or regulated in any way except by the laws inherent in the new system of production.
☐ . . . ni controlada en forma alguna más que por las leyes inherentes al nuevo sistema de producción.

☐ . . . o controlada en ninguna forma excepto por las leyes propias al nuevo sistema de producción.

☐ . . . o regulada en ninguna forma excepto por leyes inherentes al nuevo sistema de producción.

c . . . the cumulative effect of the introduction of mechanical improvements provoked an upheaval affecting the community at all levels.

☐ . . . el efecto acumulativo de los adelantos mecánicos provocó un cataclismo que afectó a la comunidad en todos sus niveles.

☐ . . . los adelantos mecánicos tuvieron un efecto que sacudió a la comunidad en todos sus niveles.

☐ . . . los adelantos logrados en la construcción de maquinaria tuvieron un efecto acumulativo que sacudió violentamente a la sociedad en todos sus niveles.

d A sense of change had been in the air for some time.

☐ Hacía tiempo que se respiraba una atmósfera de cambio.

☐ Hacía tiempo que soplaron vientos de cambio.

☐ Una sensación de cambio había prevalecido por algún tiempo.

e It was stimulated from many sources, . . .

☐ El estímulo provenía de muchas fuentes, . . .

☐ Era estimulada por muchas fuentes, . . .

☐ Muchas fuentes lo estimularon, . . .

f . . . the American example in setting up . . .

☐ . . . el ejemplo americano de establecer . . .

☐ . . . el ejemplo de los Estados Unidos al establecer . . .

☐ . . . el ejemplo dado por los Estados Unidos al establecer . . .

III Write sentences in English using each of the phrases given below. Then translate your sentences into Spanish.

a about the end of the XIXth century

b the transition from . . . to . . .

c inherent in

d interest in

IV Compare the meaning of the following pairs of words:

emergence	emergencia
community	comunidad
native	nativo

V Translate the passage into Spanish.

45 Me voy pa'l pueblo[22]

Los hijos del asfalto y el cemento, los hombres y mujeres de las grandes ciudades que vieron una gallina por primera vez a[23] los cinco años y creyeron que era un perro con plumas, sienten cada vez con más fuerza la llamada del pueblo. Muchos que emigraron a la ciudad, vuelven generaciones más tarde, a comprar su casa en el pueblo del que huyeron. Las viejas y encantadoras casonas pueblerinas[24] constituyen cada vez más la segunda vivienda de todos aquellos que aprovechan los días libres para huir de la ciudad. Es algo más que una moda: es casi una necesidad para recuperar los raices y encontrar esa identidad que se pierde en la gran ciudad. Para muchos, cada vez, poseer una segunda residencia en el pueblo en el que uno es reconocido como 'don Pablo', 'don Carlos', o 'doña Cristina' tiene más alicientes que poseer el clásico chalet en una prefabricada urbanización de chalets.

Hay casas de pueblo en Aragón, Cataluña, Andalucía, Guadalajara y Extremadura que se venden por relativamente poco dinero (desde 300,000 pesetas). Casi todas tienen patio, huerta, cuadra, o terreno fácilmente convertible en sencillo jardín. El problema es <u>reformar</u> y modernizar el interior y restaurar la fachada.

Cambio 16

I Read the passage carefully, then answer the following question in English. What are the chief reasons why people from the towns are buying houses in the country in increasing numbers?

II Mark the following translations 1, 2, 3, in order of your preference in the context. Mark X any you consider unacceptable. Give a better version if one occurs to you.

a a los cinco años
- ☐ at five years old
- ☐ when they were five years old
- ☐ at the age of five

b cada vez con más fuerza
- ☐ every time with more force
- ☐ with more and more force
- ☐ more and more strongly

c pueblo
- ☐ village
- ☐ people
- ☐ country

d Las viejas y encantadoras casones pueblerinas
- ☐ The charming old village houses
- ☐ The old and charming village houses
- ☐ The old and charming houses of the village

e reformar
- ☐ remodel
- ☐ reform
- ☐ improve

III Translate the passage into English.

46 Country diary

Trudging through[25] *the moorland snow I came to the wreck of a house.*[26] It is a shepherd's house I have known[27] for forty years and it has been empty all that time. When I first saw it there was a roof on it. But time and the upland weather have pulled it apart stone by stone and slate by slate. After the people had gone a pair of barn owls lived there for over twenty years until the rafters fell in. *Such has been the fate not just of this house but of countless others all over the moorland Wales up to about 1,600 feet.* Above that no one lived, for human endurance had its limits even in the harsh poverty of the nineteenth century. And as soon as conditions improved in the twentieth, *humanity ebbed out of*[25] *the uplands with the force of a spring tide* and has never gone back.

So the houses go on mouldering into the ground and already some are only names *to be handed down the generations.*

The Guardian

I   Read the passage carefully, then answer the following questions in English:
What words or phrases are likely to cause trouble when translating? Why?
What is the meaning here of the words: *people, such humanity*?

II   What are the main difficulties in translating the italicized expressions? Is construction or usage the chief problem? Think out three different alternatives to each of them, going from the more literal to the more natural.

III   Translate the passage into Spanish.

Further Exercises

1.   The following verbs denote a certain kind of movement:

crawl	ebb	flow	hobble	ooze	plod	stagger
stride	stroll	tramp	trample	trudge		

Supply the correct form of the appropriate verb in the sentences below.

a   The cows got into the farmer's field, ... through the corn and ruined it.

b   When the tide . . . . we'll be able to walk out to the island.

c   The small child . . . . along patiently beside her grandmother.

d   When James discovered what had happened he was furious and . . . . out of the room in a great rage.

e   The soldiers . . . . along wearily through the deep snow.

f   Keeping under cover of the trees they . . . . round to the back of the house.

g   It was impossible to cross the river at that point; the current . . . . too swiftly.

h   The old man was hungry and weary; he . . . . all the way from London, a distance of some 25 miles.

i   The boy . . . . into the room; he had been shot in the arm and already blood . . . . through the hastily improvised bandage.

j   When Brian saw them they . . . . down the street as though they had all the time in the world.

2.   Translate the above sentences into Spanish.

3.   Translate into English:

a   Me gusta su casa cada vez más.

b   Se pone cada vez más enojado.

c   Las ondas vinieron golpeándo las rocas cada vez con más fuerza.

d   Cada uno prefería la suya.

e   Cada uno tiene que traer cuaderno, lápiz y goma.

Notes

1   See **Pronouns**, Appendix A5.
2   See **The Verb — Tense**, Appendix A7a.
3   See **Prepositions**, Appendix A6.
4   See **Connectives**, Appendix A2.
5   See **Determiners**, Appendix A3.
6   What is the meaning of this phrase?
7   In what sense is *mill* used here?
8   See **Determiners**, Appendix A3.
9   While this could be translated as *Sombre Panorama*, the title *Gloomy Outlook* conveys the idea more clearly and vividly to the English or American reader. Similarly, *periódicamente* is well conveyed by the expression *from time to time*. Note this type of change.
10   See **The Verb — Spanish Reflexive**, Appendix A7d.
11   See **Nouns**, Appendix A4.
12   Note word order.
13   See **Omissions and Insertions**, Appendix B4.
14   See **Adjectives**, Appendix A1.
15   In Spanish a verb would normally be added after *developments*.
16   *economía agrícola y artesanal*
17   *de 1880 en adelante*
18   *el ritmo y la magnitud del cambio*
19   See **The Verb — Tense**, Appendix A7a.
20   *se había vuelto*. Note reflexive form of verb.
21   See **Prepositions**, Appendix A6.
22   Find a colloquial equivalent in English.
23   See **Prepositions**, Appendix A6.
24   Watch word order here.
25   See above, Unit 1, note 9.
26   See **Modulation**, Appendix B6.
27   Watch the translation of verb tenses in this passage.

Unit XII Reviews

47 Un crimen impune

La película así titulada está basada — o acaso solamente inspirada[1] — en una novela de María Luisa Pinares, escritora[2] de brillantes méritos, que imprime siempre a sus relatos un apasionante interés. Pero <u>el traslado de esta novela a la pantalla</u> no ha sido todo lo afortunado que[3] era de esperar.[4] La novela queda como <u>deshilvanada</u>, como se hubiese perdido la <u>vertebración</u> narrativa y la fuerza dramática. En una palabra: carece de ese <u>incentivo inquietante</u> que suele ser inalienable característica[2] de la inteligente narradora.

Los personajes son todos seres de compleja y, en ocasiones, turbia condición. Seres extravagantes o introvertidos, 'snobs', artistas excéntricos, etc. Todos se hallan reunidos en una isla del <u>sudeste español</u>, en donde llevan una vida que tiene más de absurdo e incoherente que de normal. De la mayor parte de ellos apenas sabemos quiénes son, qué hacen o a qué aspiran. Sólo los isleños, que viven abiertamente del contrabando, llevan una vida transparente. . .

Por[5] la técnica entrecortada que ha empleado el director, por las fugaces visiones de una *dolce vita* muy poco comprensible en sitio tan inhóspito, por la singular condición de la mayor parte de los protagonistas, es evidente que nos encontramos ante una película concebida deliberadamente como de *vanguardia*, aunque en este caso la novedad radique más bien en la oscuridad del relato que en el interés artístico del film.

Para llevar a la pantalla esta obra, ha sido reclutado un excelente equipo artístico del que pudo haberse sacado mucho mayor partido. Pero el director no ha conseguido que ninguno de ellos rebase, en cuanto a esfuerzo representativo, un nivel mediocre.

La Vanguardia Española, Barcelona, España (adapted)

I Read the review carefully and summarize for yourself the writer's opinion of the film. Many of the words are used figuratively. Think out exactly what they mean in this context.

II Mark the following translations 1, 2, 3, in order of your preference in this context. Mark X any you consider definitely unacceptable. Give a better version if one occurs to you.

a el traslado de esta novela a la pantalla
  □ the transfer of this novel to the screen
  □ the filming of this novel
  □ the screening of this novel
b deshilvanada
  □ disjointed
  □ disconnected
  □ incoherent
c vertebración
  □ vertebration
  □ articulation
  □ thread
d incentivo inquietante,
  □ disturbing incentive
  □ stimulating motivation
  □ provoking stimulus
e sudeste español
  □ Spanish southeast
  □ southeastern Spain
  □ the southeast of Spain

III Translate the passage into English.

48 *Tarka the Otter* is a very *worthy* but rather <u>dull</u> summary of Henry Williamson's book — worthy because animal photography is extremely difficult and here <u>painstakingly</u> *encompassed* by Terry Channell, John McCallum and Slim MacDonnell; dull because David Cobham, producer, director and screenplay writer with Gerald Durrell, has never quite managed to get fully into Williamson's *lovingly detailed natural world.*[6] Perhaps, in fact, the film was virtually impossible to make. Even so, to add a commentary from Peter Ustinov seems rather unnecessary. If a film needs a story-teller at all, it is *tantamount* to admitting that it can't quite *do the job for itself.*[7]

On the other hand the necessary *skinning* of the story does not do irreversible harm, the river world is skilfully *summoned up* and Tarka himself (Spade) gives a performance of considerable <u>elan</u>. The humans on view[8] are a great deal less attractive (of the unspeakable type, hot in pursuit of the inedible and surely pretty harmless) so that we know whose side we are on[7] from the start.

The children will enjoy it, but you'll have to accompany the younger ones because of the certificate. It is a film that cannot possibly do any harm. But one does wonder, half way through, whether its[9] imagination isn't a poor thing compared with that of Williamson. His words[10] fill in the blank spaces between his images and our own in a way this sort of *literal exposition* can never do on the screen without resort either to *animation* or a more positive, less reverential approach.

Manchester Guardian Weekly

I Read the passage carefully, then answer the following questions in Spanish:
¿ Cuáles son los elementos que el autor elogia?
¿ Cuáles son los que critica?
¿ Qué encuentra el crítico en el libro de Williamson que para él falta en la película?

II   The author uses some words in a rather unusual way to create the effects he wants. Consider carefully the meaning of the italicized words and think of other ways of expressing the same idea.

III   Mark the following translations 1, 2, 3, in order of your preference in this context. Mark X any you consider unacceptable. Give a better version if one occurs to you.

a   dull
   ☐ aburrido
   ☐ insípido
   ☐ pesado
b   painstakingly
   ☐ laboriosamente
   ☐ conscienzudamente
   ☐ con esmero

c   elan
   ☐ brillo
   ☐ pasión
   ☐ entusiasmo

IV   Translate the passage into Spanish.

49   *La comedia sin título*[11] es un intento radicalmente nuevo en la obra de Lorca y en esa novedad consiste el progreso que Martínez Nadal, legatario[11] fiel y exegeta[12] devoto de un texto dificilísimo, echa aquí en falta. Federico escribe en plena conciencia de las limitaciones que se impone: los hambrientos — Marx había insistido en ello[13] —, carecen de sentidos para percibir la belleza de una barca surcando el mar o la fragancia de una flor.

Por eso tantea otro camino, y hace decir al Autor, protagonista de su drama: "El autor no quiere que os sintáis[14] en el teatro sino en mitad de la calle: y no quiere por tanto[15] hacer poesía, ritmo, literatura, quiere dar una pequeña lección a vuestros corazones, para eso es poeta, pero con gran modestia (. . .). El autor sabe hacer versos, los ha hecho a mi juicio bastante buenos y no es mal nombre de teatro, pero ayer me dijo que en todo arte había una mitad de artificio que por ahora le molestaba, y que no tenía gana de traer aquí el perfume de los lirios blancos o la columna salomónica turbia de palomas de oro."

Gaceta Illustrada, F. Lázaro Carreter

I   Read the passage carefully and answer the following questions in English:
What new approach to the theatre does the writer find in Lorca's *Comedia sin título*?
What elements is Lorca proposing to omit?

II   Mark the following translations 1, 2, 3, in order of your preference in this context. Mark X any you consider unacceptable. Give a better version if one occurs to you.

a   echa aquí en falta
   ☐ finds lacking here
   ☐ misses here
   ☐ finds fault with here

b   conciencia
   ☐ conscience
   ☐ consciousness
   ☐ awareness

c surcando el mar
- [ ] furrowing the sea
- [ ] ploughing through the sea
- [ ] sailing on the sea

d hacer versos
- [ ] to make verses
- [ ] to write verses
- [ ] to write poetry

e no es mal nombre de teatro
- [ ] isn't a bad name in the theatre
- [ ] has quite a reputation in the theatre
- [ ] has quite a reputation as a playwright

III Translate the passage into English

50 *Bitter Apples* is a musical about *coming to terms with*[16] the 'seventies having experienced the 'sixties. *It's set in Liverpool*[16] and the cluttered stage, front door to old, large house, living-room and band pushed to the far corner, amply illustrates the mess we thought we could eradicate but now have to face.

The musical makes a plea for positive action[17] despite the destruction of all that seemed so fruitful. It traces the development of Mary, a sixteen-year-old girl who comes into contact with a group of poets and musicians who call themselves the Liverpool Liberation Army. Ironically, when we meet them ten years later — in 1978 — the group is still fighting for freedom *whereas*[18] Mary has already attained it, having started from a far less promising *stand-point*.

It begins *somewhat unsteadily* with the arrival of the group and their habitation of a flat next door to the working-class Leitrim family. Mary Leitrim *builds up a relationship* with Theo, the politically-orientated poet, much to the chagrin of[17] her dominant father who sees any such association as a step backwards. Marching ostensibly forwards with the ten million French workers in Paris, 1968, Theo leaves Mary to fulfill his revolutionary dreams.

Bitter Apples,
Plays and Players, Lucia Crothall

I Read the passage carefully, then answer the following questions in Spanish.
¿ De qué se trata la comedia musical *Bitter Apples*?
¿ Qué le pasa a María?
¿ Cómo empieza la acción?

II Think out carefully the meaning of the italicized expressions. You may need to think of other ways of expressing the same idea.

III Translate the passage into Spanish.

51 En *Las amables veladas con Cecilia* la serie de relatos tiene como denominador común,[19] aparte de Cecilia, oyente silenciosa, las andanzas y el trajín que se trae el narrador por las tierras ibéricas; pueblos y paisajes son escenarios de situaciones y sucesos, cuya descripción refleja la vida desabrida y trágica de la reputada 'áspera y espléndida España' por Camile Mauclair,[19] la 'España negra' — una capa sedimentaria de España — , que asoma en los textos medievales y que toma cuerpo en la novela picaresca, en Quevedo y Cervantes, y que continúa como un guadiana literario[20] hasta nuestro día con Ciro Bayo, Solana, Noel, por citar algunos nombres y más cerca de nosotros, Camila José Cela. Ramón Ayerra, que continúa esta tradición insigne de la estética de lo feo sin caer en el remedo, no desmerece de los más preclaros cultivadores del género. En esta visión esperpéntica de España, cada escritor da su interpretación personal, aunque todos ellos coinciden en algunas características: la expresión descarada, la complacencia en lo sórdido, la propensión a la deformación caricaturesca,[21] todo lo cual implica, sin necesidad de tergiversar la realidad, una selección de materiales y una identificación, a mi juicio, entre las formas de la vida que se quiere reflejar y el empleo del lenguaje. Un lenguaje literario culto, con una riqueza de léxico, giros, modismos y locuciones que adquieren su máximo vigor expresivo en sus contactos con las fuentes del idioma, con el habla de las gentes del estado llano, que aún conserva la fragancia de las significaciones primigenias.

Manuel Cerezales
(ABC, Madrid)

I   Read the passage carefully, then answer the following questions in English.
What is the subject of *Las amables veladas con Cecilia*?
What aspect of Spanish life is described?
What does the critic say about the author's use of language?

II   Which do you consider the best translation of the following words? Why?

a	oyente			b	desabrida		
	hearer	listener	auditor		bleak	hard	dull

III   Translate the passage into English.

52   Not only was Mariano Azuela the first to write about the Revolution and its effects, but in doing so he broke with the novelistic tradition so long in vogue in his country and initiated a new treatment of the novel. In *Los de abajo*, Azuela *etches an approach and a style* that will characterize the cascade of works comprising the Novel of the Mexican Revolution, an output which rather completely dominated the novel from 1925 until about 1945. *Attuned in remarkable degree to the military struggle* and the social upheaval it attempts to mirror and interpret, *Los de abajo* is of course set in the historical reality of the Revolution and is narrated in terse, simple, colloquial language.

Uncomplicated both as to style and to plot, this novel truly reflects the Revolution as it was. And all of the novelists of the Revolution who came after Azuela have continued to tell it the same way. Action takes precedence over description and characterization, conciseness and directness replace the verbosity and sermonizing of the past. As a result, the twentieth-century Mexican novel *emerges with legitimacy and is able to stand on its own feet*.

Not often does one man exert such an influence on the literature of a country. While Azuela was to produce more than twenty novels, it is safe to affirm that his influence on other novelists of the Revolution would have been much the same had he written only *Los de abajo*. And this is not at all intended to downgrade the value and importance of some of his other works. It is simply that *Los de abajo* stands forth from the outset as the bellwether[22] of the novel of the Mexican Revolution.

The Mexican Novel Comes of Age, Walter M. Langford

I   Read the passage carefully, then answer the following questions in Spanish:
¿ Por qué ocupa *Los de abajo* una posición tan importante en la novela mexicana del siglo XX?
¿ En qué consiste la novedad de *Los de abajo*?
¿ Cuáles son los rasgos más importantes de la novela de la Revolución Mexicana?

II   Think out carefully the meaning of the italicized expressions. Which of the following translations of *cascade* is most suitable here? Why?

cascada   volumen   chorro

Notes

1   You will need to include the preposition in English.
2   Definite or indefinite article?
3   See **Transposition**, Appendix B5.
4   See **The Verb — Mood and Modals**, Appendix A7b.
5   Think out your English sentence before deciding which preposition to use.
6   This will need rephrasing.
7   See **Modulation**, Appendix B6.
8   See **Transposition**, Appendix B5.
9   What does *its* refer to?
10   You will need to make clear whose words are referred to.
11   See **Determiners**, Appendix A3.
12   *commentator*
13   See **Pronouns**, Appendix A5.
14   See **The Verb — Mood and Modals**, Appendix A7b.
15   See **Connectives**, Appendix A2.
16   See **Modulation**, Appendix B6.
17   See **Transposition**, Appendix B5.
18   See **Connectives**, Appendix A2.
19   See **Transposition**, Appendix B5.
20   See **Adaptation**, Appendix B7.
21   See **Omissions and Insertions**, Appendix B4.
22   *lit.* the leading sheep of the flock, *fig.* leader.

PART II   Longer Passages for Translation

This section deals with the translation of rather longer passages where language is used mainly to communicate ideas. It contains extracts from topical articles, commentaries, history, philosophy, literary criticism and so forth.

Here the emphasis will be on the accurate translation of the ideas and clear communication of the meaning. As many of the passages are argumentative, students should note the use of balanced sentences, of repetition and contrast, as well as the way sentences are linked. Again, the selection of lexical equivalents for words or phrases will be important as well as the construction of the sentences in the language of the translation.

The passages are arranged in pairs, one Spanish and one English, on similar themes or of a similar type. Students should read both passages and note the differences in the English and Spanish ways of approach before starting to translate. When translating it may be necessary to express the idea in a different way, however the full, exact meaning must be kept. To make sure of the author's meaning it is often useful for the translator to ask 'Who . . . ? What . . . ? When . . . ? Where . . . ? Why . . . ?'

Notes on each passage, with references to the Appendices where appropriate, follow each pair of passages (A and B).

Contents of Part II

A, B   *El sentimiento trágico de la vida*, Miguel de Unamuno

C,   *The Classical Tradition*, Gilbert Highet

1A   'En ninguna forma el tema . . .', Augusto Monterroso, *Plural*

1B   *Scientific and Technical Translation*, Isadore Pinchuck

2A   *La democracia en México*, P. González Casanova

2B   *Democracy*, John Dewey

3A   '1900 el año del optimismo', Mayo Antonio Sánchez

3B   *The Groundwork of British History*, Warner and Marten

4A *El perfil del hombre y la cultura en México*, Samuel Ramos

4B *A History of Latin America*, George Pendle

5A *El pensamiento latinoamericano*, Leopoldo Zea

5B *South America*, Lewis Hanke

6A *Historia general de México*, Lorenzo Meyer

6B *A Shortened History of England*, G. M. Trevelyan

7A *México en una nuez*, Alfonso Reyes

7B *The Aztecs of Mexico*, G. C. Vaillant

8A '¿Quién es ese Huitzilopochtli . . . ?', Ignacio Bernal

8B *The X in Mexico*, Irene Nicholson

9A 'Vivir no consiste sólo en pensar', Juan José Lopez Ibor

9B *The Mind of Man*, Gilbert Highet

10A 'No eran afortunados', Angel Palomino

10B *Selected Essays*, Joyce Cary

11A *Traducción y literalidad*, Octavio Paz

11B *Interpretations of Poetry and Religion*, George Santayana

12A *El arco y la lira*, Octavio Paz

12B *El Hamlet de Shakespeare*, Salvador de Madariaga

12C *The Classical Tradition*, Gilbert Highet

12D *The Wheel of Fire*, G. Wilson Knight

13A *Hacia un concepto de la literatura española*, Guillermo Diaz-Plaja

13B *The Classical Tradition*, Gilbert Highet

14A 'Don Francisco de Goya y los retratos de gran penetración', Antonio Méndez Casal

14B *The Story of Art*, E. H. Gombrich

15A *Lima la horrible*, S. Bondy

15B *Tradition*, T. S. Eliot

Compare the original texts below with the translations which follow them and note the various problems of the translator and how he solves them.

A Hagamos que la nada, si es que nos está reservada, sea una injusticia; peleemos contra el destino, y aun sin esperanza de victoria; peleemos contra él quijotescamente.

Y no sólo se pelea contra él anhelando lo irracional, sino obrando de modo que nos hagamos insustituibles, acuñando en los demás nuestra marca y cifra; obrando sobre nuestros prójimos para dominarlos, dándonos a ellos, para eternizarnos en lo posible.

Ha de ser nuestro mayor esfuerzo el de hacernos insustituibles, si de hacer una verdad práctica el hecho teórico — si es que esto de hecho teórico no envuelve una contradicción *in adiecto* — de que es cada uno de nosotros único e irremplazable, de que no pueda llenar otro el hueco que dejamos al morirnos.

Cada hombre es, en efecto, único e insustituible; otro yo no puede darse; cada uno de nosotros — nuestra alma, no nuestra vida — vale por el Universo todo. Y digo el espíritu y no la vida, porque el valor, ridículamente excesivo, que concedan a la vida humana los que no creyendo en realidad en el espíritu, es decir en su inmortalidad personal, peroran contra la guerra y contra la pena de muerte, v.gr., es un valor que se lo conceden precisamente por no creer de veras en el espíritu, a cuyo servicio está la vida. Porque sólo sirve la vida en cuanto a su dueño y señor, el espíritu, sirve, y si el dueño perece con la sierva, ni uno ni otro valen gran cosa.

Y el obrar de modo que sea nuestra aniquilación una injusticia, que nuestros hermanos, hijos y los hijos de nuestros hermanos y sus hijos, reconozcan que no debimos haber muerto, es algo que está al alcance de todos.

El sentimiento trágico de la vida, Miguel de Unamuno

If it is nothingness that awaits us, let us make an injustice of it; let us fight against destiny, even though without hope of victory; let us fight against it quixotically.

And not only do we fight against destiny in longing for what is irrational, but in acting in such a way that we make ourselves irreplaceable, in impressing our seal and mark upon others, in acting upon our neighbours in order to dominate them, in giving ourselves to them in order that we may eternalize ourselves so far as we can.

Our greatest endeavour must be to make ourselves irreplaceable; to make the theoretical fact — if this expression does not involve a contradiction in terms -- the fact that each one of us is unique and irreplaceable, that no one else can fill the gap that will be left when we die, a practical truth.

For in fact each man is unique and irreplaceable; there cannot be any other I; each one of us — our soul, that is, not our life — is worth the whole Universe. I say the spirit and not the life, for the ridiculously exaggerated value which those attach to human life who, not really believing in the spirit — that is to say, in their personal immortality — tirade against war and the death penalty, for example, is a value which they attach to it precisely because they do not really believe in the spirit of which life is the servant. For life is of use only in so far as it serves its lord and master, spirit, and if the master perishes with the servant, neither the one nor the other is of any great value.

And to act in such a way as to make our annihilation an injustice, in such a way as to make our brothers, our sons, and our brothers' sons, and their sons' sons, feel that we ought not to have died, is something that is within the reach of all.

The Tragic Sense of Life, Miguel de Unamuno,
(Translator anonymous)

Here the writer is trying to persuade the reader to share his opinion and to modify his approach to life. His position is closely argued as he builds up his case. Note how the translator has conveyed this in English. Note the clarity and force given to the appeal of the first sentence by the shift in position of the 'if' clause and the inclusion in it of 'nothingness'; the use of 'nothingness' rather than 'nothing' also adds weight. The repetition in 'let us make . . .', 'let us fight . . .', 'let us fight . . .' gives emphasis, and the translation of 'y aun' as 'even though' strengthens the appeal still further.

In paragraph 2 the continuity of the argument is preserved in English by the translation of the impersonal 'se pelea' by 'we fight'. Since English 'it' is unemphatic the translator has repeated the word 'destiny' to give the force of the emphatic 'él'. Note also the repetition of the preposition: 'in acting . . .', 'in impressing . . .', 'in giving . . .'.

The repetition of 'fact' to translate the Spanish 'de que' in paragraph 3 and the placing of 'a practical truth' at the end of the sentence give the English passage greater coherence. The translation of 'otro yo no puede darse' as 'there can be no other I', 'peroran contra la guerra' as 'tirade against war' and 'a cuyo servicio está la vida' as 'of which life is the servant' are also worth noting.

B   Y en la segunda mitad del pasado siglo XIX, época infilosófica y tecnicista, dominada por especialismo miope y por el materialismo histórico, ese ideal se tradujo en una obra no ya de vulgarización sino de avulgaramiento científico — o más bien pseudo-científico — que se desahogaba en democráticas bibliotecas baratas y sectarias. Quería así popularizarse la ciencia como si hubiese de ser ésta la que haya de bajar al pueblo y servir sus pasiones, y no el pueblo el que debe subir a ella y por ella más arriba aún, a nuevos y más profundos anhelos.

Todo esto llevó a Brunetière a proclamar la bancarrota de la ciencia, y esa ciencia o lo que fuere, bancarroteó en efecto. Y como ella no satisfacía, no dejaba de buscarse la felicidad; sin encontrarla en la riqueza, ni en el saber, ni en el poderío, ni en el goce; ni en la resignación, ni en la buena conciencia moral, ni en la cultura. Y vino el pesimismo.

El progresismo no satisfacía tampoco. Progresar, ¿para qué? El hombre no se conformaba con lo racional, el *Kulturkampf* no le bastaba; quería dar finalidad final a la vida, que esta que llamo la finalidad final es el verdadero ὄντως ὄν. Y la famosa *maladie du siècle*, que se anuncia en Rousseau, y acusa más claramente que nadie al *Obermann* de Sénancour, no era ni es otra cosa que la pérdida de la fe en la inmortalidad del alma, en la finalidad humana del Universo.

El sentimiento trágico de la vida, Miguel de Unamuno

And in the second half of the nineteenth century, an age essentially unphilosophical and technical, dominated by a myopic specialism and by historical materialism, this ideal took a practical form, not so much in the popularization as in the vulgarization of science — or, rather, of pseudo-science — venting itself in a flood of cheap, popular, and propagandist literature. Science sought to popularize itself as if it were its function to come down to the people and subserve their passions, and not the duty of the people to rise to science and through science to rise to higher heights, to new and profounder aspirations.

All this led Brunetière to proclaim the bankruptcy of science, and this science — if you like to call it science — did in effect become bankrupt. And as it failed to satisfy, men continued their quest for happiness, but without finding it, either in wealth, or in knowledge, or in power, or in pleasure, or in resignation, or in a good conscience, or in culture. And the result was pessimism.

Neither did the gospel of progress satisfy. What end did progress serve? Man would not accommodate himself to rationalism; the *Kulturkampf* did not suffice him; he sought to give a final finality to life, and what I call the final finality is the real ὄντως ὄν. And the famous *maladie du siècle,* which announced itself in Rousseau and was exhibited more plainly in Sénancour's *Obermann* than in any other character, neither was nor is anything else but the loss of faith in the immortality of the soul, in the human finality of the Universe.

The Tragic Sense of Life, Miguel de Unamuno

Here, again, the writer is concerned with expressing ideas, so the task of the translator is to communicate these fully and <u>clearly</u>. Notice how 'el pasado siglo XIX' is translated by the more natural English 'the nineteenth century', and note the addition of 'essentially' in the next phrase whereas this is only implied in the Spanish. Observe that words which are similar in root and form do not always have the same significance in the two languages: e.g. 'vulgarización' / 'popularization', and 'avulgaramiento' / vulgarization'. See also 'democráticas bibliotecas baratas y sectarias' / 'cheap, popular and propagandist literature'. Note how 'a lo que fuere' is translated by 'if you like to call it so' and how in 'no dejaba de burscarse' the Spanish reflexive, which has no parallel English construction, is rendered by '*men* continued their quest for'.

C   Translation, that neglected art, is a far more important element in literature than most of us believe. It does not usually create great works; but it often helps great works to be created. In the Renaissance, the age of masterpieces, it was particularly important. . . . . .

The intellectual importance of translation is so obvious that it is often overlooked. No language, no nation, is sufficient unto itself. Its mind must be enlarged by the thoughts of other nations, or else It will warp and shrivel. In English, as in other languages, many of the greatest ideas we use have been brought in through translation. The central book of the English-speaking peoples is a translation — although it comes as a shock to many to realise that the Bible was written in Hebrew and Greek, and translated by a committee of scholars. There are many great books which none but specialists need read in the original, but which through translation have added essential ideas to our minds: Euclid's *Elements*, Descartes' *Discourse on Method*, Marx's *Capital*, Tolstoy's *War and Peace*.

The artistic and linguistic importance of translation is almost as great as its importance in the field of ideas. To begin with, the practice of translation usually enriches the translator's language with new words. This is because most translations are made from a language with a copious vocabulary into a poorer language which must be expanded by the translator's courage and inventiveness.

The Classical Tradition, Gilbert Highet

La traducción, ese arte rezagado, se antoja como elemento mucho más importante en la literatura de lo que muchos creemos. No suele generar grandes obras, pero con frecuencia contribuye a crearlas. Durante el Renacimiento — época de obras maestras — desempeñó un papel primordialmente importante.

La trascendencia intelectual de la traducción es tan obvia, que a menudo se la pasa por alto. Ninguna lengua, ninguna nación es autosuficiente. Cada pueblo debe enriquecerse con el pensamiento de otras naciones, so pena de desvirtuarse y marchitarse. En inglés, como en otras lenguas, muchas de las ideas capitales que manejamos fueron introducidas al través de la traducción. La obra cardinal de los pueblos anglófonos es una traducción aunque muchos se sientan sacudidos al percatarse de que la Biblia fue escrita en hebreo y griego y traducida por un conjunto de eruditos. Bastantes obras hay que sólo los especialistas requieren leer en el original y que, mediante la traducción, nos han enriquecidos con ideas esenciales: los *Elementos*, de Euclides, el *Discurso del método*, de Descartes, *El capital*, de Marx, y *Guerra y paz*, de Tolstoy.

La trascendencia artística y linguística de la traducción es casi tan grande como su importancia en el campo de las ideas. En primer término, la práctica de la traducción suele enriquecer la lengua del traductor con nuevos vocablos. Por ello, la mayor parte de las traducciones provienen de un idioma con copioso vocabulario a otra lengua más pobre a la que el valor y la inventiva del traductor deben ampliar.

La tradición clásica, Gilbert Highet,
(translated by Raul Ortiz y Ortiz)

This text is an excerpt from a very erudite chapter the author dedicates to translation in his book *The Classical Tradition*. The paragraphs we have selected concern the importance of translation in shaping up languages and ideas. The statements are very clear and do not appear to present problems of interpretation. However you will notice that some turns of phrase, typical of English, have been somewhat altered in Spanish. In getting away from a literal rendering of such expressions, the translator has attempted to state the identical concepts by means of turns of phrase which would suggest themselves more naturally to the Spanish speaker.

Consider the convenience of using 'so pena de' for 'or else'. Why do you think the translator has preferred 'manejamos' to 'usamos'?

Is it impossible to say 'el libro central'? If not, what, in your opinion, made the translator choose the expression 'la obra cardinal'?

The original does not mention in this sentence the verb 'enrich'. Was it necessary to have used it in Spanish? Had this sentence been translated as 'suele enriquecer el léxico del traductor . . .' would it have made any difference to the meaning?

1A En ninguna forma el tema de estas lineas serán[1] las divertidas equivocaciones en que con frecuencia incurren los traductores.[2] Se ha escrito ya tanto sobre esto que ese mismo hecho demuestra la inutilidad de hacerlo de nuevo. La experiencia humana no es acumulativa. Cada dos generaciones se plantearán y discutirán los mismos problemas y teorías, y siempre habrá tontos que traduzcan bien y sabios que de vez en cuando metan la pata.

Desde que por primera vez traté de traducir algo me convencí de que si con alguien hay que ser paciente y comprensivo es con los traductores, seres por lo general más bien melancólicos y dubitativos. Cuando digamos en media página me encontré consultando el diccionario en no menos de cinco ocasiones, sentí tanta compasión por quienes viven de ese trabajo que juré no ser nunca uno de ellos, a pesar de que finalmente he terminado traduciendo más de un libro.

Estamos en un mundo de traducciones del que hoy ya no podemos escapar. Lo que para Boscánera un pasatiempo cortesano, para Unamuno resultaba un imperativo ineludible. En el siglo XVI Boscán se afanaba en dar a conocer a los españoles las leyes que dictan los buenos modales, puestas en orden por Baltasar Castiglione: Unamuno, en el XX, las que rigen el comportamiento humano, según Arturo Schopenhauer. O sea la diferencia que va de moverse en un salón de baile a hacerlo en el Universo.

Plural, Augusto Monterroso

I Read the passage carefully, then consider the following questions.
Why does the writer feel sympathy for translators?
How has the general attitude towards translation changed in the last four centuries?
What is the subject of each sentence? Consider the normal English order of words and phrases. Are there any words in Spanish which could be omitted from the English version *without changing the meaning*? Is it necessary to add any words in English to make the meaning clear?

II Mark the following translations 1, 2, 3, in order of your preference in the context. Mark X beside any you consider unacceptable. Give a better version if one occurs to you.

a se plantearán . . . los mismos problemas
    ☐ the same problems will arise
    ☐ the same problems will be discussed
    ☐ the same problems will come up

b metan la pata
    ☐ put their foot in it
    ☐ make silly mistakes
    ☐ poke their noses into it

c comprensivo
    ☐ comprehensive
    ☐ sympathetic
    ☐ understanding

d se afanaba en
    ☐ struggled to
    ☐ strove hard to
    ☐ exerted himself to

III Translate the passage into English.

1B There are also a number of problems of a more practical nature. When Ortega speaks of the 'misery and splendour' of translation, he is thinking mainly of literary work. Technical translation *would seem on the face of it*[3] to have more misery than splendour about it. It is not as exciting as literary translation, which is a creative, artistic activity. It does not offer the most glamorous of careers. This is one reason why there is a shortage of properly qualified technical translators. Another reason is the incorrect conception of translating prevalent among the general public, which tends to lower the status of technical translators. In fact technical translation demands high qualifications *if it is to be done properly.*[4] *While*[5] it is no more to be compared with aesthetic translation than the writing of a scientific paper is to be compared with writing a poem, *it does*[6] *have* a creative element; it demands intelligence, ingenuity and a great deal of knowledge. *While*[5] it involves much routine work, *it does*[6] *have* its moments of 'splendour'. Since it is primarily concerned with the transfer of information, *it goes without saying* that any specialized knowledge is a great advantage for translating — in that field, and perhaps in related fields. Naturally one must also have a good knowledge of one's own language and the foreign language. There is also such a thing as a *flair* for translating, though this is hard to define.

Scientific and Technical Translation, Isadore Pinchuck

I   Read the passage carefully, then answer the following questions in Spanish:
¿ Por qué, según el autor, hay una insuficiencia de personas capacitadas para traducir materia técnica?
¿ Cuáles son las cualidades que debe poseer un experto en traducción técnica?

II   Think out carefully the Spanish equivalents of the italicized expressions.

III   Translate the passage into Spanish.

Notes

1   Watch word order.
2   See **Transposition**, Appendix B5.
3   See **Transposition**, Appendix B5.
4   This sentence will need rephrasing.
5   What is the meaning of *while* here?
6   How can you convey in Spanish the emphasis given to the English by *does*?

2A   Evidentemente la ideología del *liberalismo*, que considera a todos los *indígenas* como iguales ante el derecho,[1] constituye un avance muy grande frente a[1] las ideas racistas prevalencientes en la colonia. En la misma forma la ideología de la revolución constituye un avance no menos importante frente a las ideas darwinistas y racistas del *porfirismo*.[2] Hoy el problema indígena es abordado como un problema cultural. Ningún investigador o dirigente nacional de México piensa — por fortuna — que sea un problema racial, *innato*. La movilidad social y política del país ha llevado a hombres de raza indígena a los más altos *cargos* y les ha permitido alcanzar el 'status' social más elevado en la sociedad mexicana. Este fenómeno se ha dado desde la independencia y, particularmente, desde la revolución. Incluso la historiografía nacional y el culto de los héroes, han colocado entre sus más altos símbolos a Cuauhtémoc, el líder de la resistencia contra los españoles y a Juárez, el presidente indio, el constructor del México moderno.

La democracia en México, González Casanova

I   Read the passage carefully and answer the following questions in English:
What is the subject of this passage?
What is the main point made by the writer?
What will be the priority of the translator?

II   Consider carefully the translation of the italicized words and make sure that the English sentences express the meaning of the original clearly.

III   Translate the passage into English.

2B   The development of political democracy came about through substitution of the method of mutual consultation and voluntary agreement for the method of subordination of the many to the few enforced from above.[3] Social arrangements which involve fixed subordination are maintained by coercion. The coercion need not be physical. There have existed, for short periods, benevolent despotisms.[4] But coercion of some sort there has been;[5] perhaps economic, certainly psychological and moral. The very fact of exclusion from participation is a subtle form of suppression. It gives individuals no opportunity to reflect and decide upon what is good for them. Others who are supposed to be wiser, and who in any case have more power decide the question for them and also decide the methods and means by which subjects[6] may arrive at the enjoyment of what is good for them. This form of coercion and suppression is more subtle and more effective than is overt intimidation and restraint. When it is habitual and embodied in social institutions, it seems the normal and natural state of affairs. The mass usually becomes unaware that they have a claim to a development of their own powers. Their experience is so restricted that they are not conscious of restriction. It is part of the democratic conception that they as individuals are not the only sufferers, but that the whole social body is deprived of the potential resources that should be at its service. The individuals of the submerged mass may not be very wise. But there is one thing they are wiser about than anybody else can be, and that is where the shoe pinches, the troubles they suffer from.

Democracy, John Dewey

I   Read the passage carefully, then answer the following questions in Spanish:
¿ Cómo se desarrolló la democracia política?
¿ Cómo lograron las autoridades mantener el despotismo?
¿ Qué pasa cuando es benevolente el despotismo?
¿ Qué es lo que sabe mejor que nadie el individuo?

II   Think about how you would translate the following words:

| Your Honour | District Attorney | Sheriff | Deputy |
| representative | Delegate | | |

In texts rich in legal terms one has to be exceedingly careful because although there may be similarities between institutions in two different countries, their nomenclature, mechanism and effects may turn out to be entirely different, or vice versa in point of fact.

Notes

1   See **Prepositions**, Appendix A6.
2   Spanish has a number of words ending in -*ismo* which have no parallel in English. Here a possible translation is *of the Porfirian period*.
3   There are rather a lot of abstract nouns with similar endings in this first sentence: *development, agreement; substitution, consultation, subordination*. Rephrase and use verbs for some of them in Spanish, for example: *Political democracy developed when* . . .
4   Here is a group of short sentences. It is better to combine some of them in Spanish.
5   The position of *there has been* makes it emphatic. How can you convey this emphasis in Spanish?
6   What is the meaning of *subjects* here?

3A   La Revolución Industrial había cambiado la faz del globo <u>al surgir el maquinismo</u>[1] que presidiría[2] cada vez más[3] la vida del hombre. También <u>se mudaron los valores espirituales con</u> teorías científicas revolucionarias, cambios radicales en la literatura, la música y la pintura, filosofías materialistas y positivistas que sacudían en sus cimientos la estructura ideológica del siglo.[4]
    . . . muchos creían adivinar <u>que todo ello no era sino</u> el prólogo de[5] lo que habría[2] de traer el siglo XX. Los prodigios del siglo XIX eran la simiente de los frutos <u>que se esperaba cosechar en el siglo venidero</u>, y así como algunas sectas religiosas creían que el fin de siglo anunciaría[2] el fin del mundo, la mayoría de los habitantes del planeta, llevada por[6] su espíritu romántico y con una deliciosa falta de lógica <u>que dejaba de lado lo</u>[7] <u>irremisible</u> de los procesos históricos, esperaba que de un modo milagroso[8] el nuevo siglo trajera automáticamente la felicidad para todos. De esa manera, aunque el año 1900 no fue básicamente distinto de 1899 o 1901, el redondeamiento de la centuria se antoja oportuno para hacer un corte transversal de la sociedad humana en un momento dado.
                    1900 el año del optimismo', *Revista de Geografía Universal,*
                                                    Mayo Antonio Sánchez

I   **Read the passage carefully and answer the following questions in English:**
What changes had taken place in the 19th century according to the author?
What did many people expect of the new century?
Why were they likely to be disappointed?

II   **Mark the following translations 1, 2, 3, in order of your preference in this context. Mark X any you consider unacceptable. Give a better alternative if one occurs to you.**
a   al surgir el maquinismo
        ☐ at the rise of machinery
        ☐ with the coming of mechanization
        ☐ with the rise of mechanism
b   . . . se mudaron los valores espirituales con . . .
        ☐ . . . spiritual values changed as . . .

☐ . . . spiritual values were changed by . . .
☐ . . . spiritual values changed with . . .
c que todo ello no era sino . . .
    ☐ that all that wasn't but . . .
    ☐ that that was all but . . .
    ☐ that all that was merely . . .
d que se esperaba cosechar en el siglo venidero
    ☐ that they hoped to harvest in the coming century
    ☐ that were to be reaped in the coming century
    ☐ that they expected to gain in the future century
e que dejaba de lado lo irremisible de . . .
    ☐ which set aside the irremissible of . . .
    ☐ which left on one side the irremissible thing about . . .
    ☐ which ignored the inexorable nature of . . .

III Translate the passage into Spanish.

3B New methods in agriculture, new inventions in manufactures,[9] improved means of communication, all had their share in developing the prosperity[10] of Great Britain, and in justifying the name usually applied to this period in England's economic history, that of the 'Industrial Revolution'. The influence of the great wars, however, in developing commerce must not be forgotten. 'War fosters commerce, and commerce fosters war', is the dictum of a distinguished historian; and though this may not apply to the modern world, this statement was true at this time of Great Britain, which was never invaded. In every war imports and exports increased; and above all *there was an immense extension of merchant shipping*, which was to become in the nineteenth century, the country's most important industry. The development of commerce was especially striking during the wars between 1793 and 1815. *British shippers had the monopoly of the carrying trade;*[10] because under no other European flag were goods even moderately safe. British manufacturers were encouraged by the needs of war and by the practical suspension of manufactures in many parts of the Continent. British farmers, *secure from foreign competition*, obtained high prices for their *corn*. Great Britain indeed obtained during these years a lead which she was not to lose for some time.

The Groundwork of British History, Warner and Marten

I Read the text carefully, then answer the following questions in Spanish:
¿ Qué factores contribuyeron a la prosperidad de la Gran Bretaña durante la Revolución Industrial?
¿ Por qué se desarrolló tan rápidamente la marina mercante británica durante ese período?
¿ Qué condiciones favorecieron a los fabricantes y a los agricultores británicos en aquella época?

II Think out carefully the meaning of the italicized expressions.

III Translate the passage into Spanish.

Notes

1 The suffix *-ismo* has a much wider range than the corresponding *-ism*. Note the difference between *machinery*, *mechanism* and *mechanization*, and choose the most suitable in the context.
2 See **The Verb — Tense**, Appendix A7b.
3 See **Adjectives**, Appendix A1.
4 This whole sentence will need rephrasing. Make sure you know what it means.
5 Watch preposition here.
6 *carried away by*
7 See **Pronouns**, Appendix A5.
8 See **Determiners**, Appendix A3.
9 See **Omissions and Insertions**, Appendix B4.
10 Rephrase.

4A En el desarrollo de la cultura en América debemos distinguir dos etapas: una primera de *trasplantación*, y una segunda de *asimilación*.[1] No todas las culturas se han creado mediante el mismo proceso genético. Algunas de ellas, las más antiguas, han germinado y crecido en el mismo suelo que sustenta sus raíces. Otras, las más modernas, se han constituido con[2] el injerto de materiales extraños que provienen de una cultura pretérita, la cual, rejuvenecida por la nueva savia, se convierte en otra forma viviente del espíritu humano. Para que podamos decir[3] que en un país se ha formada una cultura derivada, es preciso que los elementos seleccionados de la cultura original sean ya parte inconsciente del espíritu de aquel país. Entendemos por cultura no solamente las obras de la pura actividad espiritual <u>desinteresada de la realidad</u>, sino también otras formas de la acción que están inspiradas por el espíritu. Desde este punto de vista,[2] la vida mexicana, a partir de la época colonial, tiende a encauzarse dentro de formas cultas traídas de Europa. Los vehículos más poderosos de esta trasplantación fueron dos: el idioma y la religión. Fueron estos los dos objectivos fundamentales de la educación emprendida por los misioneros españoles que, <u>en una hazaña memorable</u>, <u>realizaron</u> en el siglo XIX la 'conquista espiritual' de México.

El perfil del hombre y la cultura en México,
Samuel Ramos

I   Read the passage carefully, then answer the following questions in English:
How does Samuel Ramos explain the two stages in the development of American culture?
Does he consider that Latin American culture is native or derivative?
What does he include in the term 'culture'?
What were the two most powerful vehicles of the transplanted culture?

II   Mark the following translations 1, 2, 3, in order of your preference in the context. Mark X any you consider unacceptable. Give a better version if one occurs to you.

a   desinteresada de la realidad
  ☐ apart from reality
  ☐ separated from reality
  ☐ detached from reality

b   en una hazaña memorable
  ☐ in a memorable achievement
  ☐ in a memorable exploit
  ☐ in a memorable deed

c   realizaron
    ☐ realised
    ☐ achieved
    ☐ carried out

III   Translate the passage into English.

4B   Until the second decade of the twentieth century there was little change in the social or political structure of any of the Latin American countries, the mass of the people continuing to regard <u>government as not for them</u>. (In many regions even now the majority, if they had the chance to express a choice, would prefer to support an effective dictatorship rather than to entrust their fate to party politicians.) Wealth and power generally remained in the hands of the landowning oligarchy and their military allies, <u>with the addition of a new class</u>, the leaders of business, whose interests sometimes conflicted with those of the landowning families but whose views on labour were usually just as conservative. In many of the republics the introduction of foreign capital and the coming of foreign immigrants had a profound effect on economic development; but the foreign investors and <u>settlers</u> naturally had a horror of any kind of social upheaval, and so their sympathies were with the local groups that resisted social change.

By the beginning of the present century 'reform' had begun to acquire a more radical meaning. Equality in law, free elections and universal education <u>would not be enough</u>. There was a growing demand for the redistribution of land, and then for the fixing of minimum wages, and for social insurance. Reformers were becoming increasingly insistent,[4] too, that the <u>hold</u> of the foreigner on the national economy must be broken. Indeed — as in other parts of the world during periods of social change — national feelings[5] frequently predominated.

'Social Reform and Revolution', in *A History of Latin America*,
George Pendle

I   Read the passage carefully, then answer the following questions in Spanish:
¿ Por qué fue lenta la evolución social y política de América Latina?
¿ Por qué prevalecieron las ideas conservadoras?
¿ Qué cambios piden los reformadores en el siglo XX?

II   Mark the following translations 1, 2, 3 etc. in order of your preference in the context. Mark X any you consider unacceptable. Give a better version if one occurs to you.

a   ... government as not for them
    ☐ el gobierno no les afectaba
    ☐ no tenían nada que ver con el gobierno
    ☐ el gobierno no era su responsabilidad

b   with the addition of a new class
    ☐ inclusive un nuevo grupo
    ☐ más una nueva clase
    ☐ y además un nuevo grupo
    ☐ con una nueva clase adicional

c settlers
  ☐ colonizadores
  ☐ inmigrantes
  ☐ colonos
d ... would not be enough
  ☐ no bastaban
  ☐ no eran suficientes
  ☐ eran insuficientes
  ☐ eran raquíticas

e hold
  ☐ dominio
  ☐ acaparamiento
  ☐ influencia
  ☐ monopolio

III Translate the passage into Spanish.

Notes

1 See **Omissions and Insertions**, Appendix B4.
2 See **Prepositions**, Appendix A6.
3 See **Transposition**, Appendix B5.
4 See **Adverbs**, Appendix A8.
5 What is the exact meaning of *national feelings* here?

5A Pero a mediados del siglo XX, y coincidiendo con el fin de la segunda gran guerra y la problemática que ésta originó en el pensamiento y filosofía de América Latina, vuelve a surgir el problema de la posibilidad o existencia de una cultura originalmente[1] latinoamericana. Por primera vez en la historia, esta América[2] y Europa se encontraban en el mismo plano, en la situación de tener que hacer o rehacer su cultura. El modelo cultural europeo no era ya un gran modelo, los mismos europeos aceptaban la fragilidad de una cultura que no había servido para evitar la catástrofe de la guerra y sus horrores. Ahora, tanto europeos como americanos,[3] tenían que preocuparse por apuntalar las bases de una cultura que fuese[4] menos frágil que la que hasta ayer parecía modelo para la eternidad. Europeos y americanos tenían que partir, no de cero, sino de las propias y concretas experiencias para no repetir errores, ni crear nuevos espejismos. La filosofía europea de la posguerra mostraba, por un lado, la relatividad de las expresiones culturales del hombre y, por el otro, la necesidad de partir del hombre mismo, como concreción,[5] como un ente en permanente rehacerse. Era menester partir del hombre en circunstancia o en situación. Será en este sentido que los latinoamericanos reinsistan, como la generación que los antecedió al inicio de nuestro siglo XX, en conocer su realidad, en buscar su propia identificación.

El pensamiento latinoamericano, Leopoldo Zea

I **Read the passage carefully, then answer the following questions in English:**
What is the question in the author's mind at the beginning of this passage?
Why were the peoples of both America and Europe disillusioned after the Second Great War?
What task did they face?

Express in your own words the idea contained in the sentence beginning 'La filosofía europea . . .'
Consider carefully the idea expressed by 'conocer su realidad'. You may find it best to translate both 'realidad' and 'identificación' by clauses.

II   **Think out carefully exactly what the author means by the following expressions:**

la problemática   problema   apuntalar   espejismos

III   **Translate the passage into English.**

5B   Writers in the twenty nations to the south of the United States have been much preoccupied with the question of what to call themselves and the lands they live in. They resent United States citizens appropriating the term 'American', and yet no general description has been devised to include Portuguese-speaking Brazil, the Spanish American Republics, and French-speaking Haiti except the term Latin America, at best a tolerated misnomer. Luis Alberto Sánchez, the Peruvian intellectual, has written a book entitled ¿ *Existe América Latina?* His conclusion is[6] that Latin America does not, in fact, exist. The culture of the area, he holds, is Indian and Iberian (Spanish and Portuguese). 'Latin America' came into vogue among the newly emancipated nations during the nineteenth century as a reaction against the mother countries,[7] and in favour of French (Latin) culture which reigned almost supreme and still greatly attracts intellectuals in many parts of the continent. Sánchez considers that 'Latin America' cannot properly be used to label an area where millions of Indians, mestizos, and Negroes live who have no connection with the 'white, European, viceregal, and absolutist tradition' which he believes the term 'Latin America' connotes.

Whatever the truth may be[8] — and there are those who challenge the statement just made — one sees in the countries of Latin America today a great surge of determination to develop their own way of life. In the past they have attempted to absorb other cultures; now they would adapt foreign techniques only in order to attain situations which express their own individualities and reflect their own realities.

'Does Latin America Exist?', in *South America*
Lewis Hanke

I   **Read the text carefully, then answer the following questions in Spanish:**
¿ Por qué no se considera apropiado el nombre 'Latin America'?
¿ Quiénes lo escogieron?
¿ Por qué circunstancias históricas optaron por esta designación?

II   **Mark the following translations 1, 2, 3 etc. in order of your preference in the context. Mark X any you consider unacceptable. Give a better version if one occurs to you.**

a   a misnomer
  ☐ un nombre erróneo

c   came into vogue
  ☐ se hizo la moda

    ☐ un nombre inapropiado   ☐ se puso de moda
    ☐ un nombre equivocado   ☐ llegó a ser la moda

b he holds   **d** challenge
    ☐ afirma   ☐ poner en tela de juicio
    ☐ opina   ☐ rechazan
    ☐ tiene   ☐ impugnan
    ☐ sostiene   ☐ desafían
    ☐ declara   ☐ controvierten

III   Translate the passage into Spanish.

Notes

1   Make sure the adverb is given its full meaning.
2   Obviously Latin America is referred to here.
3   See **Stock Phrases**, Appendix B8.
4   See **The Verb — Mood and Modals**, Appendix A7b.
5   What is the meaning of *concreción* here? You may need a phrase to translate.
6   See **Transposition**, Appendix B5.
7   What is the meaning of *mother countries* here?
8   See **Pronouns**, Appendix A5.

6A   La tranquilidad social en el campo mexicano a partir de la Revolución fue[1] en buena medida producto de la reforma agraria. La gran masa campesina quedó dividida entre los ejidatarios[2] y los minifundistas por un lado, y los jornaleros sin tierra por el otro; los primeros neutralizaron el descontento y acción que podían haber surgido de los segundos debido al hecho de que habían sido incorporados, aunque en medida muy precaria, al[3] sistema de privilegios. Frente a[4] ellos se desarrolló una 'gran propiedad', nunca tan extensa como la antigua hacienda pero relativamente capitalizada y[5] que se convirtió en la principal fuente de los productos demandados por los mercados urbanos y de exportación. Hasta 1970 se habían repartido 80 millones de hectáreas, la tierra aún afectable era ya poca; de ahí que[6] la masa no beneficiada por la reforma agraria aumentara[1] a un ritmo más rápido que la otra. Un fenómeno semejante ocurrió con los marginados de las zonas urbanas. Las tendencias del crecimiento demográfico y del desarrollo de la economía hicieron que su importancia relativa fuera en aumento.

    El problema de la incorporación al proceso productivo de una población siempre en aumento tuvo repercusiones no sólo en los grupos marginales, sino que pareció afectar incluso a sectores de las clases medias. Estas, con una capacidad mayor para articular sus demandas, fueron las que provocaron algunos de los conflictos políticos más espectaculares del período. Empezaron a surgir en la década de los cincuenta entre algunos de los sectores obreros más organizados y privilegiados, como los ferrocarrileros, y grupos de clase media particularmente vulnerables, como los maestros de enseñanza primaria. Las manifestaciones de descontento continuaron en la década siguiente y culminaron con las demostraciones antigubernamentales masivas en la capital durante el verano de 1968.

Historia general de México, Lorenzo Meyer

I   Read the passage carefully, then answer the following questions in English:
Why has the situation in the Mexican countryside been comparatively peaceful since the Revolution?
What supplied the demands of the urban and export markets?
Why did the numbers not affected by the agrarian reform increase more rapidly?
Which classes became more active in their protests? Why?

II   Mark the following translations 1, 2, 3, in order of your preference in this context. Mark X any you consider unacceptable. Give a better alternative if one occurs to you.

a   debido al hecho de que habían sido incorporados
   ☐ due to the fact that they had been incorporated
   ☐ due to their having been incorporated
   ☐ because they had been incorporated

b   hicieron que su importancia relativa fuera en aumento
   ☐ increased their relative importance
   ☐ made their relative importance increase
   ☐ caused their relative importance to increase

c   en la década de los cincuenta
   ☐ in the fifties
   ☐ in the decade of the fifties
   ☐ in the fifties' decade

III   Translate the passage into English.

6B   Indeed, the great interest that most required protection in the first years of the new century was agriculture. Ever since 1875 foodstuffs from America and all over the world had come flooding into Great Britain on a scale never foreseen in the day of Cobden and Peel, when prices <u>had been steadied, not smashed</u>, by free importation from Europe. But, with the prairies and the pampas developed as Britain's food farm, it was becoming impossible to grow food at a profit in the island. English farm hands, badly paid and housed even in good times, were now deserting the land for the cities at an appalling rate. Great Britain was on the way to becoming urbanized altogether, unlike any other country in the world. A check ought to have been put to this catastrophe,[7] which would be irremediable when once complete. Unfortunately the protection of British agriculture was the proposal that politicians were most afraid to advocate, though something might be done <u>under cover of Colonial Preference</u>. The Free Trade system under which Britain had so long flourished had little regard for agriculture. Food was the currency in which foreign nations and our own Dominions paid for British manufactured goods. And cheap corn and meat was of great value to the wage-earning community. The absence of a democratic peasant-proprietorship like that of the European Continent made it difficult to advocate agricultural Protection. The <u>field labourer, long ill-used by the farmer</u>, scarcely knew whether he wished agriculture to be protected; he could slip off to the nearest town or mining district and get a better wage and eat his cheap food there. The most effective popular appeal of Chamberlain's opponents was <u>the unsavory memory</u> of the old Corn Laws, the fear of dear foodstuffs and the cry of the 'small loaf'. So it is only after the Great War had shaken party traditions and old economic doctrines, and the German submarine had shown the use of the plough in Britain,[8] that any attempt, and that quite insufficient, was made by subsidies and control of imports to maintain food production within the island and so save a little of what is still left of country life, while securing by statute a minimum wage to the field labourer.

A Shortened History of England, G.M. Trevelyan

I   Read the passage carefully, then answer the following questions in Spanish:
¿ Por qué era difícil vivir de la agricultura en Inglaterra durante los primeros años del siglo XX?
¿ Por qué emigraron del campo a las ciudades los jornaleros sin tierra?
¿ Por qué no introdujo el Gobierno leyes para proteger la agricultura?
¿ Cuándo tomó medidas el Gobierno?   Qué medidas tomó?

II   Mark the following translations 1, 2, 3 etc. in order of your preference in the context. Mark X any you find unacceptable. Give a better version if one occurs to you.

a   had been steadied not smashed
☐ se habían controlado no estrellado
☐ se habían estabilizado no aplastado
☐ se habían regularizado no alzado
☐ se habían equilibrado no inflado

b   under cover of Colonial Preference
☐ bajo cubierta de preferencias coloniales
☐ al abrigo de prerrogativas coloniales
☐ encubierto por las prioridades coloniales

c   field labourer
☐ campesino
☐ peón
☐ jornalero
☐ trabajador de campo

d   long ill-used by the farmer
☐ desde tiempo inmemorial maltratado por el granjero
☐ ... por el latifundista
☐ ... por el hacendado

e   unsavory memory
☐ amargo resabio
☐ ingrato recuerdo
☐ insípida memoria

III   Translate the passage into Spanish.

Notes

1   Watch tense
2   those who worked on the *ejidos*
3   Watch preposition here.
4   See **Prepositions**, Appendix A6.

5   Translation of *y* omitted in English.
6   What is the best connective to use here?
7   Rephrase.
8   What is the literal meaning of this metaphorical statement?

7A   Los Aztecas, raza <u>militar</u>, dominaban por el terror a un conjunto de <u>pueblos</u> heterogéneos, y sólo escapaban a su imperio los muy alejados o los muy bravos, como la altiva república de Tlaxcala, cuyos hijos preferían cocinar sus alimentos sin sal a tener trato con los tiranos de Anáhuac.[1] Los Aztecas vivían sobre los despojos de civilizaciones vetustas y misteriosas, cuya tradición ellos mismos habían comenzado a no entender, vaciándola poco a poco de su contenido moral.

Los pueblos americanos, aislados del resto del mundo, habían seguido una evolución diferente a la de Europa, que los colocaba, respecto a ésta, en condiciones de notoria inferioridad. Ignoraban la verdadera metalurgia y desconocían el empleo de la bestia de carga, <u>que era sustituída por el esclavo.</u>[2] Celebraban contratos internacionales para hacerse la guerra de vez en cuando, y tener víctimas humanas que ofrecer a sus dioses. Su sistema de escritura jeroglífica no admitía la fijación de las formas del lenguaje, de suerte que su literatura sólo podía perpetuarse por tradición oral. Ni[3] física ni moralmente podían <u>resistir el encuentro con</u> el europeo. Su colisión contra los hombres que venían de Europa, vestidos de hierro, armados con pólvora y balas y cañones, montados a caballo y sostenidos por Cristo, fue el choque del jarro contra <u>el caldero.</u>[4] El jarro podía ser muy fino y muy hermoso, pero era el más quebradizo.

México en una nuez, Alfonso Reyes
(Fondo de Cultura Economica, Mexico)

I   Read the passage carefully and answer the following questions in English:
What does the author tell us about the Indians who inhabited Mexico at the time of the Conquest?
Which of the nearby tribes managed to escape the rule of the Aztecs? How?
By what disadvantages were the Indians of America hampered in their struggle with the invading Europeans?

II   Mark the following translations 1, 2, 3, in order of your preference in the context. Mark X any that you consider unacceptable. Give a better version if one occurs to you.

a   militar
  ☐ military
  ☐ warlike
  ☐ of soldiers

b   pueblos
  ☐ peoples
  ☐ tribes
  ☐ towns

c   que era sustituída por el esclavo
  ☐ which was substituted by the slave
  ☐ for which they substituted slaves
  ☐ using slaves instead

d   resistir el encuentro con
  ☐ stand up against
  ☐ resist
  ☐ withstand the encounter with

e   el caldero
    ☐ the boiler
    ☐ the cauldron
    ☐ the copper boiler

III   Translate the passage into English.

7B   The most violent clash between the Indians and the Europeans took place in the Valley of Mexico during the early summer of 1520, <u>when Cortés and his Spaniards achieved the Conquest of Mexico and overthrew the Aztec civilization,</u> the most advanced Indian culture at that time. Cortés' success was the loadstone which drew to the Americas the *iron might* of Europe. Stone could not withstand steel, and *the days of the Indian were numbered*. The history of the Aztecs and their forebears is a synopsis of the rise of Indian civilization and its doom.

The Aztecs were a numerous group of independent Indian tribes who occupied *a restricted section* of central Mexico. Their history and *social customs* are better known than their neighbours' because their conquest *had such a far-reaching significance* for the European world. Spanish observers of military, priestly and civil status wrote careful accounts of the Aztec life and history, and Indian authors a generation later augmented these records, drawing on[5] the *tribal lore* still only *thinly veneered by Christianity*.

Most of the American Indian tribes had not *developed writing*, so[6] that archaeology is the one available medium for reconstructing their past, and the Aztec records reveal only a few centuries in the life of a single trible.

The Aztecs of Mexico, G.C. Vaillant

I   Read the passage carefully, then answer the following questions in Spanish:
¿ Cuándo occurrió el choque más violento de los españoles con los indios?
¿ Dónde tuvo lugar?
¿ Por qué nos es más conocida la cultura azteca que la de sus vecinos?
¿ Por qué es tan importante la arqueología para reconstruir la vida de los indios de la Preconquista?

II   Think out carefully the meaning of the italicized expressions and determine the best way of expressing the meaning in Spanish.

III   Choose the best translation:
. . . when Cortés and his Spaniards achieved the Conquest of Mexico and overthrew the Aztec civilization, . . .
☐ . . . cuando Cortés y los españoles lograron alcanzar la conquista de México y derrocar la civilización azteca, . . .
☐ . . . cuando Cortés y los españoles al derrocar la civilización azteca, . . . lograron la conquista de México.
☐ . . . cuando Cortés y los españoles lograron la conquista de México y derrocaron la civilización azteca, . . .

☐ . . . cuando Cortés y los españoles derrocando la civilización azteca, . . .
lograron la conquista de México.
Find a synonym of the word 'loadstone'.

IV   Translate the passage into Spanish.

Notes

1   In translating the first sentence, note that the word order will depend on the English
constructions used. Get all your facts clear before attempting to translate.
2   See **Transposition**, Appendix B5.
3   Remember the English construction of sentences beginning with *Neither*. See
Connectives, Appendix A2.
4   See **Adaptation**, Appendix B7.
5   What is the meaning of *drawing on* here?
6   What is the best connective to use here?

8A   Ya es tiempo de preguntarnos ¿ quién es ese[1] Huitzilopochtli que a través
de siglos guía[2] a su <u>pueblo</u> convirtiéndolo en un 'pueblo elegido'? En las crónicas
siempre aparece como el dios supremo cuya voz es escuchada con temor y
reverencia por los sacerdotes. Evidentemente se trata de un pequeño, muy
pequeño grupo — tal vez no más de cuatro personas — de <u>sacerdotes-directores</u>
que usando del artificio de la voz divina guían[2] a su pueblo y forman el destino
de los mexica. Lo interesante del caso[3] es que desde el principio de su historia
se obtiene la[4] impresión muy clara de <u>un verdadero programa preestablecido</u>,
programa que se desarrollará a través de siglos; de una concepción de gobierno
brutal pero genial que, seguida al pie de la letra[5] por esta pequeña indomable
élite, llevará a su pueblo a través de miles de peligros, privaciones y sacrificios,
hasta obtener el triunfo final, el imperio. El pueblo es empujado sin
consideración a su cansancio o a su hambre, con todo[6] y las mujeres y los hijos
que se mueren, contra todo, hacia el destino que esta élite le ha prometido. Claro
que es imposible pensar en que los mismos dirigentes pudieran haber establecido
y seguido este plan, casi diabólico, a través de tanto tiempo. Pero los primeros
formaron el 'tipo' que fue seguido por sus descendientes hasta el fin.
Huitzilopochtli habla sin descanso, en todas las ocasiones importantes, como el
más cruel pero como el más hábil de los políticos. Nunca se cansa, nunca se
detiene, nada le basta. Durante quince generaciones su voz temible abruma al
pueblo de trágicos consejos de violencia sin un minuto de reposo.

Tenochtitlán en una isla, Ignacio Bernal

I   Read the passage carefully and answer the following questions in English:
What part does the god Huitzilopochtli play in the history of the Mexicas?
How are his commands conveyed to the people?
What concept of this god emerges?

**II   Mark the following translations 1, 2, 3 etc. in order of your preference in
this context. Put an X beside any you consider unacceptable. Give a better
version if one occurs to you.**

a   pueblo
☐ people
☐ tribe
☐ race
☐ nation
b   sacerdotes-directores
☐ director-priests
☐ priest-rulers
☐ priestly leaders
c   un verdadero programa preestablecido
☐ a pre-establishing of a real programme
☐ the pre-establishment of a real programme
☐ a genuine programme pre-established

III   Translate the passage into English.

8B   The question 'who was Quetzalcóatl?' becomes irrevelant when we turn to the myth itself,[7] whose very existence proves that a great religious innovator did[8] at some time establish his doctrine in Mexico. In his symbolic representation he was water, earth (in the crawling snake), and bird. Add to this that he was described as being the colour of jade or of some precious stone; that he was the wind god and the god's messenger and road-sweeper; that he discovered maize which allowed man in his fullness to come into being; that his heart was consumed by the flames of a funeral pyre which he himself built, whence it rose to become the planet Venus;[9] and that he has also been identified with the later Aztec sun-god Huitzilopochtli: and we have in this composite symbol a description of the basic materials of creation. Quetzalcóatl is a kind of ladder, extending downward from man into animal, water and mineral; and upward to the planets, the star at their centre, and the god creators. This is a ladder which, in its fairy-tale way, is similar to the steps leading from crystals to life as described by the modern palaeontologist Pierre Teilhard de Chardin. It might be equated with the seven powers of nature described in ancient Oriental texts, and it echoes Picco della Mirandola's description of ideal man, 'the intermediary between creatures . . . intimate with the gods above, as he is lord of the beings below'.

The X in Mexico, Irene Nicholson

I   Read the text carefully, then answer the following questions in Spanish:
¿ Qué es lo que se sabe acerca de Quetzalcóatl?
¿ Qué proceso encarna el símbolo de Quetzalcóatl a los ojos de la autora?

II   What is the full significance of *road-sweeper* here? How would you translate it into Spanish?

III   Which of the following translations do you consider most appropriate in the context?

a becomes irrelevant
   ☐ carece de importancia
   ☐ pierde importancia
   ☐ se torna intrascendente
b whose very existence
   ☐ cuya existencia
   ☐ cuya mera existencia
   ☐ cuya misma existencia
   ☐ cuya existencia misma

c at some time
   ☐ en tiempos pasados
   ☐ en el pasado
   ☐ en algún tiempo
   ☐ en algún pasado remoto
d man in his fullness to come into being
   ☐ la creación del hombre en toda su plenitud
   ☐ que el hombre lograra una existencia completa
   ☐ que permitió al hombre florecer en todo su esplendor
   ☐ que el hombre desarrollara todo su ser

IV Translate the passage into English.

Notes

1 Does *ese* mean *that* or *this* here?
2 Watch tense. See **The Verb — Tense**, Appendix A7a.
3 See **Pronouns**, Appendix A5.
4 Watch articles here. Definite or indefinite article in English?
5 See **Modulation**, Appendix B6.
6 *in spite of everything*
7 See **Adjectives**, Appendix A1.
8 Note the emphasis here. How will you convey this in Spanish?
9 Rephrase to retain in Spanish the elegance of the English.

9A Resulta natural pensar que el hombre se ha de mover según la idea que se ha hecho de su mundo. El problema no es tan sencillo. Las ideas tienen una fuerza operacional sobre el hombre mayor o menor. Y no según su <u>rigor lógico</u>, sino según su poder seductor. ¿De dónde procede su poder seductor? ¿Dónde está la clave que nos explique esa aparente antinomia de que el hombre se siga moviendo por ideas que, examinadas por su fría razón,[1] considera ya sin valor o equivocadas?

La clave está en la vida misma. La operación de vivir <u>es</u> anterior y <u>más sustancial</u> que la operación de pensar. El pensar asienta sobre la <u>actividad vital.</u> Cuanto más alto se eleva el pensamiento en la esfera de la especulación, <u>posee menos poder configurador de la vida.</u>

¿Puede pensarse en más bello ideal que conformar la vida humana y el curso de la Historia según la razón? Cuando en lenguaje coloquial decimos que 'hay que vivir con la cabeza' nos mostramos fervientes ciudadanos de la Revolución francesa y adoradores de la *diosa Razón*. Pero la razón, construyendo una humanidad ideal, se mostró cruelmente traidora. Y de su <u>lema</u> seductor: 'libertad, igualdad y fraternidad' se desprendieron una serie de espantosos crímenes.

Desde entonces la Humanidad ha vivido como nunca en esa situación ambivalente y dual que ahora adquiere caracteres trágicos. Por un lado el hombre quiere conformar su propio destino con su razón y voluntad; por otro, se encuentra temeroso ante los abismos que, merced a su propio y voluntario caminar,[2] está abriendo continuamente ante sí.

Y es que aquella operación primaria del pensar sobre la circunstancia se halla envuelta en una operación más vigorosa, que es la de *estar inmerso en ella*. Esta es una forma primaria de establecer contacto que, si quisiéramos traducir a una palabra psicológica de nuestro lenguaje habitual, es la de sentir. *Vivir no es sólo pensar, sino sobre todo sentir*, dotando a este vocablo de su máxima área significativa.

'Vivir no consiste sólo en pensar', Juan José López Ibor
(ABC, Madrid)

I   Read the passage carefully, then answer the following questions in English:
What, in the opinion of the writer, determines the effect of man's ideas upon his behaviour?
How has the 'goddess Reason' failed humanity?
Why does the writer think that man does not live by ideas alone?
What else does he consider an essential part of man's life?

II   Mark the following translations 1, 2, 3, in order of your preference in the context. Mark X any that you consider unacceptable. Give a better version if one occurs to you.

a   rigor lógico
   ☐ logical accuracy
   ☐ strict logic
   ☐ logical rigour

b   es . . . más sustancial . . .
   ☐ is more substantial . . .
   ☐ carries more weight . . .
   ☐ is of more importance . . .

c   actividad vital
   ☐ vital activity
   ☐ living activity
   ☐ activity of living

d   posee menos poder configurador de la vida
   ☐ the less can it shape life
   ☐ the less effect it has on life
   ☐ the less power it has to shape life

e   lema
   ☐ motto
   ☐ slogan
   ☐ theme

III   Translate the passage into English.

9B   Strange, unfathomable happiness: the happiness of thinking, of seeking knowledge for its own sake. So much of our life is spent on solving problems to avoid immediate pain or to bring immediate profit; so much of our training is aimed at bringing 'practical' or 'pragmatic' effects, designing and running machines, buying, selling, cooking, furnishing, investing, spending; so many worthy results are obtained by purposeful planning and directed thinking — that we forget how true and inexhaustible is the happiness of pure knowing. Everyone has tasted it. It is born in children. It goes to school with them, and is too often killed there by tired or 'practical' teachers. But in some it survives, and unlike other delights it endures for the whole of life. To spend fifty or sixty years in studying the structure of fishes, or the relation between logic and language, or the history of the Incas, or the routes of comets, or the geometry of non-Euclidean space, or the literature of Iceland, or the anatomy of the brain; to acquire and systematize and record new knowledge on any of these subjects without any expectation of benefiting mankind except by extending its range of understanding: that is to pass a happy and valuable life, usually <u>tempered at the close by regret that another fifty years could not be added</u>, in which to learn more, and still more. It is the purest and least selfish satisfaction known to man, except those of creating a work of art and healing the sick. And it is, as Aristotle said, to share the activity of God Himself: his eternal life of pure contemplation.

The Mind of Man, Gilbert Highet

I   Read the passage carefully, then answer the following questions in Spanish:
¿ Por qué, según el autor, saborea el hombre sólo escasas veces la felicidad de pensar?
¿ Qué ventaja tiene este placer respecto a otros?

II   Which of the following translations do you consider most appropriate in the context?
a   Strange, unfathomable happiness.
   ☐ Singular e insondeable deleite.
   ☐ Raro deleite sin fondo.
   ☐ Extraña felicidad insondeable.
b   the happiness of pure knowing
   ☐ la felicidad de la sabiduría pura
   ☐ la felicidad de la mera sapiencia
   ☐ la felicidad del saber puro
   ☐ el deleite del saber puro
c   is too often killed there by tired or 'practical' teachers
   ☐ para allí perecer a manos de maestros 'prácticos' o cansados
   ☐ donde maestros 'prácticos' o cansados lo matan
d   tempered at the close by regret that another fifty years could not be added
   ☐ templada en el ocaso por la añoranza de que no puedan sumarse más cincuenta años
   ☐ atemperada en la clausura por el arrepentimiento de que otros cincuenta años no se hayan podido añadir

III   Translate the passage into Spanish.

Notes

1   See **Modulation**, Appendix B6.
2   See **Transposition**, Appendix B5.

10A   Tenemos que estudiar otra vez la asignatura de las Islas Canarias; partir de cero, olvidar lo que nos han contado, examinarnos y saber dónde y por qué *nos vienen el afecto, el orgullo, la alegría de saberlas España.* De verdad, aquellos españoles necesitan *constancia* física, palpable, de *solidaridad.* Están lejos, sin salir de la Patria, más lejos que nadie de la Puerta del Sol; son más que periféricos; son la única Europa de total europeidad que tenemos en esos paralelos que hilvanan Africa y América cerca ya de la cintura del trópico.

Siete islas. Bien contadas, la cuenta llega hasta trece;[1] más la de San Borondón, que surge y se desvanece para evitar malos farios.[2] Siete islas principales todas con su *talante* diferente; siete mundos; siete aires y modos de ser canario y una sola manera de ser españoles, de ser rabiosamente españoles. A dos mil kilómetros de la Puerta del Sol, *se sienten como necesitados* de gritar[3] que son España. Y cuanto más se ven empujados a toda vela por los vientos europeos, cuanto más hacen y dan y arriesgan por ser pilar económico de España en Europa, más se duelen de su españolidad aislada, lejana, sola.

No podemos, tranquilamente, sentarnos ante el cliché y el 'slogan': Islas Afortunadas, jardín de las Hespérides, 'Europa tiene una España y España tiene un jardín que son las Islas Canarias'. Todo eso es muy bonito, pero la vida no es un pasodoble, ni un cartel, ni un corro cascabelero y folklórico. Hay que ver al canario haciendo el jardín, el verdadero, no el del pasodoble, sobre la escoria volcánica; hay que ver cómo el jardín es cualquier cosa menos un regalo de los dioses. Para describir las Canarias no valen los 'fox movietones' de los mares del Sur; el jardín lo están haciendo aquellos españoles únicos, irrepetibles, que ponen en el nombre de la Patria el dulce son, la casi música del habla hispano-americana; hay que ver cómo y con qué arrestos *han puesto la proa en la punta de flecha del viento turístico*[1] *y, pisando a fondo todos los aceleradores* del riesgo y la creatividad, se adelantan a la gran demanda, al gran desafío que la Humanidad plantea a la industria del tiempo libre, que es, además, tan industria como la siderurgia o la electrónica, solo que más ecológica que, por chiripa, ha inventado el hombre.

'No eran afortunados', Angel Palomino
(ABC, Madrid)

I   Read the passage carefully and answer the following questions in English:
Why is it necessary to revise the generally accepted idea of the Canaries?
What are some of their problems?
Why are the Spaniards proud of the fact that the Canaries are Spanish?

II   Think out carefully the exact meaning of the words and expressions in italics and consider how this can best be conveyed in English.

III   Translate the passage into English.

10B   So, for good or evil, the name of a country becomes one of the most powerful symbols in the world; men will die for its glory who do not care in the least for their own.[4] They will also commit the worst of crimes if some dictator can persuade them that the name has been insulted.

Many people have come to hate patriotism as the <u>seedbed</u> of hatred and war.

But you can't abolish so fundamental and primitive an attachment[5] as the love of home. You can only pervert it. Neither is patriotism necessarily an evil or a weakness. Its quality depends on the values embodied in the symbolic name.

My <u>feeling</u> for England is especially deep and conscious because I was born in Ireland to[6] an Anglo-Irish family, long settled there. [7]My earliest memories are of Donegal, its <u>wild</u> hills and the great sea loughs of Foyle and Swilly. I loved the country and the people, spoilers of children. But my heroes were the great men of English history, many of them Anglo-Irishmen like myself; and English history is world history. My imagination played on a world <u>stage</u>. I was <u>engaged for</u>[8] England; I triumphed in her glories and suffered in her defeats and shames.

I was, like my family, sharply critical of the English and often of English policy, but my anger was that of a lover. I could not bear that England should be betrayed by her own children or by party politicians with narrow views and mean aims. I had, that is, a far more definite and romantic idea of England than the average born Englishman.

Selected Essays, Joyce Cary

I   Read the passage carefully, then answer the following questions in Spanish:

¿ Qué es la actitud del autor hacia patriotismo?

¿ Qué son sus emociones con respecto a Inglaterra?

¿ A qué atribuye la intensidad de estas emociones?

II   Which of the following translations do you consider most appropriate in the context?

a   seedbed
   ☐ semillero
   ☐ fuente
   ☐ origen

b   feeling
   ☐ amor
   ☐ sentimiento
   ☐ cariño

c   wild
   ☐ desierto
   ☐ borrascoso
   ☐ selvático

d   stage
   ☐ tablado
   ☐ escenario
   ☐ teatro

e   engaged for
   ☐ comprometido en la causa de
   ☐ dedicado a
   ☐ parte de

III   Translate the passage into Spanish.

Notes

1   See **Modulation**, Appendix B6.
2   A colloquial expression meaning *bad things, evils*.
3   See **Transposition**, Appendix B5.
4   Watch the tense, adjectives and pronouns to be used here.
5   See **Omissions and Insertions**, Appendix B4.
6   Watch preposition here.
7   A number of short sentences follow. Combine some of them in Spanish.
8   What is the meaning of *engaged for* here?

11A   Una <u>reflexión</u> del Doctor Johnson en el curso de un viaje expresa muy bien la nueva actitud: 'A blade of grass is always a blade of grass, whether in one country or another. . . Men and women are my subjects of inquiry; let us see how these differ from those we have left behind.' La frase del Doctor Johnson tiene dos sentidos y ambos prefiguran el doble camino que había de emprender la edad moderna. El primero se refiere a la separación entre el hombre y la naturaleza, una separación que se transformaría en oposición y combate: la nueva misión del hombre no es salvarse sino dominar la naturaleza; el segundo se refiere a la separación entre los hombres. El mundo deja de ser un mundo, una totalidad indivisible, y se escinde en naturaleza y cultura: y la cultura se parcela en culturas. <u>Pluralidad de</u> lenguas y sociedades: cada lengua es una visión del mundo, cada civilización es un mundo. El sol que canta el poema azteca es distinto al sol del himno egipcio, aunque <u>el astro sea el mismo</u>. Durante más de dos siglos, primero los filósofos y los historiadores, ahora los antropólogos y los lingüistas, han acumulado pruebas sobre[1] las irreductibles diferencias entre los individuos, las sociedades y las épocas. La gran división, apenas menos profunda que la[2] establecida entre naturaleza y cultura, es la que separa a los primitivos de los civilizados; en seguida, la variedad y heterogeneidad de las civilizaciones. En el interior de cada civilización <u>renacen</u> las diferencias: las lenguas que nos sirven para comunicarnos también nos encierran en una malla invisible de sonidos y significados, de modo que las naciones son prisioneras de las lenguas que hablan. Dentro de cada lengua se reproducen las divisiones: épocas históricas, clases sociales, generaciones. En cuanto a las relaciones entre individuos aislados y que pertenecen a la misma comunidad: cada uno es un emparedado vivo en <u>su propio yo</u>.

Traducción y literalidad, Octavio Paz

I   **Read the passage carefully and answer the following questions in English:**
What does Dr. Johnson imply?
What divisions does the writer mention in this passage?
Why is each man a 'living sandwich'?

II   **Mark the following translations 1, 2, 3, in order of your preference in the context. Mark X any you consider unacceptable. Give a better version if one occurs to you.**

a   reflexión
  ☐ remark
  ☐ observation
  ☐ reflection
b   Pluralidad de
  ☐ a plurality of
  ☐ many
  ☐ diverse
c   el astro sea el mismo
  ☐ the star is the same
  ☐ it's the same star
  ☐ it's the same heavenly body

d   renacen
  ☐ are reborn
  ☐ spring up again
  ☐ again arise
e   su propio yo
  ☐ his own being
  ☐ himself
  ☐ his own individuality

III   Translate the passage into English.

11B   The <u>stuff</u> of language is words, and the <u>sensuous</u> material of words is sound; if language therefore is to be made perfect, its materials must be made beautiful by being themselves subjected to a measure and endowed with a form. It is true that language is a symbol for intelligence rather than a stimulus to sense, and accordingly the beauties of discourse which commonly attract attention are merely the beauties of the objects and ideas signified; yet the symbols have a <u>sensible</u> reality of their own, a euphony which appeals to our senses if we keep them open. The tongue will choose those forms of utterance which have a natural grace as mere sound and sensation; the memory will retain these <u>catches</u>, and they will pass and repass through the mind until they become types of instinctive speech and standards of pleasing expression.

The highest form of such euphony is song; the singing voice gives to the sounds it utters the thrill of tonality. . . But this kind of euphony and sensuous beauty, the deepest that sounds can have, we have almost wholly surrendered in our speech. Our intelligence has become complex, and language, to express our thoughts, must commonly be more rapid, copious, and abstract than is compatible with singing.

Interpretations of Poetry and Religion, George Santayana

I   Haga un breve resumen en español de las ideas del autor sobre el lenguaje.

II   Which of the following translations do you consider most appropriate in the context?

a   stuff
- ☐ estofa
- ☐ materia
- ☐ material
- ☐ trama

b   sensuous
- ☐ sensual
- ☐ palpable
- ☐ perceptible

c   sensible
- ☐ sensible
- ☐ sensorial
- ☐ sensitivo

d   catches
- ☐ tonadillas
- ☐ trampas
- ☐ refranes

III   Translate the passage into Spanish.

Notes

1   Watch preposition here.
2   See **Determiners**, Appendix A3.

12A   El lugar <u>que ocupan</u>[1] Dios y el libre albedrío en el teatro español, la libertad y el Destino en el griego, <u>lo tiene</u>[1] en el inglés la naturaleza humana.

Mas el carácter sagrado de la naturaleza no proviene de Dios ni de la legalidad cósmica, sino de ser una fuerza que se ha rebelado contra esos[2] antiguos poderes. Tamerlán, Macbeth, Fausto y el mismo Hamlet pertenecen a una raza blasfema que no tiene más ley que sus pasiones y deseos. Y esa ley es terrible porque es la de una naturaleza que ha abandonado a Dios y se ha consagrado y ungido a sí misma. Los isabelinos acaban de descubrir al hombre. La marea de sus pasiones arroja a Dios de la escena. Los héroes de Shakespeare y de Webster están solos, en el sentido más radical de la palabra, porque sus gritos se pierden en el vacío: Dios y el Destino han deshabitado sus cielos. Con la desaparición de los dioses el cosmos pierde coherencia y el hombre se vuelve juguete del azar.

El Arco y la Lira, Octavio Paz (adapted)

(Fondo de Cultura Economica, Mexico)

I How does the English Theatre differ from the Spanish and from the Greek?

II Translate the passage into English.

12B Es evidente que el príncipe es un hombre hondamente desdichado. El dolor de su padre asesinado y la humillación indirecta que implica la segunda boda de su madre han sido sin duda golpes duros; pero, desde el principio, Shakespeare da la impresión de que lo que importa más no son los golpes[3] sino la resonancia que provocan en el alma de Hamlet. ¿Por qué es tan desdichado? Los dos hechos de que sufre hubieran podido hacerle[4] montar en cólera en lugar de deprimirlo a la melancolía. Tampoco cabe atribuir este estado mental a flaqueza o a enfermedad mental; ya que Hamlet no tiene nada de débil y en cuanto a la enfermedad mental no es asunto para un autor trágico sino para el hospital. La única conclusión que cabe es que Hamlet era un hombre desdichado antes de enterarse por el Fantasma de que su padre había muerto asesinado. Bien es cierto que le constaba la prisa indecorosa con que su madre había contraído segundas nupcias, pero por razones que más adelante se darán, no podía bastar este hecho para explicar su desdicha.

El Hamlet de Shakespeare, Salvador de Madariaga

I Read the passage carefully and answer the following questions in English:
What is the passage about?
To what is Hamlet's sadness usually attributed?
What is this critic's conclusion?

II Mark the following translations 1, 2, 3, in order of your preference in the context. Mark X any you consider unacceptable. Give a better version if one occurs to you.

a desdichado
  ☐ wretched
  ☐ miserable
  ☐ unhappy
b hechos
  ☐ facts
  ☐ events
  ☐ deeds

c le constaba
  ☐ was a fact
  ☐ had its effect upon him
  ☐ he had evidence for

III Translate the passage into English.

12C Shakespeare's great tragedies are dominated by a hopeless fatalism which is far more pessimistic than the purifying agonies of Greek tragedy, and almost utterly <u>godless</u>. None of them shows any belief in 'the righteous government of the world', except in so far as successful evildoers are later punished for their own cruel schemes. Sometimes his tragic heroes <u>speak of life as ruled by</u> fate inhuman, unpredictable and meaningless; and sometimes, more bitterly, <u>cry out against</u> <u>vicious mankind</u> which is unfit to live, and cruel gods who 'kill us for their sport'. That much of this hopeless gloom came from Shakespeare's own heart, no one can doubt; but he found it expressed decisively and eloquently in the stoical pessimism of Seneca.

The Classical Tradition, Gilbert Highet

I **From the following translations, choose the one most appropriate in the context. Give a better version if one occurs to you.**

a godless
  ☐ casi de todo privada de Dios
  ☐ casi de todo descreída
  ☐ casi de todo atea
b speak of life as ruled by . . .
  ☐ afirman que la vida está
    gobernada por . . .
  ☐ hablan de la vida como si
    estuviera gobernada por . . .
  ☐ describen la vida como
    gobernada por

c cry out against
  ☐ lloran contra
  ☐ claman contra
  ☐ gritan contra
d vicious mankind
  ☐ el vicioso género humano
  ☐ la malévola humanidad
  ☐ el género humano pervertido

II **Translate the passage into Spanish.**

12D <u>Our attention is early drawn to the figure of Hamlet</u>. Alone in the gay glitter of the court, silhouetted against brilliance, <u>robustness</u>, health and happiness, is the pale, black-robed Hamlet, <u>mourning</u>. When first we meet him, his words point the essential inwardness of his suffering. When he is alone, he reveals his <u>misery</u> more clearly. To Hamlet the light has been extinguished from the things of earth. He has lost all sense of purpose. We already know one reason for Hamlet's state: his father's death. Now, during Hamlet's soliloquy, we see another reason: disgust at his mother's second marriage. These two concrete embodiments of Hamlet's misery are closely related. He suffers from misery at his father's death and agony at his mother's quick forgetfulness: such callousness is infidelity, and so impurity, and, since Claudius is the brother of the King, incest. It is reasonable to suppose that Hamlet's state of mind, <u>if not wholly</u> <u>caused by these events</u>, is at least definitely related to them. Of his two loved parents, one has been taken for ever by death, the other dishonoured for ever by her act of marriage.

'Hamlet's Mental Suffering', *The Wheel of Fire*
G. Wilson Knight (adapted)

I From the following translations, choose the one most appropriate in the context.

a Our attention is early drawn to the figure of Hamlet.
- ☐ La figura de Hamlet pronto atrae nuestra atención.
- ☐ Nuestra atención atrae temprano a la figura de Hamlet.
- ☐ Nuestra atención es concentrada desde el principio por la figura de Hamlet.

b robustness
- ☐ vigor
- ☐ robustez
- ☐ enjundia

c mourning
- ☐ de luto
- ☐ que se conduele
- ☐ enlutado

d misery
- ☐ miseria
- ☐ dolor
- ☐ aflicción

e if not wholly caused by these events
- ☐ si bien no del todo causado por estos acontecimientos
- ☐ si no enteramente causado por estos acontecimientos

II Translate the passage into Spanish.

Notes

1 Notice the balance between *que ocupan* and *lo tiene*. How can you keep this in English?
2 See **Determiners**, Appendix A3.
3 Watch word order here.
4 See **The Verb — Mood and Modals**, Appendix A7b.

13A Se nace, decía Coleridge, aristotélico o platónico. De Grecia nos llega esta bifurcada posibilidad de concebir el mundo del espíritu, y la tradición grecolatina en que vivimos hace llano que[1] los conceptos fundamentales de nuestra vida ideal fluctúen entre uno y otro polo. Así la poesía. Si partimos de los conceptos de poesía de Aristóteles y Platón observaremos que caben en ellos todas las concepciones de la lírica posterior. Para Aristóteles la poesía es una *mimesis*, una imitación; para Platón es una embriaguez que arrebata al poeta. Con esto puede quedar deslindado el campo de los que ven en la poesía un ejercicio en el que cuenta la habilidad, y el de los que la conceptúan como una enajenación en la que cuenta la inspiración. No es difícil seguir el rastro de ambas tendencias a lo largo de nuestra literatura. En el siglo XV — siglo de encrucijada — oímos al marqués de Santillana decir — aristotélicamente — que la poesía es una 'fermosa cobertura' mientras Juan Alfonso de Baena asevera — platónicamente — que la poesía es una 'gracia infusa del Señor Dios'. En adelante, todas las épocas neoclásicas (en el sentido amplio de la palabra) considerarán la poesía según la primera de estas tendencias. Nuestro Ortega y Gasset está, acaso sin proponérselo, transido de esta tradición cuando afirma que 'poesía es eludir el nombre cotidiano de las cosas'.

Pero, paralelamente, el otro concepto de poesía va haciendo su fortuna en todas las épocas que preside el sentimiento, que no sabe razonar ni medir. Para nuestros místicos la poesía tiene un origen celestial y sirve para devolver el espíritu a Dios. Todo ello según fuente platónica.

Hacia un concepto de la literatura española,
Guillermo Diaz-Plaja

I   Read the passage carefully and answer the following questions in English:
What is Aristotle's concept of poetry?
How do Plato's ideas of poetry differ from Aristotle's?
Name some poets who follow the ideal of Aristotle.
Name some who are governed by Plato's ideas.

II   Mark the following translations 1, 2, 3, in order of your preference in the context. Mark X any you consider unacceptable. Give a better version if one occurs to you.

a   Así la poesía.
  ☐ So is poetry.
  ☐ It's the same with poetry.
  ☐ Poetry is like that.
b   caben en ellos
  ☐ are contained in these
  ☐ are contained here
  ☐ fit in them
c   embriaguez
  ☐ drunkenness
  ☐ intoxication
  ☐ rapture

d   transido
  ☐ governed
  ☐ filled
  ☐ inspired
e   según fuente platónica
  ☐ according to Plato
  ☐ according to Platonic sources
  ☐ according to Plato's ideas

III   Translate the passage into English.

13B   Long before the Renaissance began, lyric poetry already existed in Europe. Provençal, French, Italian, English, German, Spanish poets had made song-patterns of much beauty and intricacy. Perhaps in the very beginning the songs of the vernacular languages had grown out of the Latin hymns of the church; but they soon left behind any link with the parent language. Therefore, when Pindar and Horace and the other classical lyrical poets were rediscovered, the discovery did not create modern lyric poetry. It was not like the theatre, where the emergence of Greek and Latin comedy and tragedy was a complete revelation of hitherto undreamed of forms and creative possibilities. Poets who already commanded the sonnet in its various shapes and many more complex stanza-forms scarcely needed to borrow many patterns from the classics.

What they did borrow was, first of all, thematic material. Not the broad subjects — love and youth and the fear of death and the joy of life — but a number of clear and memorable attitudes to the subjects of lyric poetry, images or turns of thought that made them more vivid; and, of course, the whole range of imagery supplied by Greco-Roman myth. More important, they enriched their language on the model of Pindar's and Horace's odes, taking it farther away from plain prose and from conventional folk-song phraseology. And in their eagerness to rival the classics, they made their own lyrics more dignified, less colloquial and song-like, more ceremonial and hymn-like. This was the most important change that classical influence brought into modern lyric: a graver, nobler spirit. To mark these debts and their general kinship with the classics, the Renaissance lyric poets frequently copied or adapted the verse forms of Pindar, Horace, and the others.

The Classical Tradition, Gilbert Highet (adapted)

I   Read the passage carefully, then answer the following question in Spanish:
¿ En qué campo influyó el pensamiento clásico en la poesía lírica del Renacimiento?

II   Would you use the same Spanish word for *borrow* in the last line of paragraph 1 and the first line of paragraph 2?

III   Which of the following translations do you consider most appropriate in the context?

a   poets had made song-patterns
  ☐ los poetas habían hecho patrones de canciones
  ☐ los poetas habían logrado consolidar formas de canción
  ☐ los poetas habían logrado consolidar canciones de forma

b   left behind
  ☐ dejaron atrás
  ☐ dejaron a la zaga
  ☐ retrasaron

c   turns of thought
  ☐ giros del espíritu
  ☐ matices del pensamiento
  ☐ vueltas del pensamiento

IV   Translate the passage into Spanish.

Notes

1   See **Pronouns**, Appendix A5.

14A   El Goya pintor de retratos no surge de súbita manera. Bien sabido es que no fue pintor precoz, y tocante el arte del retrato, vivió largo período de tanteo, aprendiendo un léxico que la permitiese producir con soltura. Y con tanto soltura se produce, al fin, que hablar de la 'técnica de Goya' equivale a demostrar, quien así dice, que no ha penetrado en la complejidad y constante mudar del arte de don Francisco.

Goya, en sus primeros años de pintor avecindado en Madrid, interpreta el retrato dentro de un barroco y rococó[1] un tanto tiepolesco.[2] Así el primer retrato del arquitecto don Ventura Rodríguez, ejecutado antes de 1770. Por[3] este tiempo pinta[4] algunos retratos oficiales, siguiendo muy de cerca a Mengs. Mas estas obras *tienen mucho de forzadas,* de industriales, y en ellas el artista no actuó libre y espontáneamente.

Ya entrado el siglo XIX, Goya, *en posesión de numerosos recursos del oficio,* pinta retratos *siguiendo la técnica, el capricho o la conveniencia de la estructura del modelo*. Unas veces se muestra rudo, con desenfadada pincelada; otras alcanza esmaltes de primitivo, borrada toda huella de pincel. Y ya entona en gris plata, bien en oro o en negro, mas siempre sin perder unidad ni grandeza. Sus retratos, tan humanos, son, no obstante, sutiles glosas de la forma del modelo, superiores a fieles copias. Son briosas y rotundas versiones del carácter fisonómico del retratado. A cada modelo lo interpreta bajo el influjo de la mayor o menor simpatía que por él siente.

De aquí que en algún retrato asome claramente el íntimo desprecio que a Goya le inspiraba el modelo. Algunos retratos de Fernando VII son caricaturas crueles. A las damas jóvenes y bellas dedicaba Goya la máxima atención en lo técnico. Es raro ver un retrato de mujer joven y hermosa ejecutado por Goya con descuido, como quien pintó por salir cuanto antes del paso. Es frecuente, en cambio — demasiado frecuente — , contemplar retratos de hombres que han sido pintados sin atención cuidada ni emoción. En los retratos de niño, Goya transmite a la obra la ternura y simpatía que le producían los pequeños modelos.

'Don Francisco de Goya y los Retratos de Gran Penetración Psicológica'

Antonio Méndez Casal

(ABC, Madrid)

I   Read the passage carefully, then answer the following questions in English:
What does the author say about Goya's portrait painting at different periods?
How does Goya show his attitude towards his models?

II   Think out carefully the meaning of the italicized expressions. Try several ways of translating them and choose the one you prefer.

III   Translate the passage into English.

14B   Among the artists of David's generation who discarded the old type of subject-matter was the great Spanish painter, Francisco Goya (1746-1828). Goya was well versed in the best tradition of Spanish painting, which had produced El Greco and Velazquez, and his group on a balcony shows that unlike David he did not renounce this mastery in favour of classical grandeur. The great Venetian painter of the eighteenth century, Giovanni Battista Tiepolo, had ended his days as a court painter in Madrid, and there is something of his radiance in Goya's painting. And yet Goya's figures belong to a different world. The two women who eye the passer-by provokingly, while two rather sinister gallants keep in the background, may be closer to the world of Hogarth. Goya's portraits which secured him a place at the Spanish court look superficially like the traditional state portraits of Vandyke or of Reynolds. The skill with which he conjured up the glitter of silk and gold recalls Titian or Velazquez. But he also looks at his sitters with a different eye. Not that these masters had flattered the mighty, but Goya seems to have known no pity. He made their features reveal all their vanity and ugliness, their greed and emptiness. No Court Painter before or after has ever left such a record of his patrons.

The Story of Art, E.H. Gombrich

I Which of the following translations do you consider most appropriate in the context?

a The two women who eye the passer-by provokingly
  ☐ Las dos mujeres que miran provocativas al transeúnte
  ☐ Las dos mujeres que ven provocadoras al transeúnte
  ☐ Las dos mujeres que, provocativas miran con fijeza al transeúnte

b recalls
  ☐ recuerda
  ☐ evoca
  ☐ trae a cuento

II Translate the passage into Spanish.

Notes

1 See **Omissions and Insertions**, Appendix B4.
2 *in the manner of Tiepolo*
3 Watch preposition here.
4 Watch verb tense.

15A Que el pasado nos atrae es algo menos de lo que en verdad ocurre: estamos _alienados_ por él, no sólo porque es la fuente de toda la cultura popular, y porque contiene una pauta de conducta para el Pobre Cualquiera que ansia ser algún día don Alguien,[1] y porque la actualidad reproduce como caricatura el orden pretérito, sino porque en esencia, parece no haber escapatoria a llevar la cabeza de revés,[2] hipnotizada por el ayer hechizo y ciego _al rumbo venidero_. El pasado está en todas partes, _abrazando_ hogar y escuela, política y prensa, folklore y literatura, religión y mundanidad. Así, por ejemplo, en labios de los mayores se repiten _rutinarias_ las consejas coloniales, en las aulas se repasan los infundios arcadios,[3] en las calles desfilan las carrozas doradas del gobierno y en los diarios reaparecen, como en un ciclo ebrio, las elegías al edén perdido. Cantamos y bailamos 'valses criollos', que ahora se obstinan en evocar el puente y la alameda tradicionales, y se imprimen libros de anécdotas y recuerdos de aquello que José Gálvez bautizó como la Lima que se va. Entre humos de fritanga se desplazan las viejas procesiones y otras nuevas, a través de idénticos vapores, remozan el gregarismo devoto. Y asistimos — ¡qué remedio queda! — a bodas y funerales de ritual _ocioso_, de hipócrita convencionalismo. La trampa de la Arcadia Colonial está en todos los caminos. No es sencillo sortearla.

Lima, la horrible, S. Bondy

I Read the passage carefully, then answer the following questions in English:
What is the passage about?
What is the general attitude towards the past?
What examples does the author give of the 'presence of the past' in our daily lives?

II **Mark the following translations 1, 2, 3, in order of your preference in this context. Put an X beside any that you consider definitely unacceptable. Give a better version if one occurs to you.**

a alienados
- ☐ put off
- ☐ alienated
- ☐ carried away

b el rumbo venidero
- ☐ the direction of the future
- ☐ the way ahead
- ☐ the route to come

c abrazando
- ☐ embracing
- ☐ including
- ☐ enfolding

d rutinarias
- ☐ routine
- ☐ mechanically
- ☐ everyday

e ocioso
- ☐ idle
- ☐ empty
- ☐ vain

III **What is the meaning of** la actualidad reproduce como caricatura el orden pretérito? **Give three possible translations and give the one you prefer.** What is the exact meaning of *Arcadia Colonial* here?

IV **Translate the passage into English.**

15B What I mean by tradition involves all those habitual actions, habits and customs, from the most significant religious rite to our conventional way of greeting a stranger, which represent the blood relationship of 'the same people living in the same place'.

We are always in danger, in clinging to an old tradition, or attempting to re-establish one, of confusing the vital and the unessential, the real and the sentimental. Our second danger is to associate tradition with the immovable; to think of it as something hostile to all change; to aim to return to some previous condition which we imagine as having been capable of preservation in perpetuity, instead of aiming to stimulate the life which produced that condition in its time.

It is not of advantage to us to indulge in a sentimental attitude towards the past. For one thing, in even the very best living tradition there is always a mixture of good and bad, and much that deserves criticism; and for another, tradition is not a matter of feeling alone. Nor can we safely, without very critical examination, dig ourselves in stubbornly to a few dogmatic notions, for what is a healthy belief at one time may, unless it is one of the few fundamental things, be a pernicious prejudice at another. Nor should we cling to traditions as a way of asserting our superiority over less favoured peoples. What we can do is to use our minds, remembering that a tradition without intelligence is not worth having, to discover what is the best life for us not as a political abstraction, but as a particular people in a particular place; what in the past is worth preserving and what should be rejected; and what conditions within our power to bring about, would foster the society that we desire.

'Tradition', *Selected Prose*, T.S. Eliot

In this passage you will need to pay special attention to the terms you will use in Spanish to translate the connectives and the words used by the author to add emphasis.

I Read the passage carefully, then answer the following questions in Spanish:
¿ Qué elementos integran el concepto que de la tradición tiene el autor?
¿ Qué amenazas se ciernen sobre la cabeza de quienes son en extremo conservadores?

II Which of the following translations do you consider most appropriate in the context?

a   What I mean by tradition
    ☐ Lo que entiendo por tradición
    ☐ Lo que quiero decir cuando hablo de tradición
    ☐ Para mí tradición es

b   We are always in danger, in clinging to an old tradition, or attempting to re-establish a new one, of confusing the vital and the unessential
    ☐ Al aferrarnos a una antigua tradición, o al intentar reinstaurarla, corremos siempre el riesgo de confundir lo vital y lo accesorio
    ☐ Siempre estamos en peligro, de aferrarnos a alguna vieja tradición o al tratar de restablecerla, de confundir lo vital y lo superfluo
    ☐ Corremos siempre el peligro, si nos aferramos a una tradición añeja, o cuando tratamos de resucitarla, de mezclar lo primordial y lo secundario

c   immovable
    ☐ inmutable
    ☐ inconmovible
    ☐ inmóvil

d   It is not of advantage to us
    ☐ No nos conviene
    ☐ No nos sirve
    ☐ No nos beneficia

e   to indulge in
    ☐ dar rienda suelta a
    ☐ regodearnos en
    ☐ refocilarnos

f   dig ourselves in
    ☐ empecinarnos
    ☐ estancarnos
    ☐ empantanarnos

III Translate the passage into Spanish.

Notes

1   See **Modulation**, Appendix B6.
2   See **Transposition**, Appendix B5.
3   *fairy tales, myths*

PART III Literary Translation

The first section of this part consists of a number of English and Spanish
originals together with translations followed by comments and questions for the
consideration of readers. The second and third sections contain a number of
passages taken from well-known Spanish and English writers to be translated.
Here, although the range is very wide and there are some fairly straightforward
passages, the emphasis is on literary translation and the comments and questions
following the texts are intended to direct the student's attention to the style of
the original, the writer's use of language to produce particular effects, and the
special problems of the translator.

Notes on each passage, with references to the Appendices where appropriate,
follow each passage in the Translations and Commentaries section. In the
Spanish and English Passages for Translation sections, the Notes appear at the
end of each section.

Contents of PART III

TRANSLATIONS AND COMMENTARIES   **109**
A   *Cien años de soledad*, Gabriel García Marquez
B   *Al filo del agua*, Agustín Yáñez
C   *Coplas por la muerte de su padre*, Jorge Manrique
D   *El ingenioso hidalgo Don Quijote de la Mancha*, Miguel de Cervantes
     Saavedra
E   *Canciones entre el alma y el esposo*, San Juan de la Cruz
F   *Amanecer de otoño*, Antonio Machado
G   *Clea*, Lawrence Durrell
H   *Under the Volcano*, Malcolm Lowry
I   'Leonardo da Vinci', Walter Pater
J   *Burnt Norton; East Coker*, T.S. Eliot
K   *The Lady's Not For Burning*, Christopher Fry

SPANISH PASSAGES FOR TRANSLATION   **131**
1   'Después de cenar. . .', Juan Antonio Payno
2   *El bordo*, Sergio Galindo

3   *Pedro Páramo*, Juan Rulfo
4A   'Daban las horas en el reloj . . .', Miguel Delibes
4B   'Sólo ésto me faltaba . . .', Miguel Delibes
5   *Los intereses creados*, Jacinto Benavente
6   *El señor de Pigmalión*, Jacinto Grau
7   'Nada dije a Alfredo . . .', Miguel Delibes
8   *Las tierras flacas*, Agustín Yáñez
9   *La familia de Pascual Duarte*, Camilo José Cela
10   *Visión de España*, Azorín
11   *En torno al casticismo*, Miguel de Unamuno
12   'No tenían cara . . .', Augusto Roa Bastos
13   *Terra Nostra*, Carlos Fuentes
14   *Los intereses creados*, Jacinto Benavente
15   *El viaje definitivo*, Juan Ramón Jiménez
Notes

ENGLISH PASSAGES FOR TRANSLATION   146

16   *A City of Bells*, Elizabeth Goudge
17   *Jane*, W. Somerset Maugham
18   'While Christopher merely recognized . . .'
19   *The Bird in the Tree*, Elizabeth Goudge
20   *Blithe Spirit,* Noel Coward
21   'The bar, she found with pleasure . . .', Elaine Feinstein
22   *The Tightening String*, Ann Bridge
23   *The Open Window*, Saki
24   *Homage to Catalonia*, George Orwell
25   *Spain*, Sacheverell Sitwell
26   *Howards End*, E.M. Forster
27   *To the Lighthouse*, Virginia Woolf
28   *The Lord of the Rings*, J.R.R. Tolkien
29   'It must have been like travelling . . .', Rumer Godden
30   *A Song for Simeon*, T.S. Eliot
Notes

Translations and Commentaries

A   Deslumbrada por tantas y tan maravillosas invenciones, la gente de Macondo no sabía por dónde empezar a asombrarse.[1] Se trasnochaban[2] contemplando las pálidas bombillas eléctricas alimentadas por la planta que llevó Aureliano Triste en el segundo viaje del tren, y a cuyo obstinante tumtum costó tiempo y trabajo acostumbrarse.[3] Se indignaron[2] con las imágenes vivas que el próspero comerciante don Bruno Crespi proyectaba en el teatro con taquillas de bocas de león, porque un personaje muerto y septultado en una película, y por cuya desgracia se derramaron lágrimas de aflicción, reapareció vivo y convertido en árabe en la película siguiente. El público que pagaba dos centavos para compartir las vicisitudes de los personajes, no pudo saportar aquella burla inaudita y rompió la silletería. El alcalde, a instancias de don Bruno Crespi, explicó mediante un bando, que el cine era una máquina de ilusión que no merecía los desbordamientos pasionales del público. Ante la desalentadora explicación, muchos estimaron que habían sido víctimas de un nuevo y aparatoso asunto de gitanos, de modo que optaron por no volver al cine, considerando que ya tenían bastante con sus propias penas para llorar por fingidas desventuras de seres imaginarios. Algo semejante ocurrió con los gramófonos de cilindros que llevaron las alegres matronas de Francia en sustitución de los anticuados organillos, y que tan hondamente afectaron por un tiempo los intereses de la banda de músicos. Al principio, la curiosidad multiplicó la clientela de la calle prohibida, y hasta se supo de señoras respetables que se disfrazaron de villanos para observar de cerca la novedad del gramófono, pero tanto y de tan cerca lo observaron, que muy pronto llegaron a la conclusión de que no era un molino de sortilegio, como todos pensaban y como las matronas decían, sino un truco mecánico que no podía compararse con algo tan conmovedor, tan humano y tan lleno de verdad cotidiana como una banda de músicos.

Cien Años de Soledad, Gabriel García Marquez

Here the author is describing the effect of various new inventions on the people of Macondo, and his style is one of simple narrative and description. García Marquez merely relates events as an observer, there is no personal comment. The language is such as might have been used by one of the characters. This gives a particular vividness to the account.

Consider the translation below and say how far the translator has used similar language to that of the original and preserved the general impression.

Dazzled by so many and such marvellous inventions, the people of Macondo did not know where their amazement began.[1] They stayed up all night[2] looking at the pale electric bulbs fed by the plant that Aureliano Triste had brought back when the train made its second trip, and it took time and effort for them to grow accustomed to its obsessive toom-toom.[3] They became indignant[2] over the living images that the prosperous merchant Bruno Crespi projected in the theatre with the lion-head ticket windows, for a character who had died and was buried in one film and for whose misfortune tears of affliction had been shed would reappear alive and transformed into an Arab in the next one. The audience, who paid two cents apiece to share the difficulties of the actors, would not tolerate that outlandish fraud and they broke up the seats. The mayor, at the urging of Bruno Crespi, explained in a proclamation that the cinema was a machine of illusions that did not merit the emotional outbursts of the audience. With that discouraging explanation many felt that they had been the victims of some new and showy gypsy business and they decided not to return to the movies, considering that they already had too many troubles of their own to weep over the acted-out misfortunes of imaginary beings. Something similar happened with the cylinder phonographs that the merry matrons from France brought with them as a substitute for the antiquated hand organs and that for a time had serious effects on the livelihood of the band of musicians. At first curiosity increased the clientele on the forbidden street and there was even word of respectable ladies who disguised themselves as workers in order to observe the novelty of the phonograph from first hand, but from so much and such close observation they soon reached the conclusion that it was not an enchanted mill as everyone had thought and as the matrons had said, but a mechanical trick that could not be compared with something so moving, so human, and so full of everyday truth as a band of musicians.

One Hundred Years of Solitude, Gabriel García Marquez,
(translated from the Spanish by Gregory Rabassa)

Notes

1   Note the changes in parts of speech in *por donde asombrarse / where their amazement began*, and the addition of *began* implied in the original.
2   Note that the longer verbs are translated by clauses: *se trasnochaban / they stayed up all night*, and *se indignaron / they became indignant*.
3   The relative clause *a cuyo obstinante tumtum costó tiempo y trabajo acostumbrarse* becomes a coordinate clause in English: *and it took time and effort for them to grow accustomed to its obsessive toom-toom*.

B   Gentes y calles absortas.[1] Regulares las hiladas de muros, a grandes lienzos vacíos.[2] Puertas y ventanas de austera cantería, cerradas con tablones macizos, de nobles, rancias maderas,[3] desnudas de barnices y vidrios, todas como trabajadas por uno y el mismo artífice rudo y exacto.[4] Pátina del tiempo, del sol, de las lluvias, de las manos consuetudinarias,[5] en los portones, en los dinteles y sobre los umbrales. Casas de las que no escapan rumores, risas, gritos, llantos; pero a lo alto, la fragancia de finos leños consumidos en hornos y cocinas, envuelta para regalo del cielo con telas de humo.[6]

En el corazón y en los aledaños el igual hermetismo. Casas de las orillas, junto al río, junto al cerro, al salir de los caminos, con la nobleza de su cantería, que sella dignidad a los muros de adobe.

Y cruces al remate de la fachada más humilde, coronas de las esquinas, en las paredes interminables; cruces de piedra, de cal y canto, de madera, de palma; unas, anchas, otras, altas; y pequeñas, y frágiles, y perfectas y toscas.[7]

Al filo del agua, Agustín Yáñez
(Editorial Porrua, S.A., Mexico)

Here, the writer is not only describing the physical aspect of the village, but creating such a word picture that the reader can see the whole in all its details in his mind's eye, and even get an impression of the stillness and the slow rhythm of life as it is lived there. The use of language is highly stylized, almost poetic. The short staccato phrases are almost like brush strokes in a painting. The frequent use of commas, separating juxtaposed words and phrases, gives a certain deliberation to the movement of the eye, and the slow rhythm checks the pace of the reader and so heightens the effect. The translator's chief priority here is to create the same impression, keeping as close as possible to the original imagery and sound patterns.

Consider the translation below, note how the translator solves the various problems and say how far you think he conveys the same impression as the original.

People and streets absorbed[1] in their own thoughts. The smooth, straight walls present a blank surface, broken only by doors and windows.[2] Doors and windows, set in plain stonework, and fastened with heavy beams of good, seasoned timber;[3] there is no varnish or glass, and all have the appearance of having been fashioned by the same craftsman, primitive and exact.[4] Time, the sun, the rain, the daily touch of hands,[5] have given a patina to the panels of the doors, to the lintels and thresholds. From these houses no sounds of voices, no laughter, no shouts, no cries escape; but above them hovers the fragrance of fine wood, burned in ovens and kitchens, wrapped like a gift from heaven in clouds of blue smoke.[6]

Inside and out the same secrecy. In the houses on the banks of the river, on the slopes of the hills, on the outskirts of the village, the noble stonework gives a certain dignity to the adobe walls.

And the lowliest house has its cross on top, and there are wreaths of coloured paper flowers at the corners and on the walls stretching endlessly into the distance; crosses made of stone, of stone and mortar, of wood, of straw. . . wide, tall, small, and fragile crosses, some crudely fashioned, others perfect in form.[7]

The Edge of the Storm, Agustin Yáñez
(translated by Ethel Brinton)

Notes

1   Here the English *absorbed* would not give the full meaning of *absortas*; it is necessary to complete the idea with a phrase, e.g. *in themselves*.

2   This sentence cannot be translated literally. The translator must visualize the picture and convey it as closely as possible to the English reader.

3   Note here the evocative importance of words; *rancio* can mean English *rancid*, but we should not use this term to refer to *seasoned timber* or *well-matured wine*. The plural *maderas* is rendered more closely by *timber*.

4   Obviously the author does not mean *rude* or *rough* here in the normal English sense, but *unskilled* or *untrained*, yet this is in some measure contradicted by *y exacto*, so *primitive* is probably closer to his meaning.

5   *las manos consuetudinarias* — English would have to bring in the idea of touch here — *the daily touch of hands*

6   *telas de humo* — We cannot speak of *sheets* or *cloths* of smoke in English. To keep the imagery of the wrapping of the gift from heaven, we might use *clouds* of smoke.

7   English seems to need a little extra weight at the end of this paragraph to compensate for finality of the sound of *perfectas y toscas*, so the translator has substituted short phrases for single words here.

C   **Coplas por la muerte de su padre**

Recuerde el alma dormida,
Abive el seso y despierte,
contemplando
cómo se pasa la vida,
cómo se viene la muerte
tan callando;
cuán presto se va el plazer,
cómo después de acordado,
da dolor,
cómo, a nuestro parescer,
cualquiera tiempo pasado
fué mejor.

Nuestras vidas son los ríos
que van a dar en la mar,
que es el morir:
allí van los señoríos
derechos a se acabar
y consumir;
allí los ríos caudales,
allí los otros medianos
y más chicos,
allegados son iguales,
los que viven por sus manos
y los ricos.

Jorge Manrique

Consider the translation below of this part of the *Coplas* of Jorge Manrique by Henry W. Longfellow. Here the American poet has translated the Spanish poem by an English poem. Note how the translation keeps the form of the original poem, 6 line stanzas, two tercets of two longer lines followed by a short line, but the rhyming pattern is slightly different. Whereas the Spanish rhyme scheme is abc, abc, the scheme of the English poem is aab, ccb. Does this change affect the atmosphere of the poem?

How closely does the translator keep to the ideas expressed in the poem? to the imagery? to the sound effects? Write an appreciation of the English poem as a translation of the Spanish poem.

Ode on the Death of his Father

O, let the soul her slumbers break!
Let thought be quickened and awake,—
    Awake to see
How soon this life is past and gone,
And death comes softly stealing on,—
    How silently!

Swiftly our pleasures glide away:
Our hearts recall the distant day
    With many sighs;
The moments that are speeding fast
We heed not; but the past — the past —
    More highly prize.

Our lives are rivers gliding free
To that unfathomed boundless sea,
    The silent grave:
Thither all earthly pomp and boast
Roll to be swallowed up and lost
    In one dark wave.

Thither the mighty torrents stray,
Thither the brook pursues its way,
    And tinkling rill.
There all are equal. Side by side,
The poor man and the son of pride
    Lie calm and still.

(Translated by Henry W. Longfellow)

D   **El ingenioso hidalgo, Don Quijote de la Mancha**

Que trata de la condición y ejercicio del famoso hidalgo Don Quijote de la Mancha.

En un lugar de la Mancha, de cuyo nombre no quiero acordarme, no ha mucho tiempo que vivía un hidalgo de los de lanza en astillero, adarga antigua, rocín flaco y galgo corredor. Una olla de algo más vaca que carnero, salpicón las más noches, duelos y quebrantos los sábados, lentejas los viernes, algún palomino de añadidura los domingos, consumían las tres partes de su hacienda. El resto della concluían sayo de velarte, calzas de velludo para las fiestas, con sus pant u flas de lo mesmo, y los días de entresemana se honraba con su vellorí de lo más fino. Tenía en su casa una ama que pasaba de los cuarenta, y una sobrina que no llegaba a los veinte, y un mozo de campo y plaza, que así ensillaba el rocín como tomaba la podadera.

Miguel de Cervantes Saavedra

Consider the three translations given below and compare them. Compare the impression created by the original with that given by each of the translations. Note the different choice of words to translate *condición, hidalgo, ejercicio*; note also the different ways in which *adarga antigua, rocín flaco, galgo corredor* and *mozo de campo y plaza* are translated. Which version do you prefer? Why?

The ingenious knight, Don Quijote de la Mancha

Which treats of the condition and way of life of the famous knight, Don Quijote de la Mancha.

In a village of La Mancha, the name of which I do not care to recollect, there lived not long ago a knight, one of those who kept lance in rack, an ancient targe, a lank stallion, and a swift greyhound.

A pot which consisted somewhat more of beef than mutton, cold spiced meat and onions on most nights, resurrection pie on Saturdays, lentils on Fridays, and some pigeon by way of a treat for Sundays, ate up three-fourths of his estate. The rest of it went in a doublet of fine cloth, breeches of velvet, and slippers of the same for Sundays, while on weekdays he dressed himself out in his finest homespun. He retained at home a housekeeper who had passed forty, a niece who had not reached twenty, and a manservant for field and market, who could saddle the rouncy as well as he could handle a bill-hook.

(Translated by A.J. Duffield, 1881)

The Adventures of Don Quixote

Which treats of the quality and way of life of the famous knight Don Quijote de la Mancha.

In a certain village in La Mancha, which I do not wish to name, there lived not long ago a gentleman — one of those who have always a lance in the rack, an ancient shield, a lean hack and a greyhound for coursing. His habitual diet consisted of a stew, more beef than mutton, of hash most nights, boiled bones on Saturdays, lentils on Fridays, and a young pigeon as a Sunday treat; and on this he spent three-quarters of his income. The rest of it went on a fine cloth doublet, velvet breeches and slippers for holidays, and a homespun suit of the best in which he decked himself on weekdays. His household consisted of a housekeeper of rather more than forty, a niece not yet twenty, and a lad for the field and market, who saddled his horse and wielded the pruning-hook.

(Translated by J.M. Cohen, 1950)

The Ingenious Gentleman Don Quijote de la Mancha

Which treats of the station in life and the pursuits of the famous gentleman, Don Quixote de la Mancha.

In a village of La Mancha the name of which I have no desire to recall, there lived not so long ago one of those gentlemen who always have a lance in the rack, an ancient buckler, a skinny nag, and a greyhound for the chase. A stew with more beef than mutton in it, chopped meat for his evening meal, scraps for a Saturday, lentils on Friday, and a young pigeon as a special delicacy for Sunday, went to account for three-quarters of his income. The rest of it he laid out on a broadcloth greatcoat and velvet stockings for feast days, with slippers to match, while the other days of the week he cut a figure in a suit of the finest homespun. Living with him were a housekeeper in her forties, a niece who was not yet twenty, and a lad of the field and market place who saddled his horse for him and wielded the pruning-knife.

(Translated by Samuel Putnam, 1953)

E   Canciones entre el alma y el esposo

Esposa

Adónde te escondiste,
Amado, y me dejaste con gemido?
Como el ciervo huiste,
habiéndome herido;
Salí tras ti clamando, y eras ido.

Pastores, los que fuerdes
Allá por las majadas al otero,
si por ventura vierdes
Aquel que yo más quiero,
Decidle que adolezco, peno y muero.

San Juan de la Cruz

Analyze carefully the two translations of the poem given below. Which do you prefer? Why?

Spiritual Canticle Between the Soul and Christ

Bride

Where hidest thou from me,
Beloved, and I left wounded here? As yon
Swift hart, so thou didst flee;
With grief I followed on,
I sought and called for thee, but thou wert gone.

Shepherds, who go up higher
Unto your folds, if you by chance espy
Him whom I most desire,
O let him not go by,
But tell him that I suffer, grieve and die.

(Translated by Jessie Read Wendell)

Songs between the soul and the bridegroom

Bride

Where hast thou hidden thee
Beloved, leaving me to mourn?
Swift as a deer did'st flee,
And left me wounded, that I yearn
And wander, calling on thee to return.

Shepherds, if as ye wend
Towards your sheepcotes perched on high,
You chance to meet my friend
And well-beloved, drawing nigh,
Tell him that here I suffer, droop and die.

(Translated by F.T. Prince)

F   Amanecer de otoño

Una larga carretera
entre grises peñascales
y alguna humilde pradera
donde pacen negros toros. Zarzas, malezas, jarales.

Está la tierra mojada
por las gotas del rocío,
y la alameda dorada,
hacia la curva del río.

Tras los montes de violeta
quebrado el primer albor;
a la espalda la escopeta
entre sus galgos agudos, caminando un cazador. .

Antonio Machado

Analyze the above poem, then analyze and comment upon the translation below.

Autumn Dawn

A highroad's barren scar
Among the grey rock-spires
And humble pastures far
Where strong black bulls are grazing. Brambles, thickets, briars.

The dew has drenched with cold
The landscape in the dark
And the poplars' frieze of gold,
Toward the river's arc.

A hint of dawn half seen
With purple crags for frame.
Beside his greyhounds keen,
His eager gun at rest, a hunter stalking game.

(Translated by Jean Rogers Longland)

G   How could I help but think of the past towards which we were returning across the dense thickets of time, across the familiar pathways of the Greek sea? The night slid past me, an unrolling ribbon of darkness. The warm sea-wind brushed my cheek — soft as the brush of a fox. Between sleep and waking I lay, feeling the tug of memory's heavy plumb-line: tug of the leaf-veined city which my memory had peopled with masks, malign and beautiful at once. I should see Alexandria again, I knew, in the elusive temporal fashion of a ghost — for once you become aware of the operation of a time which is not calendar-time you become in some sort a ghost. In this other domain I could hear the echoes of words uttered long since in the past by other voices. Balthazar saying: 'This world represents the promise of a unique happiness which we are not well-equipped enough to grasp.' The grim mandate which the city exercised over its familiars, crippling sentiment, steeping everything in the vats of its own exhausted passions. Kisses made more passionate by remorse. Gestures made in the amber light of shuttered rooms. The flocks of white doves flying upwards among the minarets. These pictures seemed to me to represent the city as I would see it again. But I was wrong — for each new approach is different. Each time we deceive ourselves that it will be the same. The Alexandria I now saw, the first vision of it from the sea, was something I could not have imagined.

It was still dark when we lay up outside the invisible harbour with its remembered outworks of forts and anti-submarine nets. I tried to paint the outlines on the darkness with my mind. The boom was raised only at dawn each day. An all-obliterating darkness reigned. Somewhere ahead of us lay the invisible coast of Africa, with its 'kiss of thorns' as the Arabs say. It was intolerable to be so aware of them, the towers and minarets of the city, and yet to be unable to will them to appear. I could not see my own fingers before my face. The sea had become a vast empty ante-room, a hollow bubble of blackness.

Clea, Lawrence Durrell

These are the silent musings of a melancholy soul who travels not only through space but also through time, dreading to discover his long forgotten identity. These meditative wanderings are somewhat reminiscent of Thomas Mendip's second monologue in *The Lady's Not For Burning*, by Christopher Fry, included in this book (see below, page **128**). Compare *The night slid past me . . .* with *the night wind passed me like a sail . . .* The style of this prose selection does not maintain the lyric vein of the verse excerpt to which we refer. Notice the variations of rhythm which naturally integrate our altogether varied pace. Images are valid in themselves as silhouettes rising on the horizon or surging in the realm of memory and imagination. The longings of the character, conveyed through the author's descriptions, do not altogether detach him from the surrounding world. He moves in two worlds: the universe of his own introspection and the images produced by his own contemplation of outward reality. Snatches of obliterated conversations, remembrances of past experiences, images of great strength are all expressed in comparatively short sentences almost telegraph-like in their directness. Compare the Spanish version with the English text and express your point of view on the results of the translator's efforts.

¿Cómo podía yo dejar de pensar en el pasado hacia el que regresábamos a través de la densa espesura del tiempo, a través de las rutas conocidas de aquel mar griego? La noche desplegaba su cinta de oscuridad y se escurría a la distancia. El cálido viento marino me rozaba la mejilla con la delicadeza de una cola de zorro. Entre el sueño y la vigilia, sentía el tirón de la plomada de recuerdo; el tirón de la ciudad inervada como una hoja que mi memoria había poblado de máscaras, malignas y hermosas a la vez. Volvería a ver Alejandría — lo sabía — como un fantasma evadido del tiempo, porque cuando uno toma por fin conciencia del funcionamiento de un tiempo que no es el tiempo del calendario, se convierte en una especie de fantasma. En esa nueva dimensión podía oír los ecos de palabras pronunciadas hacia mucho tiempo, en el pasado, por otras voces, la de Balthazar cuando decía: 'Este mundo constituye la promesa de una felicidad única que no estamos suficiente preparados para comprender.' El inflexible dominio que la ciudad ejercía sobre sus criaturas, sentimiento mutilador que saturaba todas las cosas en los abismos de sus propias pasiones exhaustas. Besos que se tornaban más apasionados por el remordimiento. Gestos esbozados a la luz ambarina de habitaciones cerradas. Las bandadas de blancas palomas volando en lo alto entre los minaretes. Aquellas imágenes representaban para mí la ciudad que volvería a ver. Pero me equivocaba, pues todo nuevo encuentro es distinto del anterior. Cada vez nos engañamos con la ilusión de que habrá de ser el mismo. La Alejandría que ahora veía, la primera visión desde el mar, era algo que jamás había imaginado.

Era todavía de noche cuando llegamos a las afueras del invisible muelle con sus recordadas fortificaciones y redes antisubmarinos. Intenté trazar mentalmente los contornos en la oscuridad. El botalón se levantaba sólo al amanecer. Reinaba una oscuridad que lo devoraba todo: En alguna parte, frente a nosotros, se tendía la invisible costa africana, con su 'beso de espinas', como dicen los árabes. Era intolerable conocer tan bien aquellas torres y minaretes de la ciudad, y no poder sin embargo hacerlos aparecer a voluntad. Ni siquiera alcanzaba a distinguir mis dedos junto a mi rostro. El mar se había transformado en una vasta antecámara vacía, una hueca burbuja de oscuridad.

Clea (translated by Matilde Horne)

H . . . Night: and once again, the nightly grapple with death, the room shaking with demonic orchestras, the snatches of fearful sleep, the voices outside the window, my name being continually repeated with scorn by imaginary parties arriving, the dark's spinnets. As if there were not enough real noises in these nights the colour of grey hair. Not like the rending tumult of American cities, the noise of the unbandaging of great giants in agony. But the howling pariah dogs, the cocks that herald dawn all night, the drumming, the moaning that will be found later, white plumage huddled on telegraph wires in back gardens or fowl roosting in apple trees, the eternal sorrow that never sleeps of great Mexico. For myself I like to take my sorrow into the shadow of old monasteries, my guilt into cloisters and under tapestries, and into the misericordes of unimaginable *cantinas* where sad-faced potters and legless beggars drink at dawn, whose cold jonquil beauty one rediscovers in death. So that, when you left, Yvonne, I went to Oaxaca. There is no sadder word. Shall I tell you, Yvonne, of the terrible journey there through the desert over the narrow gauge railway on the rack of a third-class carriage bench, the child whose life its mother and I saved by rubbing its belly with tequila out of my bottle, or of how, when I went to my room in the hotel where we once were happy, the noise of slaughtering below in the kitchen drove me out into the glare of the street, and later, that night, there was a vulture sitting in the washbasin? Horrors portioned to a giant nerve! No, my secrets are of the grave and must be kept. And this is sometimes how I think of myself, as a great explorer who has discovered some extraordinary land from which he can never return to give his knowledge to the world: but the name of this land is hell.

Under the Volcano, Malcolm Lowry

Under the Volcano is undoubtedly one of the outstanding masterpieces of twentieth century fiction. After a series of vicissitudes, the novel has finally gained general universal admiration on account both of its structural innovations and of the beauty of style which expresses a pathos unparalleled in literature. The excerpt included here is part of 'the letter', one of the most moving testimonies of human suffering, in Chapter 1.

Note the careful choice of words selected by the novelist to produce the impression of despair, despondency and hopelessness. Analyze his combination of sounds and rhythmic effects: study carefully his handling of images, his masterly metaphors and pace of language. Compare the Spanish and English versions and try to enumerate some criticisms on the correspondences or differences you discover between the two texts. Do you think the Spanish version conveys the cycle of this long clause, only occasionally — and perhaps unnecessarily — punctuated, which starts on a moan of agony with the dreaded mention of *Night* and winds its way through painful recollections until it reaches final liberation in the sentence: *but the name of this land is hell?* Are you aware of the effects in the English text? Has the translator, in your opinion, transferred them successfully into an altogether different vehicle — the Spanish language, which has its own pace, imposed by such features as syntax, length of words, etc.

. . . Noche: y una vez más el nocturno combate con la muerte, el cuarto que se cimbra con demoníacas orquestas, las ráfagas de sueño aterrado, las voces fuera de la ventana, mi nombre que repiten con desdén imaginarios grupos que van llegando — espinetas de la oscuridad. ¡como si no hubiera bastantes ruidos reales en estas noches de color canoso! No semejantes al desgarrador tumulto de las ciudades norte-americanos, el ruido que produce el desvendar gigantes agónicos, sino el aullido de perros callejeros, a los gallos que anuncian el alba toda la noche, al tamborileo, a los quejidos que más tarde habrán de descubrirse, verde plumaje acurrucado en los alambres telegráficos de los jardines ocultos, a aves perchadas en manzanos — a la eterna tristeza del gran México que nunca duerme. En cuanto a mi, me gusta abrigar mi tristeza en la penumbra de antiguos monasterios, mi culpa en los claustros y bajo los tapices y entre las misericordias de inconcebibles 'cantinas', donde alfareros de rostro entristecido y mutilados pordioseros beben al despuntar el alba cuya fría belleza de junquillo volvemos a descubrir en la muerte. Así es que, cuando te fuiste, Yvonne, me marché a Oaxaca. ¡No hay palabra más triste! ¿Quieres que te relate, Yvonne, aquel terrible viaje: la travesía por el desierto en el angosto ferrocarril, sentado en el potro del asiento de un vagón de tercera clase?, ¿del niño cuya vida salvamos su madre y yo sobándole la barriga con tequila de mi botella?, ¿o cómo, cuando entré a mi cuarto en el hotel donde una vez fuimos felices, el ruido de la matanza, abajo, en la cocina, me hizo salir al resplandor de la calle?, ¿y cómo, más tarde, encontré aquella noche un zopilote posado en la palangana? ¡Horrores a la medida de los nervios de un gigante! No, mis secretos son de ultratumba y deben permanecer como tales. Y así, a veces me veo como un gran explorador que ha descubierto algún país extraordinario del que jamás podrá regresar para darlo a conocer al mundo: porque el nombre de esta tierra es el infierno.

Bajo el volcán, Malcolm Lowry
(translated by Raul Ortiz y Ortiz)

I   The presence that rose thus so strangely beside the waters, is expressive of what in the ways of a thousand years men had come to desire. Hers is the head upon which all 'the ends of the world are come,' and the eyelids are a little weary. It is a beauty wrought out from within upon the flesh, the deposit, little cell by cell, of strange thoughts and fantastic reveries and exquisite passions. Set it for a moment beside one of those white Greek goddesses or beautiful women of antiquity, and how would they be troubled by this beauty, into which the soul with all its maladies has passed! All the thoughts and experience of the world have etched and moulded there, in that which they have of power to refine and make expressive the outward form, the animalism of Greece, the lust of Rome, the mysticism of the middle age with its spiritual ambition and imaginative loves, the return of the Pagan world, the sins of the Borgias. She is older than the rocks among which she sits; like the vampire, she has been dead many times, and learned the secrets of the grave; and has been a diver in deep seas, and keeps their fallen day about her; and trafficked for strange webs with Eastern merchants, and, as Leda, was the mother of Helen of Troy, and, as Saint Anne, the mother of Mary; and all this has been to her but as the sound of lyres and flutes, and lives only in the delicacy with which it has moulded the changing lineaments, and tinged the eyelids and the hands. The fancy of a perpetual life, sweeping together ten thousand experiences, is an old one; and modern philosophy has conceived the idea of humanity as wrought upon by, and summing up in itself, all modes of thought and life. Certainly Lady Lisa might stand as the embodiment of the old fancy, the symbol of the modern idea.

'Leonardo da Vinci', in *The Renaissance*,
Walter Pater

This happens to be one of the most complex paragraphs of what is generally known as 'impressionist prose'. The author has carefully handled his choice of words and combination of sounds as well as the variety of metaphors and rich imagery he uses. His syntax is deliberately recherché and yet it conveys the feeling of an almost burnished translucent surface. Note the frequent omission of auxiliary verbs. Any Spanish translator of this piece of sheer brilliance would realize forthwith the difference his choice of tenses will make in the general effect of the vision as it rises from the vicinity of the invisible waves. For the sentence *She is older than the rocks among which she sits*, a version which attempts to keep the beauty of the original must re-create the image and express it in terms of a similar poetic nature as the author does in the original. How absurd a literal translation of this image would sound! *En más vieja que la rocas entre las que está sentada.* What do you think the author means by the *fallen day*? Note how the translator conveys the image in Spanish.
In *The fancy of a perpetual life, sweeping together* . . . note the way in which the translator has rendered into Spanish the two impulses entailed in the underlined expression.
Who or what is the passage about?

La presencia que así surgía en modo tan insólito a la orilla del agua expresa cuanto el hombre llegó a desear en el transcurso de un milenio. Suyo es el rostro donde convergen 'todos los extremos del mundo' y los párpados son un tanto melancólicos. Trátase de una belleza labrada desde dentro sobre la carne, depósito célula tras célula, de reflexiones extrañas, ensueños fantásticos y pasiones exquisitas. Colóquesela un instante junto a una de esas blancas diosas griegas o al lado de las mujeres hermosas de la antigüedad y ¡cómo se turbarían ante esta belleza, en la que se ha vertido el alma con todas sus dolencias! Todos los pensamientos y la experiencia del mundo han grabado y moldeado ahí, en cuanto poseen de fuerza para refinar y expresar la forma externa, el animalismo de Grecia, la sensualidad de Roma, el misticismo del medioevo con su ambición espiritual y amores imaginativos, el retorno del mundo pagano, los pecados de los Borgia. Es más antigua que las rocas que la rodean; como el vampiro, ha muerto muchas veces y aprendido los secretos de ultratumba, y ha buceado en mares profundos cuya penumbra crepuscular la envuelve; traficó en exóticos tejidos con mercaderes orientales; y, como Leda, fue madre de Helena de Troya; como Santa Ana, madre de María, y todo eso no ha sido para ella sino como música de liras y flautas, y perdura sólo en la delicadeza con que ha moldeado los cambiantes rasgos y matizado los párpados y las manos. El anhelo de una vida eterna que barre, juntandolas, diez mil experiencias es antiguo, y la filosofía moderna ha concebido la idea de la humanidad como forjada por todas las formas del pensamiento y vida, a las que resume. Sin duda doña Lisa podría pasar como encarnación del antiguo anhelo, símbolo de la idea moderna.

(Translated by Raul Ortiz y Ortiz)

J   Here are two extracts from the work of T.S. Eliot. The transparent simplicity in Eliot's use of language leads us through an extremely complex world, rich in meaning and profound in philosophical concepts. His mastery of classical versification integrates in both excerpts a combination of metres that weave intricate patterns of rhythmic surfaces, terse and smooth, which flow with an ease typical of the everyday spoken word. For the translator both texts represent a challenge and hold out a possibility, since the ambivalence of language reaches its peak here, and there are numerous opportunities for finding alternative moulds for the English blank verse.

    Read both texts and their Spanish versions aloud and compare the various effects produced in each language. Formulate your own criticisms and explain why you either accept or reject the solutions given in these translations. In case you have other options which you deem preferable, propose them to your fellow students and discuss them in class.

Burnt Norton

Time present and time past
Are both perhaps contained in time future,
And time future contained in time past.
If all time is eternally present
All time is unredeemable.
What might have been is an abstraction
Remaining a perpetual possibility
Only in a world of speculation.
What might have been and what has been
Point to one end, which is always present.
Footfalls echo in the memory
Down the passage which we did not take
Towards the door we never opened

Into the rose-garden. My words echo
Thus, in your mind.

                    But to what purpose
Disturbing the dust on a bowl of rose-leaves
I do not know.

                    Other echoes
Inhabit the garden. Shall we follow?
Quick, said the bird, find them, find them,
Round the corner. Through the first gate,
Into our first world, shall we follow
The deception of the thrush? Into our first world.

                                  T.S. Eliot

Tiempo presente y tiempo pasado
acaso estén ambos presentes en el tiempo futuro,
y el tiempo futuro contenido en el tiempo pasado.
Si todo tiempo es eternamente presente
todo tiempo es irremisible.
Lo que pudo haber sido es abstracción
que permanece como perpetua posibilidad
sólo en un mundo de especulación.
Lo que pudo haber sido y lo que ha sido
apuntan a un fin único, que está siempre presente.
Resuenan pisadas en la memoria
por el sendero que no tomamos
hacia la puerta que nunca abrimos
para el jardín de rosas. Mis palabras resuenan
así, en tu mente.

                    Pero, ¿a qué
perturbar el polvo en un tazón de pétalos de rosa?
No lo sé yo.

                    Otros ecos
habitan el jardín. ¿Seguiremos?
Rápido, dijo el pájaro, búscalos, búscalos,
a la vuelta de la esquina. Por la primera puerta,
hacia nuestro primer mundo, ¿seguiremos
el engaño del tordo? Hacia nuestro primer mundo.

                (Translated by Raul Ortiz y Ortiz)

East Coker

In my beginning is my end. In succession
Houses rise and fall, crumble, are extended,

Are removed, destroyed, restored, or in their place
Is an open field, or a factory, or a by-pass.
Old stone to new building, old timber to new fires,
Old fires to ashes, and ashes to the earth
Which is already flesh, fur and faeces,
Bone of man and beast, cornstalk and leaf.
Houses live and die: there is a time for building
And a time for living and for generation
And a time for the wind to break the loosened pane
And to shake the wainscot where the field-mouse trots
And to shake the tattered arras woven with a silent motto.

In my beginning is my end. Now the light falls
Across the open field, leaving the deep lane
Shuttered with branches, dark in the afternoon,
Where you lean against a bank while a van passes,
And the deep lane insists on the direction
Into the village, in the electric heat
Hypnotised. In a warm haze the sultry light
Is absorbed, not refracted, by grey stone.
The dahlias sleep in the empty silence.
Wait for the early owl.

T.S. Eliot

En mi principio está mi fin. Sucesivamente
álzanse y caen las casas, se desmoronan, se acrecientan
son removidas, se destruyen, se restauran, o en su sitio
queda un campo abierto o una fábrica o una desviación.
Piedra vieja en edificio nuevo, viejo leño en fuegos nuevos,
viejos fuegos en cenizas, y cenizas en tierra
que es ya carne, pelaje y heces,
hueso de hombre y bestia, tallo y hoja de maíz.
Las casas viven y mueren; hay un tiempo para construir
y un tiempo para vivir y para procrear
y un tiempo para que el viento arranque de la vidriera el cristal flojo
y sacuda el friso donde corretea el ratón de campo
y sacuda el harapiento tapiz tejido con lema silencioso.

En mi principio está mi fin. Ahora la luz
atraviesa el campo abierto y abandona la profunda senda
cubierta de ramas, oscura en el atardecer,
donde uno se apoya en el talud mientras un camión pasa,
y la profunda senda insiste en dirección
a la aldea, hipnotizada

en el calor eléctrico. En una bruma tibia
la piedra gris absorbe, sin reflejarla, la bochornosa luz.

Las dalias duermen en el silencio vacío.
Aguarda el buho tempranero.

(Translated by Raul Ortiz y Ortiz)

Compare the following translations with the foregoing ones. Say which you prefer and why.

East Coker

En mi principio está mi fin. En sucesión
Las casas se levantan y se caen, se desmoronan, se extienden,
Son trasladadas, destruídas, restauradas,
o en su lugar
Existe un campo abierto, o un taller, o una travesía
Vieja piedra para un nuevo edificio, vieja
leña para nuevos fuegos.
Viejos fuegos para cenizas, y cenizas para la tierra.
Que es ya carne, piel, heces.
Hueso de hombre y de bestia, tallo de maíz y hoja.
Las casas viven y mueren: hay un tiempo para edificar
Y un tiempo para la vida y la generación
Y un tiempo para que el viento rompa la
desvencijada ventana
Y sacuda el entarimado por donde trota el ratón
Y sacuda el harapiento Arras tejido con
un silencioso lema.
En mi principio está mi fin. Ahora la luz desciende
A través del campo abierto, dejando al callejón profundo
Cerrado de ramas, oscuro en la tarde.
Allá donde tú te reclinas en una loma
mientras un carro pasa.
Y el profundo callejón insiste en su dirección.
Hacia la aldea, hipnotizado
Por el calor eléctrico. En una bruma
ardiente la luz bochornosa
Es absorbida, no refractada, por la piedra gris.
Aguarda a la temprana lechuza.

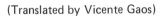

(Translated by Vicente Gaos)

Burnt Norton

El presente y el pasado
Serán tal vez presente en el futuro

Y el futuro esté contenido en el pasado.
Si todo tiempo está eternamente presente
Todo tiempo es irredimible.

Lo que pudo haber sido es una abstracción
Que sigue siendo posibilidad perpetua
Solamente en un mundo de especulación.

Lo que pudo haber sido y lo que ha sido
Apuntan a un mismo punto, siempre presente.

El eco de pisadas resuena en la memoria
A lo largo del corredor que no seguimos
Hacia la puerta que jamás abrimos
Al jardín de las rosas. Así el eco de mis palabras
En tu mente, resuena.
Pero con qué fin
Inquietan así polvo en un tazón de pétalos de rosa
No lo sé,
Otros ecos
Habitan el jardín. ¿Los seguiremos?
Pronto, dijo el pájaro, encuéntralos, encuéntralos,
A la vuelta de la esquina. Atravesando la primera verja,
Para entrar a nuestro primer mundo, ¿ sequiremos
El engaño del tordo? A nuestro primer mundo.

(Translated by Isabel Fraire)

Burnt Norton

El tiempo presente y el tiempo pasado
Están tal vez ambos presentes en el tiempo futuro,
Y el tiempo futuro contenido en el tiempo pasado.
Si todo tiempo es eternamente presente
Todo tiempo es irredimible.
Lo que podría haber sido es una abstracción
Que permanece como perpetua posibilidad
Sólo en un mundo de especulación.
Lo que podría haber sido y lo que ha sido
Apuntan a un fin único, que es siempre presente.
Resuenan pisadas en la memoria
Por el sendero que no recorrimos
Hacia la puerta que no abrimos nunca
En el jardín de rosas. Mis palabras resuenan
Así, en tu mente.
Mas con qué propósito
Remueven el polvo del cuenco de hojas de rosa
Yo no lo sé.
Otros ecos
Habitan el jardín, ¿Continuaremos?

De prisa, dijo el pájaro, descúbrelos, descúbrelos,
Junto al rincón. Tras la primera puerta,
En nuestro primer mundo, ¿seguiremos
a decepción del tordo? En nuestro primer mundo.

Translated by Vicente Gaos

K Here are two extracts from *The Lady's Not For Burning* by Christopher
Fry. Both the speeches selected for this book are deemed by the translator to
be amongst the most beautiful lyric passages in contemporary English literature.
In the twentieth century we find a medieval hero who speaks in a language until
now heard only on the lips of the loftiest Shakespearean protagonists, and who
expresses contemporary man's lyricism and *angst*. Thomas Mendip's language
and imagery are rich in meaning; his vocabulary flows through metaphors of
extreme complexity and, with the subtle auditive effects achieved by the author,
provides an almost insurmountable challenge for the translator.

We have striven to keep — as far as possible — a <u>similar</u> pace and rhythm to
those displayed in such a masterly fashion in the original. It has also been
necessary to consider, in the case of a play, whether the new version in another
language will function dramatically on stage, i.e. whether the lines lend themselves to dramatic delivery, and whether they can be grasped by the public.

Try to compare and analyze the effects sought for in the Spanish version, and
formulate your observations on achievements or failures.

Thomas   Guilty
Of mankind. I have perpetrated[1] human nature.
My father and mother were accessories before the fact,
But there'll be no accessories after the fact,
By my virility there won't! Just see me
As I am, me like a perambulating
Vegetable, patched with inconsequential
Hair, looking out of two small jellies for the means
Of life, balanced on folding bones, my sex
No beauty but a blemish to be hidden
Behind judicious rags,[2] driven and scorched
By boomerang[3] rages and lunacies which never
Touch the accommodating artichoke
Or the seraphic strawberry beaming in its bed:
I defend myself against pain and death by pain
And death, and make the world go round, they tell me,
By one of my less lethal appetites:
Half this grotesque life I spend in a state
Of slow decomposition, using
The name of unconsidered God as a pedestal
On which I stand and bray that I'm best
Of beasts, until under some patient

Moon or other I fall to pieces, like
A cake of dung. Is there a slut would hold
This in her arms and put her lips against it?

The Lady's Not For Burning, Christopher Fry

Thomas   Culpable
de humanidad. He perpetrado[1] la naturaleza humana.
Mi padre y madre fueron cómplices antes el hecho,
pero cómplices no habrá después del hecho,
¡por mi virilidad, no los habrá! Contémplame
tal cual soy, ambulante
vegetal, parchado de pelo
intrascendente que escudriña desde dos diminutas gelatinas
en busca de sustento, equilibrado sobre huesos plegadizos;
mi sexo que dista de ser bello, mas es baldón que he de ocultar
bajo andrajos circunspectos,[2] aguijoneado y abrasado
por furores y locuras de búmerang[3] que nunca
afectan a la alcachofa complaciente
ni a la fresa que, seráfica, brilla en su lecho:
me defiendo del dolor y muerte con dolor
y muerte, y hago girar la tierra, — se me dice —
merced a uno de mis menos letales apetitos:
la mitad de esta vida tan grotesca me transcurre en un estado
de lenta decomposición, e invoco
el nombre de un dios que me es indiferente como pedestal
desde done me yergo y rebuzno que soy yo la mejor
bestia, hasta que bajo alguna u otra luna tolerante
me desmorone, cual
montón de estiércol. ¿Acaso habrá ramera alguna
dispuesta a estrechar todo esto entre sus brazos y a posar sus labios sobre ello?

Que no quemen a la dama, Christopher Fry,
(translated by Raul Ortiz y Ortiz)

Thomas
I've been cast adrift on a raft of melancholy.
The night-wind passed me, like a sail across
A blind man's eye.[4] There it is,
The interminable tumbling of the great grey
Main of moonlight,[5] washing over
The little oyster-shell of this month of April:
Among the raven-quills of the shadows
And on the white pillows of men asleep:
The night's a pale pastureland of peace,

And something condones the world, incorrigibly.
But what, in fact, is this vaporous charm?
We're softened by a nice conglomeration
Of the earth's uneven surface, refraction of light,
Obstruction of light, condensation, distance,
And that sappy upshot of self-centred vegetablism
The trees of the garden. How is it we come
To see this as a heaven in the eye?
Why should we hawk and spit out[6] ecstasy
As though we were nightingales, and call these quite
Casual degrees and differences
Beauty? What guile recommends the world
And gives our eyes the special sense to be
Deluded, above all animals? — Stone me, Richard!
I've begun to talk like that soulless girl, and she
May at this moment be talking like me! I shall go
Back into the garden, and choke myself with the seven
Sobs I managed to bring with me from the wreck.

The Lady's Not For Burning, Christopher Fry

Thomas
Fui lanzado a la deriva a bordo de una balsa de melancolía.
El viento de la noche me pasó de largo, cual vela que surcara ante
el ojo de un ciego.[4] Helo allí,
el interminable embate del gris e inmenso
plenilunio[5] que barre
el minúsculo nácar de este abril:
entre sombras oscuras cual corvino plumaje
y sobre las blancas almohadas de los hombres que duermen
es la noche, pálida pradera de paz,
y algo indulta al mundo, incorregiblemente.
Mas ¿qué es, de hecho, este encantamiento vaporoso?
Nos enternece la suave conglomeración
de la desigual faz terrestre, refracción de luz,
obstrucción de luz, condensación, distancia,
y aquel jugoso retoño de egocéntrico vegetalismo:
los árboles del jardín, ¿Por qué artes llegamos
a sentir esto cual paraíso en nuestros ojos?
¿Por qué pregonar y vomitar[6] éxtasis
cual si fuésemos ruiseñores, y llamar belleza
a estos grados y diferencias asaz
casuales? ¿Qué trampa recomienda el mundo
y da a nuestra mirada el singular sentido para engañarnos
más que a ningún otro animal? — ¡Apedréame, Richard!
Comienzo a hablar como esa moza desalmada, y ella

tal vez ahora mismo esté hablando como yo. Volveré
al jardín a ahogarme con los siete
sollozos que lograra traer del naufragio.

Que no quemen a la dama, Christopher Fry,
(translated by Raul Ortiz y Ortiz)

Notes

1   Note the use of the verb *to perpetrate*, reserved exclusively for a direct object of a criminal nature, referring here to mankind as though it were a crime. The translator has kept this specific and unusual turn of phrase.

2   Note how the translator has rendered the lines from . . . *my sex no beauty* to . . . *judicious rags* in order to follow the trend and movement of the verse in the English original.

3   As there is no original Spanish equivalent of the word *boomerang* (native name, New South Wales), the translator finds it legitimate to give it the Spanish spelling, the more so since the word is now in current use in Spanish-speaking countries.

4   Note how the noun *vela* in the context of *the blind man's eye* might be misleading in Spanish; hence to avoid ambiguity the translator has used the verb *surcar* in Spanish, which the reader will associate with a boat that sails (*surca*).

5   *The interminable tumbling of the great grey main of moonlight*: although it is impossible to render exact equivalents in an alliteration of this nature, the translator has striven to reproduce as many effects as the text in Spanish allows without losing clarity in meaning or vividness in imagery.

6   Why do you suppose the translator chose *vomitar* for *spit out*?

Spanish Passages for Translation

1   Después de cenar se reunieron en torno al fuego. Comentaron incidencias del paseo. Se comunicaban los mejores sitios que cada uno había descubierto. Chisporroteaban los leños. A ratos sonó el acordéon de Luis, templado por el cansancio. Las voces fueron[1] decayendo hasta cesar. Luego todo permaneció en silencio. Silencio olvidado de todo, fuera de todo. Era el verdadero descanso, el descansado de lo conocido, el[2] que llega al trasplantarse a un sitio sin antecedentes ni consiguientes, sin relaciones, ni problemas.[3] El[2] que viene de sumergirse en un vacío, sin futuro ni pasado, donde nada ata a uno ni uno cuenta para nada.[3]

Juan Antonio Payno

I   Read the passage carefully, then answer the following questions in English:
What kind of 'paseo' is suggested by the context? You will need to be specific in English.
What impression of the scene does the writer convey?
What kind of atmosphere does he create? How does he do this?

II   Mark the following translations 1, 2, 3, in order of your preference in the context. Mark X any you consider unacceptable. Give a better version if one occurs to you.

a   chisporroteaban
  ☐ sputtered
  ☐ threw out sparks
  ☐ crackled
b   templado
  ☐ tempered
  ☐ muted
  ☐ softened

c   olvidado de todo
  ☐ forgetful of everything
  ☐ forgotten by everything
  ☐ forgetting everything
d   relaciones
  ☐ relations
  ☐ connections
  ☐ ties

III   Translate the passage into English.

2   Alejandro entró con un atado de leños y ella le pidió que encendiera el fuego. En realidad no hacía falta; la atmósfera era agradable, pero <u>antes de una hora – con el anochecer</u> –, descendería el frío.[4] Vió[5] como el viejo iba colocando los leños uno sobre otro,[6] en una especie de tejido[7] y cómo <u>éstos ardían</u> inmediatamente, al primer cerillo.

  — Tan secos[8] – dijo Alejandro.
  — Sí . . . Arderán demasiado aprisa.
  — ¿Traigo más?
  — Sí. Traiga.
Alejandro desapareció.
  — <u>Eres más friolenta que yo</u> – comentó Esther.
  — No. . . No soy mucho, pero <u>el fuego me da alegría</u>. ¡Es tan bonito!
Las dos se quedaron contemplando las llamas que minuto a minuto adquirían más intensidad.
Lorenza se metió las manos entre el pelo[9] y preguntó:
  — ¿En qué piensas?
  — En Cuernavaca, en mamá, en nada . . . Es bonito el fuego.
Siguió un largo silencio en el cual Esther estuvo a punto de decir: "En Hugo. . ." Pero mientras más[10] se agrandaba ese silencio más díficil parecía decir el nombre de su marido e iniciar una confidencia, a pesar de que el momento era propicio. Fué Lorenza quien lo usó.
  — . . . Y no es que quiera impresionarte, es que. . . así soy. Suena estúpido, pero es verdad. Cuando dije lo de las mentiras no hablaba por hablar,[9] tengo mis razones. . . .
Se puso a contarle lo de la fiesta de fin de año, lo del vestido. . . Pero sin pensar en ello, recordando otra mentira, otra <u>encubierta ignominia</u>, la muerte de su padre. Por exceso de bebida, por falta de alimento, por miseria, había muerto de tuberculosis. Cuando el doctor les dijo de qué enfermedad se trataba lo apartaron a un cuartito pequeño que había arriba, en aquella estrecha casa del callejón de Rojas – última posesión de los Landero. – El doctor era amigo de ellos y no lo contó a nadie. Pero no era necesario contarlo: todo el mundo lo sabía.

El bordo, Sergio Galindo
(Fondo de Cultura Economica, Mexcio

I   Try to picture the scene and hear the conversation. What kind of atmosphere does the author create? Can you re-create this in your translation?

II   Mark the following translations 1, 2, 3, in order of your preference in the context. Mark X any you consider unacceptable. Give a better version if one occurs to you.

a   antes de una hora — con el anochecer
  ☐ in an hour — at nightfall
  ☐ in an hour — when it got dark
  ☐ within an hour — with the dusk

b   éstos ardían
  ☐ these were burning
  ☐ they caught fire
  ☐ they blazed up

c   Eres más friolenta que yo
  ☐ You feel the cold more than I do
  ☐ You are more shivery than I am
  ☐ You are more sensitive to cold than I am

d   El fuego me da alegría
  ☐ The fire gives me pleasure
  ☐ The fire looks cheerful
  ☐ I like the look of the fire

e   encubierta ignominia
        ☐ concealed shame
        ☐ shameful secret
        ☐ hidden ignominy

III   Translate the passage into English.

3   Vine a Comala porque me dijeron que acá vivía mi padre, un tal Pedro Páramo.[11] Mi madre me lo[12] dijo. Y yo le prometí que vendría[13] a verlo en cuanto ella muriera. Le apreté sus manos en señal de que lo haría; pues ella estaba por morirse y yo en un plan de prometerle todo. "No dejes de ir a visitarlo — me recomendó —, Estoy segura de que le dará gusto conocerte." Entonces no pude hacer otra cosa sino decirle que así lo haría, y a tanto de círselo se lo seguí diciendo aun después que a mis manos les costó trabajo zafarse de sus manos muertas.
        Todavía antes me había dicho:
        — No vayas a pedirle nada. Exígele lo nuestro. Lo que estuvo obligado a darme y nunca me dió. . . El olvido en que nos tuvo, mi hijo, cóbraselo caro.
        — Así lo haré, madre.
        Pero no pensé cumplir mi promesa. Hasta que ahora pronto comencé a llenarme de sueños, a darle vuelo a las ilusiones. Y de este modo se me fue formando un mundo alrededor de la esperanza que era aquel señor llamado Pedro Páramo, el marido de mi madre. Por eso vine a Comala.
        Era ese tiempo de la canícula, cuando el aire de agosto sopla caliente, envenenado por el olor podrido de las saponarias. El camino subía y bajaba; "sube o baja según se va o se viene. Para él que va, sube; para él que viene, baja."
        — ¿Cómo dice usted que se llama el pueblo que se ve allá abajo?
        — Comala, señor.

Pedro Páramo, Juan Rulfo
(Fondo de Cultura Economica, Mexico)

I   Read the passage carefully, then answer the following questions in English:
What is the general effect of this passage on the reader?
How does the author create this?
What do you notice about his choice of words?
How will you re-create the total effect in your translation?

II   Mark the following translations 1, 2, 3, in order of your preference in the context. Mark X any you consider unacceptable. Give a better version if one occurs to you.
a   en cuanto ella muriera
        ☐ as soon as she died
        ☐ as soon as she should die
        ☐ as soon as she was dead
b   Así lo haré
        ☐ I will do it
        ☐ I will
        ☐ So I will

c   envenenado por el olor podrido de las saponarias
  ☐ foetid with the stench of the soapwort
  ☐ infected with the decaying smell of the soapwort
  ☐ poisoned by the rank smell of the soapwort

III   Translate the passage into English.

4A   Daban las horas en el reloj[14] de la Catedral y Sebastián contó mentalmente las campanadas. Eran las seis. Aún faltaba una hora para acudir a[15] casa del señor Sixto, y le disgustaba volver a enfrentarse con la Orencia y responder a sus nerviosas[16] interrogantes. Se detuvo en medio de la plaza y, como advirtiese que una vendedora de pan blanco se dirigió hacia él, aturdido e inconsciente, cruzó la calle, empujó el portón claveteado del Convento de los Capuchinos y entró en él.

Era la primera vez que Sebastián cruzaba aquellos recios muros, y al verse arropado en el ambiente espectral del templo sintió una rara impresión de frío.

C.P.E., June 1977, Miguel Delibes (adapted)

I   Translate the passage into English, trying to convey the sequence of events presented by the writer as *naturally* as possible.

4B   — Sólo ésto me faltaba . . ¡Este maldito se ha propuesto darme guerra, pero si quiere guerra la tendrá! ¡Vaya que sí![17]

— ¿Qué es ello, don Saturnino? — Luis, el mayor de los hermanos, se aproximó a él.

— ¿Qué ha de ser? Este bribón[18] de Hugo, que es un sinvergüenza[18] de siete suelas. Pero ya le voy a dar yo citaciones, ya. . . Esgrimía de nuevo al papelito blanco, sin el sobre ahora. — Me ha llevado el muy pillo[18] a la Magistratura. . . ¡Excuso decirles a ustedes! Yo un escándalo en la Magistratura del Trabajo, cuando soy un padre para mis subordinados, cuando. . .

Don Arturo intentó aplacarle.

— ¡No hace falta que me calme nadie, anótelo bien! Yo sólo quiero saber quién, además de usted, está dispuesto a atestiguar la verdad. . .

C.P.E., June 1977, Miguel Delibes (adapted)

I   Translate the passage into English, trying to match the very colloquial and forceful language of the original.

5

Leandro y Crispín que salen por la segunda izquierda.[19]

Leandro   Gran ciudad ha de ser ésta, Crispín; en todo se advierte su señorío y riqueza.

Crispín   Dos ciudades hay. Quiera el Cielo que en la mejor hayamos dado!

Leandro	¿Dos ciudades, dices, Crispín? Ya entiendo, antigua y nueva, una de cada parte del río.[20]
Crispín	¿Qué importa el río ni `la vejez ni la novedad? Digo dos ciudades como en toda ciudad del mundo: una para el que llega con dinero, y otra para el que llega como nosotros.
Leandro	¡Harto es haber llegado <u>sin tropezar con la justicia</u>! Y bien quisiera detenerme aquí algún tiempo,que[21] ya me cansa tanto correr tierras.
Crispín	A mí no,que[21] es condición de los naturales, como yo, del libre reino de Picardía no hacer asiento en parte alguna, si no es forzado y en galeras, que es duro asiento. Pero ya que sobre esta ciudad caímos y es plaza fuerte a lo que se descubre, tracemos como prudentes capitanes nuestro plan de batalla, si hemos de conquistarla con provecho.
Leandro	¡<u>Mal pertrechado ejército venimos</u>!
Crispín	Hombres somos, y con hombres hemos de vernos.[20]
Leandro	Por todo caudal, nuestra persona. <u>No quisiste que nos desprendiéramos de</u> estos vestidos, que,[21] <u>malvendiéndolos</u>, hubiéramos podido juntar algún dinero.
Crispín	¡Antes me desprendiera yo de la piel que de un buen vestido!Que[21] nada importa tanto como parecer, según va el mundo, y el vestido es lo que antes parece.

Los intereses creados, Jacinto Benavente

I   Read the dialogue carefully, then answer the following questions in English:
What do you learn about the speakers? About their relationship to each other? What are they talking about? What does Crispin mean by 'el libre reino de Picardía'?
What do you notice about the language they are using? How can you convey the same impression in English? You may have to change constructions more than in translating a straight prose passage.

II   Mark the following translations 1, 2, 3, in order of your preference in the context. Mark X any you consider unacceptable. Give a better version if one occurs to you.

a   sin tropezar con la justicia
   ☐ without falling into the hands
     of the law
   ☐ without running up against
     the law
   ☐ without running into justice
b   ¡Mal pertrechado ejército venimos!
   ☐ A badly equipped army we are!
   ☐ A nicely equipped army we are!
   ☐ A fine army we are!

c   No quisiste que nos desprendiéramos de . . .
   ☐ You didn't want us to get rid
     of . . .
   ☐ You wouldn't part with . . .
   ☐ You refused to sell . . .
d   malvendiéndolos
   ☐ selling them cheaply
   ☐ selling them at a loss
   ☐ getting a poor price for them

III   Translate the passage into English.
Read your translation aloud and listen to how it sounds.

6

Capitán	¡Basta ya![22] Esta es la ocasión de escaparse![23]
Urdemalas	¡Y tanto! Llega, por fin, la oportunidad de emanciparnos y perdéis el tiempo peleándoos.
Capitán	Cierto. Huyamos.
Muñecas	(A coro,) Libertad, libertad.
Juan	(Saltando regocijadísimo.[24]) Cu, cu, cu, cu.
Pero Grullo	Calla, tú, tontuelo. ¿Quién va a sustituir a Pygmalión para dirigirnos?
Mingo Revulgo	Yo me encargo de administraros y exhibiros por el mundo.
Don Lindo	Como si tuvieras tú el talento de Pygmalión.
Mingo Revulgo	Para eso tenemos a Urdemalas de consejero.
Pero Grullo	Y yo, ¿qué?[22] ¡Puede prescindirse de mí en ese gobierno?
Urdemalas	(Disimulando una sonrisa.) De ninguna manera. Tú serás nuestro diplomático y representante entre los hombres. Estás lleno de dignidad, y no te equivocas nunca.
Pero Grullo	Exacto. Me gusta mucho que me hagan justicia.
Urdemalas	No perdamos más tiempo.
Capitán	Muy bien hablado. Voy a preparar la fuga en el acto[22] y a enardeceros a todos.
Juan	(Muy alegre.) Cu, cu, cu, cu.
Capitán	(Sacando el sable y blandiéndolo en el aire.) Venid aquí. Escuchadme atendedme. (Continúa empuñando con la diestra el sable, y recoge del suelo, con la izquierda, la linterna que dejó el Conserje, contemplándola detenidamente. Rodéanle muñecos[25] y muñecas. Accionando, ya con el sable, ya con la linterna.) ¡Os hablo en nombre de nuestra conveniencia y más sagrados intereses!
Urdemalas	(Yendo cerca del Capitán.) Sé breve.
Capitán	Ya, ya. Fíjaos bien todos en esa ventana. (Volviéndose y señalándola con el sable.) ¡Fíjaos bien! (Los muñecos miran a la ventana.) Tras esa ventana está el fin de nuestra esclavitud.
Pero Grullo	(Adelantando un paso y alzando solemnemente el brazo.) Y el principio de nuestra libertad.
Urdemalas	¡Eso es! ¡Bravo!

El señor de Pigmalión, Jacinto Grau

I Read the scene carefully, then answer the following questions in English:
What do you learn about the attitudes of the different characters?
What is the general impression created by the scene? How can you convey this in English?

II Mark the following translations 1, 2, 3, in order of your preference in the context. Mark X any you consider unacceptable. Give a better version if one occurs to you.

a Me gusta mucho que me hagan justicia
☐ I do like to have justice
☐ I do like to be given my due
☐ I very much like justice to be done

b Yendo cerca del Capitán
☐ Approaching the Captain
☐ Going up to the Captain
☐ Drawing near the Captain

III   Translate the passage into English.

7   Nada dije a Alfredo de mi descubrimiento del día de Navidad. Lo contrario hubiese equivalido a poner las cosas peor de lo que estaban, ya que hay cosas que se soportan mejor en la penumbra que perfiladas en toda su ingrata sinceridad. A Alfredo la cabía aún la duda que afectaba no sólo a la relación de su madre con 'el hombre', sino a toda posible relación irregular, en abstracto, entre cualquier hombre y cualquier mujer. Dejé por ello correr los días sin dejarme ganar por la vanidad de partir con mi amigo un descubrimiento que le tocaba tan de cerca.

Por otra parte, las conversaciones sobre nuestras familias iban espaciándose cada vez más,[26] sin que ni nosotros mismos nos percatáramos de que era nuestra propia vida, la vida que vivíamos, la que desplazaba de nuestras mentes la idea de toda otra preocupación. Tampoco su madre ni mi tío, aparentaban por otra parte, ningún interés en evitar este apagamiento de nuestra admiración y cariño hacia ellos. Vivían su vida con absoluta independencia. Ambos faltaban de Ávila, casi sin interrupción, desde nuestros respectivos internamientos en casa de don Mateo. La madre de Alfredo no asomó por allí pasadas las Navidades, y mi tío, aparte una relampagueante visita en el mes de marzo, apenas si volvió a acordarse de que, a retaguardia de sus ocupaciones y devaneos, quedaba un sobrino y pupilo a quien, siquiera por ley, tenía la obligación de controlar y educar. Alfredo recibía cartas con relativa frecuencia; yo, tan de tarde en tarde, que terminé por perder el poco gusto con que antes recibiese la correspondencia de mi tío, y, algunas veces, dejé transcurrir varias semanas sin abrir, ni picarme la tentación de hacerlo siquiera, las cartas que mi tío pergeñaba en Barcelona.

Fruto lógico de esta tibieza hacia ellos fue el fomento de la amistad recíproca que nos unía a Alfredo y a mí. De mi parte puedo afirmar que experimentaba casi de una manera física el acercamiento creciente de nuestros espíritus. El día que, por cualquier circunstancia, nos fallaba alguno de los habituales ratos de expansión confidencial, me parecía que me obligaban a cargar con un lastre insoportable que impedía el ascenso normal del globo de mi optimismo pueril. Estábamos ya hechos como la mano y el guante, para encontrar uno en el otro la forma y, otro en el uno, el calor.

D.E.S. June 1976, Miguel Delibes

I   Mark the following translations 1, 2, 3, etc. in order of your preference in the context. Mark X any you consider unacceptable. Give a better version if one occurs to you.

a   lo contrario
- ☐ the opposite
- ☐ otherwise
- ☐ to have done so
- ☐ if I had

b   ingrata
- ☐ unwelcome
- ☐ unpleasant
- ☐ ungrateful
- ☐ disagreeable

c   educar
- ☐ educate
- ☐ bring up
- ☐ care for

d   de tarde en tarde
- ☐ from time to time
- ☐ infrequently
- ☐ occasionally

e   pergeñaba
    ☐ scribbled off
    ☐ dashed off
    ☐ scrawled

II   Translate the passage into English.

This is a straightforward account of the speaker's memories of a certain period of his youth. The translator will try to keep the simplicity of the style in English.

8   Caminábamos[27] y caminábamos hablando no más de la tierra. Yo era el nieto consentido de mi abuelo. Casi desde que nací me sacó a sus andanzas de todos los días; primero abrazándome;[28] luego, en la cabeza de la silla; después a enancas. Si no el mero día de mi nacimiento, sí a la siguiente semana, o a lo sumo antes de cumplir un mes de nacido. Si no puedo decir que nací a caballo, sí me crié a caballo, y a caballo crecí. El mismo día que yo, nació un potrillo de la yegua más fina y lo apartó mi abuelo para mí; lo cuidó tanto como a mí, como si fuéramos gemelos, o todavía más: una sola persona. Era mi tocayo y el Tocayo se le quedó por nombre. . . .

Entre mi abuelo y el Tocayo me enseñaron[29] a entender el idioma en que habla la tierra, sus gustos y caprichos, que[30] también los tiene. Paraba el caballo las orejas como diciéndome: — oye, y yo me quedaba oyendo; hacía esfuerzos para oír; primero no más oía[31] el zumbar del aire, de los animales voladores, de los árboles, y los ruidos del rancho, de los animales caseros, de los arroyos, de las lluvias, del trueno; me fijé en que el Tocayo paraba las orejas antes de que se produjeran los ruidos y cuando pasábamos por sitios en que alguien había sido muerto; más tarde comencé a oír el crecimiento de las yerbas, de las milpas, y el paso de las hormigas, de los gusanos, de los microbios y plagas, debajo de la tierra o adentro de los capullos, de las hojas de los elotes, de las vainas del frijol y los chícharos, o escondidos en los codos de retoños. Cada cosa se la iba preguntando al abuelo: — qué dice el aire cuando ni hay viento, y las moscas y las mariposas cuando están paradas no más, y los perros cuando aúllan distinto a sus ladridos de costumbre, y por qué para las orejas el Tocayo si enfrente no hay nada extraño.

Las tierras flacas, Agustín Yáñez

(Editorial Joaquin Mortiz, Mexico

How would you describe this passage? What are the elements of the style which you will try to preserve in your translation? What do you notice about the author's use of language?

Note the passages where you will need to use a different construction in English. Are there any difficult words? Try to find more than one English equivalent for each and choose the most suitable in the context.

I   Translate the passage into English.

Read your translation without looking at the Spanish. Does it convey the same impression?

9   Mi madre, al revés de mi padre, no era gruesa, aunque andaba muy bien de estatura;[32] era larga y chupada y no tenía aspecto de buena salud,[33] sino que, al contrario, tenía la tez cetrina[33] y las mejillas hondas y toda la presencia de estar o tísica o de no andarle muy lejos;[34] era también desabrida y violenta, tenía un humor que se daba a todos los diablos[35] y un lenguaje en la boca que Dios le haya perdonado, porque blasfemaba las peores cosas[33] a cada momento y por los más débiles motivos. Vestía siempre de luto y era poco amiga del agua, tan poco que si he de decir la verdad, en todos los años de su vida que yo conocí, no la vi lavarse más que en una ocasión en que mi padre la llamó borracha y ella quiso como demostrarle que no le daba miedo el agua. El vino en cambio ya no le disgustaba tanto y siempre que apañaba algunas perras, o que le rebuscaba el chaleco al marido,[35] me mandaba a la taberna por una frasca que escondía, porque no se la encontrase mi padre, debajo de la cama. Tenía un bigotillo cano por las esquinas de los labios, y una pelambrera enmarañada y zafia que recogía en un moño, no muy grande, encima de la cabeza.

La familia de Pascual Duarte, Camilo José Cela

The translator's main aim here will be to see the picture of the speaker's mother as he describes her, and convey this picture in English.

I   **Mark the following translations 1, 2, 3, in order of your preference in the context. Mark X any you consider unacceptable. Give a better version if one occurs to you.**

a   gruesa
  ☐ big
  ☐ fat
  ☐ stout

b   desabrida
  ☐ insipid
  ☐ disagreeable
  ☐ surly

c   apañaba algunas perras
  ☐ collected some dogs
  ☐ got together a few coppers
  ☐ got hold of a few cents

II   **Translate the passage into English.**

10   La vida de una pequeña ciudad tiene un ritmo acompasado y monótono. Todos los días, a las mismas horas, ocurre lo mismo. Si habéis pasado vuestra niñez y vuestra adolescencia en el tráfago y el bullicio, mal os acomodaréis de la existencia uniforme, gris, de una vieja casa en una vieja ciudad. Hagáis lo que hagáis, no podréis engañaros; sea cualquiera lo que arbitréis para ilusionaros a vosotros mismos, siempre os vendrá al espíritu el recuerdo de aquellos pintorescos y bulliciosos días pasados. Por la mañana, en la ciudad vetusta, las campanas de la catedral se mezclan las campanaditas cristalinas argentinas, de los distintos y lejos conventos. Un mostranquero[36] echa su pregón[37] en la calle desierta. Luego un ermitaño pide su limosna "Den por Dios para la lámpara de la señora Santa Lucía, que les conserve la vista!" Un mes sucede a otro; los años van pasando; en invierno las montañas vecinas se tornan blancas; en verano el vivo resplandor de sol llena las plazas y callejas; las rosas de los rosales se abren fragantes en la primavera; caen lentas, amarillas, las hojas en el otoño. . . De tarde en tarde, Costanza recuerda los años pasados, allá en su mocedad, en el mesón del *Sevillano*.

Visión de España, Azorín

As you read this passage, listen to the sound of it. Note the rhythm of the prose and the atmosphere created and try to achieve the same effect in English.

I Mark the following translations 1, 2, 3, etc. in order of your preference in the context. Mark X any you consider unacceptable. Give a better version if one occurs to you.

a acompasado
- ☐ slow
- ☐ regular
- ☐ measured
- ☐ deliberate

b tráfago
- ☐ traffic
- ☐ drudgery
- ☐ hustle
- ☐ intense activity

c espíritu
- ☐ spirit
- ☐ soul
- ☐ mind

III Translate the passage into English.

11 La población se presenta, por lo general, en el campo castellano, recogida en lugares, villas o ciudades, en grupos de apiñadas viviendas, distanciados de largo en largo por extensas y peladas soledades. El caserío de los pueblos es compacto y recortadamente demarcado, sin que[38] vaya perdiéndose y difuminándose en la llanura con casas aisladas que lo rodean, sin matices de población intermedia, como si las viviendas se apretaran en derredor de la iglesia para prestarse calor y defenderse del rigor de la Naturaleza, como si las familias buscaran una segunda capa, en cuyo ambiente aislarse de la crueldad del clima y la tristeza del paisaje. Así es que los lugareños tienen que recorrer a las veces en su mula no chico trecho hasta llegar a su labranza, donde trabajan, uno aquí, otro allá, aislados, y los gañanes no pueden hasta la noche volver a casa, a dormir el reconfortante sueño del trabajo sobre el escaño duro de la cocina. ¡Y[38] que es de verlos <u>a la caída de la tarde</u>, bajo el cielo blanco, dibujar en él sus siluetas, montados en sus mulas, dando al <u>aire sutil</u> sus cantares lentos, monótonos y tristes, que se pierden en la infinita inmensidad del campo lleno de surcos!

Mientras ellos están en la labor, sudando sobre la dura tierra, hacen la suya <u>las comadres</u>, <u>murmurando</u> en las solanas en que gozan del breve día. En las largas veladas invernales suelen reunirse amos y criados <u>bajo la ancha campana del hogar</u>, y bailan éstos <u>al compás de la seca pandereta</u> y al de un viejo romance no pocas veces.

Penetrad en uno de esos lugares o en una de las viejas ciudades amodorradas en la llanura, donde la vida parece discurrir calmosa y lenta en la monotonía de las horas, y allí dentro hay almas vivas, con fondo transitorio y fondo eterno y una intra-historia castellana.

En torno al casticismo, Miguel de Unamuno

I Read the passage carefully and try to picture the Castillian country side as Unamuno describes it. Answer the following questions in English:
What do you notice about the style of the passage? Can you keep this in English?
How will you express the progression of 'lugares, villas o ciudades' in English?

II Mark the following translations 1, 2, 3, in order of your preference in the context. Mark X any you consider unacceptable. Give a better version if one occurs to you.

a   a la caída de la tarde
  ☐ at nightfall
  ☐ at sunset
  ☐ as evening falls
b   el aire sutil
  ☐ the subtle air
  ☐ the soft air
  ☐ the thin air
c   las comadres
  ☐ their wives
  ☐ the village women
  ☐ the women

d   murmurando
  ☐ murmuring
  ☐ gossiping
  ☐ criticizing
e   bajo la ancha campana del hogar
  ☐ in the wide-spreading shelter of the home
  ☐ under the wide dome of the hearth
  ☐ under the sloping rafters of the farmhouse
f   al compás de la seca pandereta
  ☐ in time to the thudding tambourine
  ☐ to the rhythm of the tambourine
  ☐ in time to the beat of the tambourine

III Translate the passage into English.

12 No tenían cara,[39] chorreados, comidos por la oscuridad. Nada más que sus dos siluetas vagamente humanas, los dos cuerpos reabsorbidos en sus sombras. Iguales y sin embargo tan distintos. Inerte el uno, viajando a ras del suelo con la pasividad de la inocencia o de la indiferencia más absoluta. Encorvado el otro, jadeante por[40] el esfuerzo de arrastrarlo entre la maleza y los desperdicios. El olor del agua estancada del riachuelo debía estar[41] en todas partes, ahora más con la fetidez dulzarrona del baldío hediondo, ese olor pastoso por la amenaza de mal tiempo que el hombre manoteaba de tanto en tanto para despegárselo de la cara.[42] Varillitas de vidrio o metal entrechocaban entre las yerbas, aunque de seguro ninguno de los dos oiría ese cántico isócrono, fantasmal. Tampoco el apagado rumor de la ciudad que allí parecía trepidar bajo tierra. Y el que arrastraba, sólo tal vez ese ruido blando y sordo del cuerpo al rebotar sobre el terreno, el siseo de restos de papeles o el opaco golpe de los zapatos contra las latas y cascotes. A veces el hombro del otro se enganchaba en las matas duras o en alguna piedra. Lo destrababa entonces a tirones, mascullando alguna furiosa interjección o haciendo a cada forcejeo el ha . . . nuemático de los estibadores al levantar la carga rebelde al hombro. Era evidente que le resultaba cada vez más pesado. No sólo por esa resistencia pasiva que se le empacaba de vez en cuando en los obstáculos. Acaso también por el propio miedo, la repugnancia o el apuro que le iría comiendo las fuerzas, empujándolo a terminar cuanto antes.

Ya habían llegado a un sitio donde la maleza era más alta. Lo acomodó como pudo, lo arropó con desechos y ramas secas. Parecía de improviso querer protegerlo de ese olor que llenaba el baldío o de la lluvia que no tardaría en caer. Se detuvo, se pasó el brazo por[40] la frente regada de sudor, escarró y escupió con rabia. Entonces escuchó[43] ese vagido que lo sobresaltó. Subía débil y sofocado del yuyal,[44] como si el otro hubiera comenzado a quejarse con lloro de recién nacido bajo su túmulo de basura.

D.E.S. June 1979, Augusto Roa Bastos

I   Read the passage carefully and answer the following questions in English:
This is a very descriptive passage. Can you visualize the scene?
What can you see of the two men? Of their surroundings and actions?

II   Translate the passage into English.

13   Necio de mí,[45] había preguntado lo que ya sabía, lo que ya veía, lo que ya sentía. Había malgastado mi única pregunta de ese primer día, abundando[46] las que podrían aclararme los misterios de esta tierra y de mi presencia en ella. Y adormecido por la comida y el humo y el viaje, recosté mi cabeza sobre el regazo de la anciana. Ella me acarició maternalmente la cabeza. <u>Dormíme.</u>

Y en mi sueño, Señor, aparecióse la señora de las mariposas. La acompañaba un monstruoso animal, idéntico a la noche, pues nada en él reflejaba luz alguna, sino que era como una sombra en cuatro patas, espesa y velluda. En vano buscaba su mirada.[47] Sólo su forma era visible. No tenía mirada, sino piel y fauces y cuatro patas torcidas, pues en vez de señalar hacia adelante, estaban dobladas hacia atrás. La mujer que yo amé junto al templo arruinado era rodeada de una luz brumosa y el animal su compañero cavaba en la tierra un hoyo; y al hacerlo gruñía espantablemente. Cuando hubo terminado su tarea, la difusa luz de ese momento de mi sueño se reunió en una oblicua columna dorada que nacía en el centro del cielo y venía a morir en el hoyo escarbado aquí por el animal. Esa amarilla e intensa luz era como un río líquido y fluyente, y a medida que empapaba las profundidades de la excavación, el animal le arrojaba tierra encima con sus patas torcidas, y mientras más tierra le echaba, más se apagaba la luz. La señora de las mariposas lloró. Espantado, yo le pedí a la vieja <u>que me arrullaba</u>:

— Madre, bésame, que tengo miedo . . .

Y ella besó mis labios, mientras la mujer de la selva se desvanecía llorando en la noche y el animal aullaba con una mezcla de alegría y desgracia.

Yo desperté.

Terra Nostra, Carlos Fuentes

I   Read the passage carefully, then answer the following questions in English:
Can you imagine what the writer saw in his dream?
What were his feelings?

II   Mark the following translations 1, 2, 3 etc. in order of your preference in
the context. Mark X any you consider unacceptable. Give a better version if
one occurs to you.

a   Dormíme
   ☐ I slept
   ☐ I fell asleep
   ☐ I was asleep

b   que me arrullaba
   ☐ who was rocking me
   ☐ who was soothing me
   ☐ who was cradling me
   ☐ who had my head on her lap

III   Translate the passage into English.

14   He aquí el tinglado de la antigua farsa, la que alivió en posadas aldeanas
el cansancio de los trajinantes, la que *embobó* en las plazas de humildes lugares a
los simples *villanos*, la que juntó en ciudades populosas a los más variados
concursos como en París sobre el puente Nuevo, cuando Tabarín, desde su
tablado de feria, solicitaba la atención de todo transeúnte: desde el espetado
doctor, que detiene un momento su docta cabalgadura para desarrugar por un
instante la frente,[48] siempre cargada de graves pensamientos, al escuchar algún
donaire de la alegre farsa, hasta el pícaro hampón, que allí divierte sus ocios
horas y horas, engañando el hambre con la risa, y el prelado, y la dama de
calidad, y el gran señor desde sus carrozas, como la moza alegre y el soldado, y
el mercader y el estudiante. Gente de toda condición, que en ningún otro lugar
se hubiera reunido, comunicábase allí su regocijo, que[49] muchas veces, más que
de la farsa, reía el grave de ver reír al risueño, y el sabio al bobo, y los pobretes
de ver reír a los grandes señores, ceñudos de ordinario, y los grandes de ver reír a
los pobretes, tranquilizada su conciencia con pensar: "también los pobres ríen!"[50]
Que[49] nada prende tan pronto de unas almas en otras como esta simpatía de la
risa. Alguna vez también subió la farsa a palacios de príncipes, altísimos señores,
por humorada de sus dueños, y no fue allí menos libre y despreocupada. Fue de
todos y para todos. Del pueblo recogió burlas, y malicias, y dichos sentenciosos;
de esa filosofía del pueblo, que siempre, dulcificada por aquella resignación de
los humildes de entonces, que no lo esperaban todo de este mundo,[51] y por eso
sabían reírse del mundo sin odio y sin amargura. Ilustró después su plebeyo
origen con noble ejecutoria: Lope de Rueda, Shakespeare, Molière, como
enamorados príncipes de cuento de hadas, elevaron a Cenicienta al más alto
trono de la poesía y del arte.

Los intereses creados, Jacinto Benavante

Read carefully. Try to picture the scene before your eyes and feel the
atmosphere. What are the chief features of the author's style? Note the effect
created by his use of old-fashioned words. How can you convey this in your
translation? Who or what is the 'Cinderella' mentioned in the last sentence?

I **Think out carefully the meaning of the italicized words.**

II **Mark the translations below 1, 2, 3, in order of your preference in the context. Mark X any you consider unacceptable. Give a better version if one occurs to you.**

a   alivió . . . el cansancio de los
    trajinantes
    ☐ eased the weariness of the
      wayfarers
    ☐ alleviated the fatigue of the
      carters
    ☐ soothed the tiredness of the
      busy

b   el espetado doctor
    ☐ the dignified doctor
    ☐ the solemn doctor
    ☐ the pompous doctor

c   cargada de graves pensamientos
    ☐ heavy with weighty thoughts
    ☐ laden with weighty thoughts
    ☐ filled with serious ideas

d   donaire
    ☐ witticism
    ☐ sally
    ☐ witty saying

d   divierte sus ocios horas y horas,
    ☐ beguiles his idle hours
    ☐ enjoys his hours of leisure
    ☐ spends his leisure hours

III **Translate the passage into English.**

15   El viaje definitivo

> . . . Y yo me iré. Y se quedarán los pájaros cantando;
> y se quedará mi huerto, con su verde árbol,
> y con su pozo blanco.
>   Todas las tardes, el cielo será azul y plácido;
> y tocarán, como esta tarde están tocando,
> las campanas del campanario.
>   Se morirán aquellos que me amaron;
> y el pueblo se hará nuevo cada año;
> y en mi rincón aquel de mi huerto florido y encalado,
> mi espíritu errará, nostáljico . . .
>   Y yo me iré, y estaré solo, sin hogar, sin árbol
> verde, sin pozo blanco,
> sin cielo azul y plácido . . .
> Y se quedarán los pájaros cantando.

Juan Ramón Jiménez

The translation of poetry is an art as well as a skill. Analyze the elements in the above poem and try to reproduce them in your English version.

Notes

1   See **The Verb — Tense**, Appendix A7a.
2   What does *el* refer to here?
3   Watch translation of *ni . . . nada . . . ni*. See **Connectives**, Appendix A2.
4   Give normal English phrase.
5   In this context *watched* rather than *saw*.
6   See **Prepositions**, Appendix A6.
7   *criss-cross pattern*
8   Supply a verb.
9   See **Modulation**, Appendix B6.
10 See **Adjectives**, Appendix A1.
11 What is the meaning of *un tal Pedro Páramo* here?
12 See **Pronouns**, Appendix A5.
13 *come* or *go*?
14 See **Modulation**, Appendix B6.
15 See **Transposition**, Appendix B5.
16 What is the best translation of *nerviosa* here: *nervous, agitated* or *impatient*?
17 How can you convey the emphasis here in English?
18 Note the three terms of abuse: *bribón, sinvergüenza, pillo*. Can you find three similar terms of abuse in English?
19 *up left*
20 See **Modulation**, Appendix B6.
21 What is the exact function of *que* here? How will you translate it?
22 See **Modulation**, Appendix B6.
23 The characters here are puppets whom Pygmalion has brought to life. He has been exhibiting them in different cities. Now they see a chance to escape.
24 See **Transposition**, Appendix B5.
25 *the puppets*
26 See **Adverbs**, Appendix A8.
27 Give full value of tense here.
28 See **Transposition**, Appendix B5.
29 Watch word order.
30 What is the function of *que* here?
31 See **The Verb — Mood and Modals**, Appendix A7b.
32 See **The Verb — Tense**, Appendix A7a.
33 See **Transposition**, Appendix B5.
34 See **Omissions and Insertions**, Appendix B4.
35 See **Modulation**, Appendix B6.
36 *street vendor*
37 See **Transposition**, Appendix B5.
38 Watch connectives.
39 See **Transposition**, Appendix B5.
40 Watch prepositions here.
41 See **The Verb — Mood and Modals**, Appendix A7b.
42 See **Omissions and Insertions**, Appendix B4.
43 *listened* or *heard*?
44 *yuyal* — from *yuyo* (herbage)
45 See **Omissions and Insertions**, Appendix B4. Also **Transposition**, Appendix B5.
46 Express by a phrase in English.
47 See **Modulation**, Appendix B6.
48 See **Transposition**, Appendix B5.
49 What is the function of *que* here? How will it best be translated?
50 The first two sentences are rather long. Where could they be divided?
51 See **Pronouns**, Appendix A5.

English Passages for Translation

16 Hugh Anthony at eight years old was compact and rounded like his grand-father. His blue, astonished eyes[1] were also like his grandfather's, but his circular face, dusted all over with golden freckles,[2] his turned-up[3] nose and flaming red hair were all his own. Quite his own, too, was his look of perpetual inquiry. His whole body seemed at times to be curved into the shape of a question-mark and the word 'why?' was seldom off his lips. The house rang with it from the moment he woke in the morning until the moment when he fell asleep with his final question still vibrating in the air of the silent unanswering night.

"Why don't you grow a beard?" he asked Jocelyn.

"I've been a soldier," said Jocelyn, "and in the Army it is the fashion to have a moustache only."

"Why?"

"To distinguish soldiers from sailors, who are either clean-shaven or have beards."

"Why?"

"It's just the fashion."

"Why?"

"I don't know."

"Why don't you know?"

Henrietta pushed Hugh Anthony face downward on the bed and seated herself upon the small of his back where, enthroned in grace,[4] she smiled sweetly at Jocelyn. She was a child of few words, but all her actions were quick, decisive and to the point.

A City of Bells, Elizabeth Goudge

Chiefly a descriptive passage. Note the extreme precision in the use of adjectives which convey an almost photographic image of the character of Hugh Anthony. The author supplements the visual impact by adding certain attitudes and particularities of speech. Here translators have to find in the spoken examples the commonplace everyday expressions which, on Hugh Anthony's lips become extremely personal.

I **Translate the passage into Spanish.**

17   Early next morning Mrs Tower rang me up and I heard at once from her voice that she was in high spirits.

"I've got the most wonderful news for you", she said. "Jane is going to be married."

"Nonsense."

"Her fiancé is coming to dine here to-night to be introduced to me and I want you to come too."

"Oh, but I shall be in the way."

"No, you won't. Jane suggested herself that I should ask you. Do come."

She was bubbling over with laughter.[5]

"Who is he?"

"I don't know. She tells me he's an architect. Can you imagine the sort of man Jane would marry?"

I had nothing to do and I could trust Mrs Tower to give me a good dinner. When I arrived Mrs Tower, very splendid in a tea gown a little <u>too young for her</u>, was alone.

"Jane is putting the finishing touches to her appearance. . . . . . <u>She's all in a flutter</u>. She says he adores her. His name is Gilbert and when she speaks of him her voice gets all <u>funny</u> and tremulous. It makes me want to laugh."

"I wonder what he's like."

"Oh, I'm sure I don't know. Very big and massive, with a bald head and an immense gold chain across an immense tummy. A large, fat, clean-shaven, red face[6] and a booming voice."

Jane, W. Somerset Maugham

What we ought to aim at in translating this selection is chiefly the agile brittle dialogue frequently achieved when in haste we 'phone our friends. Words, nevertheless, in this package have been very carefully selected to give the final lackadaisical impression full of implications and different states of mind between the characters who speak in this text.

I   **Which of the following translations would you select in this context? Mark your preferences with an X.**

a   too young for her
    □ demasiado joven
    □ demasiado juvenil

b   She's all in a flutter
    □ está completamente agitada
    □ está muy emocionada
    □ está muy nerviosa

c   The adjective 'funny' in English can be very ambivalent. In this particular instance it has a very specific connotation which, notwithstanding, is not at all clear in Spanish.

funny
- ☐ cómica
- ☐ graciosa
- ☐ chistosa
- ☐ extraña
- ☐ rara

II Translate the passage into Spanish.

18 While Christopher merely recognized in Viertel 'the face[7] of Central Europe', Viertel recognized in Christopher — from that very first moment, I believe — the exceedingly odd kind of individual his temperament required as a working companion.

Christopher was an amateur,[8] in both senses of the word. A lover of movies since childhood, he was also eager to learn the craft of film writing and prepared to begin at the beginning. Why shouldn't he play the <u>humble novice</u>? It caused him no pain to do so, for his arrogance as a novelist was wrapped protectively around his ego. Viertel was subtle enough to understand this. He addressed him as 'Master', in the humourous tone of a fellow artist whose embarrassment mocks his sincere admiration. Meanwhile he trained the film-writer with the impatient patience of a <u>craftsman</u> who has to make the best of a slow-witted apprentice.

C.P.E. December 1979

This is an example of classical prose conceived and achieved by a very modern mind. Elegant in his turns of phrase, the author is exceedingly precise and demanding in his syntax. Try to create a Spanish version of this very concise text which will produce a similar elegance and precision. Note the irony of the entire second paragraph. Your Spanish version has to have a similar tone.

I   Which of the following best conveys the sarcasm of the phrase *humble novice*?
- ☐ novato humilde
- ☐ humilde novato
- ☐ principiante humilde
- ☐ humilde principiante
- ☐ humilde novicio
- ☐ novicio humilde

II   Consider and comment on the translation below:
Le decía maestro con el tono irónico de un colega que, conturbado, hace mofa de una genuina admiración a la vez que la imita.

III   Choose the Spanish word you find most accurate for *craftsman* **in this context:**
☐ artesano   ☐ artífice   ☐ maestro   ☐ maese

IV   Translate the passage into Spanish.

19   Meanwhile Lucilla, the children's grandmother, sat having tea with her maid Ellen in her fire-lit drawing-room.[9] Her daughter Margaret was at a meeting at the Vicarage, and the children had gone to meet David, so only Ellen was with her. She liked this, for <u>a strange peace came over her</u> when she and Ellen were alone. They had been together for sixty years now, ever since Lucilla had come back from her honeymoon, and what they didn't know about each other wasn't worth knowing. It was their utter knowledge that gave them their happiness together; that and the fact that they saw eye to eye in the matter of[10] always having the window open a little bit, but not too much, and always having a wood fire burning in the grate unless there was actually a heat wave on. More happy homes have been wrecked, Lucilla was apt to say, by not seeing eye to eye about how much window to have open than by any other controversy known to man. It is quite possible to live happily with a person who does not think as you do about the eternal verities, but it is not possible to live happily with someone who wants the window open when you want it shut, or with someone who likes a fire when you don't. Lucilla and Ellen were utterly at one about the fire. The drawing-room was beautiful, but it was damp, and it was no good saying it wasn't. Lucilla and Ellen didn't say it wasn't. . . They lit the fire.

The Bird in the Tree, Elizabeth Goudge

   This text does not present major problems from the linguistic standpoint. Yet the great challenge for a translator resides in conveying into another language the exquisite refinement of the atmosphere created by words in this apparently simple passage and the remote irony that permeates the prose you are about to translate. Here translators ought to concentrate mainly on atmosphere.

I   Select the best translation in this context.
   a strange peace came over her
   ☐ una extraña paz flotó sobre su cabeza
   ☐ una paz extraña la asaltó
   ☐ una inusitada paz la invadió
   ☐ una extraña sensación de tranquilidad la invadió
   ☐ una extraña paz la invadió

II   Translate the passage into Spanish.

20

Ruth	Would you say the evening had been profitable?
Charles	Yes — I suppose so.
Ruth	I must say it was extremely funny at moments.
Charles	Yes — it certainly was.
Ruth	What's the matter?
Charles	The matter?

Ruth   Yes — you seem odd somehow — do you feel quite well?
Charles   Perfectly. I think I'll have a drink. (*Moves up stage to drinks table and pours whisky-and-soda.*) Do you want one?
Ruth   No, thank you, dear.
Charles   (*pouring himself out a drink*) It's rather chilly in this room.
Ruth   Come over by the fire.
Charles   I don't think I'll make any notes to-night — I'll start fresh in the morning.
(*Charles turns with glass in hand, sees Elvira and drops his glass on the floor.*)
Charles   My God!
Ruth   Charles!
Elvira   That was very clumsy, Charles dear.
Charles   Elvira! — then it's true — it was you!
Elvira   Of course it was.
Ruth   (*starts to go to Charles*) Charles — darling Charles — what are you talking about?
Charles   (*to Elvira*) Are you a ghost?
Elvira   (*crosses below sofa to fire*) I suppose I must be — it's all very confusing.
Ruth   (*comes to right of Charles, becoming agitated*) Charles — what do you keep looking over there for? Look at me — what's happened?
Charles   Don't you see?
Ruth   See what?
Charles   Elvira.
Ruth   (*staring at him incredulously*) Elvira!
Charles   (*with an effort at social grace*) Yes — Elvira, dear, this is Ruth — Ruth, this is Elvira.

Blithe Spirit, Noël Coward

Translating for the theatre requires an altogether different technique. Anybody who attempts a Spanish version of this excerpt, for instance, must bear in mind how any such version is going to sound on the stage. Turns of phrase which, to an English ear, sound like household words may, if translated literally into some other language, appear stilted, affected, unreal, and the overall effect will be one of utter inaccuracy. The opening lines of this dialogue could not be easier to render into Spanish; yet try to be literal at first, and then analyze the stiff effect.

Consequently, the translator has to discover the customary language used by native Spanish-speakers in similar circumstances to express conversational overtones, even if other words have to be used in order to convey the same literary atmosphere expressed in the English dialogue, so that it will sound believable on a Spanish-speaking stage. Consider the following example:

Ruth   ¿Dirías que la velada fue provechosa?
Charles   Supongo que sí.
Ruth   Me pareció graciosísima a ratos.
Charles   Ya lo creo.

I Translate the dialogue into Spanish.

21 The bar, she found with pleasure, could offer drinks of green and red and every shade of glowing brown from the palest to the most coppery. She wanted to choose something she normally couldn't afford. And <u>had just settled for</u> a Grand Marnier, when she found Max beside her again.

"Good," he said, "most of your generation prefer to <u>pickle their livers</u> without considering their tongues."
Emily only saw the laugh she seemed to provoke in him.

"Look, what's so funny about me," she demanded.

"I don't know," he admitted, "you aren't the prettiest girl in the room, certainly. Look at that one, for instance. And you're gawky."

"I am not," said Emily, "we just have different styles of dancing."

"Gauche, then. And" (as Emily asked for another drink in a larger glass) "I think you probably drink too much. But, yes, you amuse me. Do you mind?"
With a rush of horror, Emily found that she liked the idea.

At the same moment she felt rather than saw the gliding prescence of Frieda reaching towards them; she felt her as a long elegantly arched hand.

"Emily, we haven't had a chance to talk for one moment. Max, you must excuse her."

"Not now," said Max firmly, "we are going to dance once more to Emily's favourite tune."

As they moved away in what Emily felt was probably an accomplished tango turn, she caught a glimpse of Frieda's face, with one hand, covered with jewels, in between her lips. Above her hand the lovely eyes shone as green and hard as the emerald on her smallest finger. The expression was one Emily had never seen before, and could not for the moment place. But she could feel those eyes on her, even at the farthest edge of the floor. Where, even as she performed a remarkable backward slide, she caught sight of her father.

D.E.S. June 1978, Elaine Feinstein

The chief goal every translator ought to aim at is to give readers the impression that what they are reading was originally written in the language into which it has been translated. There is perhaps no worse evil than a translation which <u>sounds</u> like a translation. This risk grows even greater when translating conversations as in this excerpt. What we have said about the previous text is equally valid for this one, though not as dramatically important, since the former text was not written to be read but to be performed on the stage where the deficiencies of the translator will be more blatant.

I Mark the following translations 1, 2, 3, 4, in order of your preference in this context. Mark X any you consider unacceptable. Give a better version if one occurs to you.

a She had just settled for . . .
- ☐ acababa de transigir en favor de . . .
- ☐ acabó decidiéndose por . . .
- ☐ se acababa de comprometer por . . .
- ☐ acababa de decidirse por . . .

b pickle their livers
- ☐ escabechar el hígado
- ☐ escabecharse el hígado
- ☐ dejar el hígado en escabeche
- ☐ dejarse carcomer el hígado

II Translate the passage into Spanish.

22 This <u>peculiar</u> region lies to the east of the Tisza, the Danube's big northern tributary — an immense, open, treeless plain, geometrically flat, unfenced and uncultivated;[11] the saltpetre in the soil prevents the growth of any crop save grass, on which tens of thousands of horses, sheep, cattle and pigs grazed in huge flocks. There were no houses or villages save round the periphery; the whole vast area, some fifty miles long by thirty wide, was empty save for the livestock and the men who tended them, and criss-crossed in every direction by rough earthen tracks used by the animals. It was studded all over by shallow blue lakes to which, in autumn, ducks and geese came flighting in; but it was so featureless, land and water so mixed up, that those who came to shoot always had to take a guide to lead them to any given mere.

In the heart of this strange place stood the *czarda*, or inn, on which the shepherds, swineherds, cowherds and horse-masters, the *Czikös*, who lived too far out from the outlying villages to ride to them, relied entirely for supplies; they both ate there, and bought their food and tobacco. This was the czarda's *raison d'être*, but there were a few bedrooms for the odd sportsman who came after duck and geese.

The Tightening String, Ann Bridge

Terms are very precise in this selection; the overall effect we perceive from the description is an almost photographic vision. If in dialogue we have frequently to *re-create*, it would be advisable in a text like this to *follow very closely* the author's syntax which is direct, concise, and does not pursue speech rhythms or effects. From the two paragraphs we perceive an entirely realistic image like those one can see in the canvasses of turn-of-the-century painters.

I Which of the following adjectives will you select to translate *peculiar*?
☐ rara ☐ extraña ☐ peculiar ☐ singular

II Translate the passage into Spanish.

23 "Do you know many of the people <u>round here?</u>" asked the niece, when she judged that they had had sufficient silent communion.[12]

"Hardly a soul," said Framton. "My sister was staying here, at the rectory, you know, some four years ago, and she gave me letters of introduction to some of the people here."

He made the last statement in a tone of distinct regret.

"Then you know practically nothing about my aunt?" pursued the self-possessed[13] young lady.

"Only her name and address," admitted the caller. He was wondering whether Mrs. Sappleton was in the married or widowed state. An undefinable something about the room seemed to suggest masculine habitation.

"Her great tragedy happened just three years ago," said the child; "that would be since your sister's time."[14]

"Her tragedy?" asked Framton; somehow in this restful country spot tragedies seemed out of place.

"You may wonder why we keep that window wide open on an October afternoon," said the niece, indicating a large French window that opened on to a lawn.

"It is quite warm for the time of the year," said Framton; "but has that window got anything to do with the tragedy?"

"Out through that window, <u>three years ago to a day</u>, her husband and her two young brothers went off for their day's shooting. They never came back. In crossing the moor to their favourite shooting ground they were all three <u>engulfed</u> in a treacherous piece of bog. It had been that dreadful wet summer, you know, and places that were safe in other years <u>gave way</u> suddenly without warning. Their bodies were never recovered. That was the dreadful part of it."

The Open Window, Saki

Saki is known mainly for his quick, poignant and extremely funny style. His stories are usually very short and hilarious; he achieves his comic effects by a concentrated wit. His characters usually speak in an affected *fashionable* style that was in vogue amongst the upper classes during the first quarter of this century. His can accurately be called a highly sophisticated witty style.

I Mark the following translations 1, 2, 3, etc. in order of your preference in the context. Mark X any you consider unacceptable. Give a better version if one occurs to you.

a   round here
   ☐ por estos contornos
   ☐ por aquí
   ☐ por estos rumbos
   ☐ en estas latitudes

b   Hardly a soul
   ☐ Ni un alma
   ☐ Ni un gato vivo
   ☐ Casi a nadie
   ☐ A nin g u no

c   three years ago to a day
   ☐ hoy día a día hace tres años
   ☐ hoy hace tres años exactamente
   ☐ hoy hace tres años y un día

d   engulfed
   ☐ engolfados
   ☐ enfrascados
   ☐ embebidos
   ☐ engullidos

e   gave way
   ☐ cedieron el paso
   ☐ dejaron pasar
   ☐ se hundieron

II Translate the passage into Spanish.

24   The train was due to leave at eight,[15] and it was about ten past eight when the harassed, sweating officers managed to marshal us in the barrack square.[16] I remember very vividly the torchlit scene[17] — the uproar and excitement, the red flags flapping in the torchlight, the massed ranks of militiamen with their knapsacks on their backs and their rolled blankets worn bandolier-wise across the shoulder; and the shouting and the clatter of boots and tin pannikins, and then a tremendous and finally successful hissing for silence;[18] and then some political commissar standing beneath a huge rolling red banner and making us a speech in Catalan. Finally they marched us to the station, taking the longest route, three or four miles, so as to show us to the whole town. In the Ramblas they halted us while a borrowed band played some revolutionary tune or other. Once again the conquering-hero stuff — shouting and enthusiasm, red flags and red and black flags everywhere, friendly crowds thronging the pavement to have a look at us, women waving from the windows. How natural it all seemed then; how remote and improbable now! The train was packed so tight with men that there was barely room even on the floor, let alone on the seats. At the last moment Williams' wife came rushing down the platform and gave us a bottle of wine and a foot of that bright red sausage which tastes of soap and gives you diarrhoea. The train crawled out of Catalonia and on to the plateau of Aragon at the normal speed of something under twenty kilometres an hour.

Homage to Catalonia, George Orwell

Although this is a straight piece of description, towards the end it gets tinged with some remote note of melancholy which the author can not avoid expressing after the downfall of the Spanish Republic and the many illusions cherished at the time by the members of international brigades who fought in Spain.

I **Mark the following translations 1, 2, 3, in order of your preference in the context. Mark X any you consider unacceptable. Give a better version if one occurs to you.**

a the conquering-hero stuff
- ☐ la estofa del heróicoconquistador
- ☐ la baladronada del héroe que se convierte en conquistador
- ☐ la verbonea acerca del héroe conquistador

b let alone on the seats
- ☐ por no hablar de los asientos
- ☐ los asientos habían quedado solitarios
- ☐ Deja solos los asientos

II **Translate the passage into Spanish.**

25 This is a town with a straight street running down to the palm trees and the harbour, with sea and palm trees below the window of the restaurant, a graceful Churriguerresque doorway to a church in the blazing sunlight, shops selling 'turrón de Jijona', a most delicious sweet made of almonds, in little wooden packing cases complete with nails; more palms and blue sea, and again, more sea and palms. Alicante could hardly[19] be pleasanter, or more delightful, or less interesting. But it is only half an hour, by road, from Elche, in a forest of palms as dense as that of Marrakesh. To the African aspect of Elche must be added the memory of the 'Madonna of Elche', the only work of art of Carthage or its colonies that is left to us. That peaked, sacerdotal headdress of a sacred prostitute, or virgin, those huge cartwheel earrings, would not be out of place in Elche, a town which has one of the most astonishingly elaborate and graceful façades in all the Levante, built in that local style that is neither quite Rococo nor Churriguerresque, but more poetical than the one and saner and more balanced than the other. It is in this church that the miracle play of Elche is performed every year in August, a religious ceremony as curious as any in Christian Europe and a procedure as 'set' and formalized as that of the dancing white Lippizaners[20] in the Winter Riding School at Vienna. It is an 'auto de fé' or sacred play in the old Limousin or 'langue d'oc' dialect, <u>of which Elche is the most southern or ultimate extension.</u> There are picturesque processions through the town, and at the climax of the play Baroque cupids in the form of living children are lowered from the ceiling.

Spain, Sacheverell Sitwell

Another descriptive paragraph where the author conveys his associations with a landscape but without the sort of imagery we have found in other texts. History and the past participate in the rather analytical account made in very concise language, the nature of which at times betrays some influence of long phrases that are so commonly found in Spanish.

I   Which of the following translations do you prefer? Why?
. . . of which Elche is the most southern or ultimate extension.
☐ . . . que en Elche llega a sus más remotos confines o más remoto alcance.
☐ . . . del que Elche es la última extensión sureña.
☐ . . . que Elche encarna como su más remota extensión sureña y definitiva.

II   Translate the passage into Spanish.

26   The funeral was over.[21] The carriages had rolled away[22] through the soft mud, and only the poor remained. They approached the newly dug shaft and looked their last[23] at the coffin, now almost hidden beneath the <u>spadefuls</u> of clay. <u>It was their moment.</u>[24] Most of them were women from the dead woman's district, to whom black garments had been served out[25] by Mr. Wilcox's orders. Pure curiosity had brought others. They thrilled with the excitement of a death, and of a rapid death, and stood in groups or moved between the graves like drops of ink. The son of one of them, a woodcutter, was perched[25] high above their heads, pollarding[26] one of the churchyard elms. From where he sat he could see the village of Hilton, strung[27] upon the North Road, with its accreting suburbs; the sunset beyond, scarlet and orange, winking at him beneath brows of gray; the church; the plantations; and behind him an unspoilt[28] country of fields and farms. But he, too, was rolling the event luxuriously in his mouth. He tried to tell his mother <u>down below</u> all that he had felt when he saw the coffin approaching: how he could not leave his work and yet didn't like to go on with it; how he had almost slipped out of the tree, he was so <u>upset</u>; the rooks had cawed, and no wonder — it was as if the rooks knew too. His mother <u>claimed</u> that prophetic power herself — she had seen a strange look about Mrs. Wilcox for some time. London had done the mischief, said others.

Howards End, E.M. Forster

Notice how the author uses words chiefly to give the reader a picture of a specific scene. Terms are direct and metaphors scarcely used. Sentences, because of their brevity, produce a striking impact on the reader and the author seems to be absent from the scene, a mere observer who takes no part in the drama.

I Mark the following translations 1, 2, 3, 4 in order of your preference in the context. Mark X any that you consider unacceptable. Give a better version if one occurs to you.

a spadefuls
- ☐ paletadas
- ☐ palas
- ☐ montones
- ☐ terrones

b It was their moment
- ☐ Había llegado su momento
- ☐ Les había llegado el momento
- ☐ Había llegado el momento de ellos
- ☐ Les había llegado su momento

c down below
- ☐ allá abajo
- ☐ que estaban a sus pies
- ☐ que se encontraba abajo
- ☐ abajo

d upset
- ☐ nervioso
- ☐ enojado
- ☐ irritado
- ☐ alterado

e claimed
- ☐ alegaba
- ☐ aseguraba
- ☐ pretendía tener
- ☐ reclamaba para sí

II Translate the passage into Spanish.

27 Night after[29] night, summer and winter, <u>the torment of storms</u>, the arrow-like[30] stillness of the weather, held their court[31] without interference. Listening (had there been anyone to listen) from the upper rooms of the empty house only gigantic chaos streaked with lightning could have been heard tumbling and tossing, as the winds and waves[32] disported[33] themselves like the amorphous bulks of leviathans whose brows are pierced by no light of reason, and mounted one on top of another, and lunged and plunged in the darkness or the daylight (for night and day, month and year[34] ran shapelessly together) in idiot games, until it seemed as if the universe were battling and tumbling in <u>brute confusion</u>[32] and <u>wanton</u> lust aimlessly by itself.

In spring the garden urns, casually filled with windblown[35] plants, were gay as ever. Violets came and daffodils. But the stillness and the brightness of the day were as strange as the chaos and tumult of the night, with the trees <u>standing there</u>,[36] and the flowers standing there,[36] looking before them,[37] <u>looking up</u>,[38] yet beholding nothing, eyeless,[38] and so terrible.

To the Lighthouse, Virginia Woolf

In reading the passage, take careful note of the special features of the author's style. Notice the way in which the author uses alliteration.

I Mark the following translations 1, 2, 3 etc. in order of your preference in the context. Mark X any you consider unacceptable. Give a better version if one occurs to you.

a   the torment of storms
- ☐ la agonía de las tormentas
- ☐ el tormento de las tormentas
- ☐ la tortura de las tempestades
- ☐ la tortura tempestuosa

b   brute confusion
- ☐ bruta confusión
- ☐ brutal confusión
- ☐ bestial confusión
- ☐ salvaje confusión
- ☐ bárbara confusión
- ☐ torpe confusión

c   wanton
- ☐ lascivo
- ☐ juguetón
- ☐ desenfrenado
- ☐ procaz

d   standing there
- ☐ allí parados
- ☐ detenidos allí
- ☐ qui allí se erguían
- ☐ allí erguidos

e   looking up
- ☐ mirando hacia arriba
- ☐ mirando intensamente
- ☐ mirando con deliberación
- ☐ mirando fijamente

II   Translate the passage into Spanish.

28   They found it was further than they thought. The ground was rising steeply still, and it was becoming increasingly stony. The light grew broader as they went on, and soon they saw that there was a rock-wall before them: the side of a hill, or the abrupt end of some long root thrust out by the distant mountains. No trees grew on it, and the sun was falling full on its stony face. The twigs of the trees at its foot were stretched out stiff and still, as if reaching out to the warmth. Where all had looked so shabby and grey before, the wood now gleamed with rich browns, and with the smooth black-greys of bark like polished leather. The boles of the trees glowed with a soft green like young grass: early spring or a fleeting vision of it was about them.

In the face of the stony wall there was something like a stair: natural perhaps, and made by the weathering and splitting of the rock, for it was rough and uneven. High up, almost level with the tops of forest-trees, there was a shelf under a cliff. Nothing grew there but a few grasses and weeds at its edge, and one old stump of a tree with only two bent branches left: it looked almost like the figure of some gnarled old man, standing there, blinking in the morning-light.

"Up we go!" said Merry joyfully. "Now for a breath of air and a sight of the land!"

They climbed and scrambled up the rock. If the stair had been made it was for bigger feet and longer legs than theirs. They were too eager to be surprised at the remarkable way in which the cuts and sores of their captivity had healed and their vigour had returned. They came at length to the edge of the shelf almost at the feet of the old stump; then they sprang up and turned round with their backs to the hill, breathing deep and looking out eastward. They saw that they had only come two or three miles into the forest: the heads of the trees marched down the slopes towards the plain. There, near the fringe of the forest, tall spires of curling black smoke went up, wavering and floating towards them.

The Lord of the Rings, J.R.R. Tolkien

You will notice in this excerpt an abundance of verbs in the English past tense. Some of these must be translated into Spanish with the co-preterite to convey the gradual pace of the action they express, some in the preterite to express the action completed altogether. Prepare two Spanish versions of this text, one by using the tense which, in your opinion, corresponds in each case, the other using the preterite only, and then analyze your own two versions. Discuss these in class.

Compare the difference in tone between the paragraphs separated by Merry's statement; the first two are beautiful descriptions in poetic prose. Discover in them alliterations and striking images. Describe in your own words how the author succeeds in producing this luminous, ethereal impression. Study his use of adjectives and note the importance of adverbs. In your *definitive* version of this text try to retain the impression of loftiness and movement upward.

I   Translate the passage into Spanish.

29   It must have been like travelling with a tribe of monkeys; we were in wild spirits and, as we got bored, boxed up in that small space for two or three days, we grew more and more restive; we would invent games to play on the upper berths, shouting across to each other, and would swing between the berths or from one to the other. When the train pulled up at a station we gave no trouble; we asked nothing better than to sit at one of the windows and watch — we were not allowed to get out and walk up and down the platform because it was so dirty, but there was much to watch.

When a poor Indian family intended to travel, it seemed to take its entire belongings and move with them and all its family members — as Father's clerks called them — into the station and camp until the right day and time arrived to take the train. They spread their mats on the platform, slept there, cooked their food over small braziers, washed under the station tap, while the coolies and other passengers and railway officials stepped round or over them; nobody seemed to mind but the platforms were crowded in a babel of noise. Not only humans used the stations: there was always a sacred bull, wandering from camp to camp and calmly helping itself to the food; there were goats, chickens, pigeons and stray dogs which were well fed compared to street ones — people threw scraps from trains. The beggar children knew this; people even threw money, perhaps because travelling was so spendthrift anyway that a pice or two more or less did not matter. Beggars were not allowed on the platform — the railways had some rules — but the children bobbed up on the other side of the train and stood between the tracks rubbing their stomachs and wailing, "No Mummy. No Daddy. No foo-oo-d" but as they wailed they laughed and pulled faces at us. All along the platform were booths, kiosks and barrow stalls that sold inviting things, especially hot good-smelling Indian food but, "Not safe," said Mam and Aunt Mary. In those days there were no ice-cream barrows but sherbet was sold, and brass trays held sticky Indian sweets. Mam brought oranges or bananas but not the open figs or dates. There were sellers of green coconuts who would obligingly hack off the top of the nut so that the customer could drink the cool juice, and sellers of soda water, lemonade and the virulently red raspberryade we always longed to try. Best of all were the toy barrows that had chip baskets of miniature brass cooking pots and ladles, or bigger baskets of wooden toys painted with bright flowers, and wooden animals and birds, all sizes, painted with flowers too: crimson daisies, green leaves, yellow roses.

D.E.S. June 1976, Rumer Godden (adapted)

This excerpt *integrates* a direct description. The words convey almost photographic impressions. The reader is not required to establish internal images through comparisons generated by similes or metaphors. Language is used to express bluntly what the author observes, no appreciation of his personal point of view is possible. In reading this text we are facing a strictly objective document which, at best, is full of local colour but does not contain any emotional element to move us. The syntax is utterly correct: nouns mean what they mean and verbs describe the action flatly; adjectives are scarce. The rare adverbs one can pluck here and there find themselves in this context just because they happen to be necessary. This selection is almost a reporter's account to be published in tomorrow morning's paper. Even the use of figurative language is almost absent from these sentences.

I   Translate the passage into Spanish.

30   A Song for Simeon

Lord, the Roman hyacinths are blooming in bowls and
The winter sun creeps by the snow hills;
The stubborn season has made stand.
My life is light, waiting for the death wind,
Like a feather on the back of my hand.
Dust in sunlight and memory in corners
Wait for the wind that chills towards the dead land.
Grant us thy peace.
I have walked many years in this city,
Kept faith and fast, provided for the poor,
Have given and taken honour and ease.
There went never any rejected from my door.
Who shall remember my house, where shall live my
        children's children
When the time of sorrow is come?
They will take to the goat's path, and the fox's home,
Fleeing from the foreign faces and the foreign swords.

T.S. Eliot

Apart from the mastery of the metaphors and similes in this poem, there is an element of beauty which issues from the various effects achieved by Eliot through his use of an extremely simple language. No alteration or deviation from a strictly logical syntax ought to be encouraged in rendering this poem into Spanish. Yet note the poet's results in his English text and try to achieve them in Spanish.

I Translate the poem into Spanish.

Notes

1   See **Adjectives**, Appendix A1.
2   Try to find an expression that will convey visually the image implied in the English description.
3   There is a specifically ready-made expression in Spanish to convey exactly the meaning of *turned up*. Find it.
4   *Sentóse sobre él, entronizada en toda su gracia, a la altura del talle.*
5   *reventaba de risa*
6   See **Adjectives**, Appendix A1.
7   What is the exact meaning of *face* in this context?
8   The author plays with the word *amateur* in this whole sentence. How are you going to achieve the same effect in Spanish?
9   Think out the order in which the various ideas expressed in this sentence will be conveyed in Spanish.
10   See **Modulation**, Appendix B6.
11   See **Adjectives**, Appendix A1.
12   How would you make this satirical statement sound equally funny in Spanish?
13   You have two ways of translating this expression: by using either an adjective or an adverb. Say which you choose and explain why.
14   How would you translate *time* in this specific context?
15   How do you translate this colloquial English expression into Spanish?
16   *organizarnos para entrar en formación en la plaza de las barracas*
17   See **Transposition**, Appendix B5.
18   *un impresionante siseo para exigir silencio que al cabo se logró*
19   *apenas*
20   White horses especially trained for performance in the Spanish Riding School of Vienna.
21   What is the most matter-of-fact way to translate this expression into Spanish?
22   Compare the difference in meaning between the verb *roll* + adverb *away*, used here, and *roll* used further down in the passage.
23   *echaron una última mirada*
24   Beware of the way you translate English possessive articles into Spanish.
25   How would you express this verb with complete accuracy in Spanish?
26   Consult dictionaries for the exact meaning of this word and find the best Spanish translation.
27   Notice the figurative sense in which this verb is used and picture the image the author is trying to convey.
28   Compare the use of prefixes and suffixes in English and Spanish.
29   What preposition do you propose to use here?
30   What is the meaning of *arrow-like*?
31   See **Modulation**, Appendix B6.
32   Try to find Spanish words that will produce alliterative effects similiar to those sought by the author of the English text.
33   What Spanish verb will you use here?
34   Read this phrase carefully. Try to re-create in Spanish the rhythmic pace of the English text.
35   Note that in some cases you have to use several words in Spanish in order to convey a concept which, in English, can be expressed in one single word.
36   To avoid repetition in Spanish use verb only once here.
37   *mirando ante sí*
38   Notice how the suffix affects the noun here. How would you express this in Spanish?

PART IV Technical Translation

Technical language is distinguished from natural language by the frequency of occurrence of terms to which meanings have been assigned within specific intellectual disciplines or fields of technology. Technical texts are also characterized by the consistent use of certain conventions of presentation. The terms of technical discourse refer to bodies of knowledge outside the general experience of the great majority of the speakers of a language, hence texts with a high density of such terms are often not immediately comprehensible to nonspecialist readers.

Throughout this introductory course, great emphasis has been placed upon full comprehension of the text as an indispensable first step in the translation process. In the case of a technical text this implies acquiring some degree of familiarity with the body of knowledge to which it refers. The use of specialized dictionaries and lexicons is obligatory, but not always sufficient. The translator should also consult specialists and study text-books and articles on the subject in question. Such reading will also acquaint the translator with the appropriate conventions of presentation.

In order to limit the need to consult a variety of technical dictionaries, the passages for translation which follow have been arranged in pairs, each serving as a source of information for the translation of the other. Both passages, together with their accompanying exercises, should be read before attempting one of them. A technical dictionary is required only in the case of the medical texts.

The texts have been chosen to illustrate very broadly the range of difficulties the technical translator must confront. Most of the texts have been edited to reduce slightly the density of unfamiliar technical terms. Awkward constructions have been preserved.

Contents of PART IV

1A   Teleprocessing
1B   Teleproceso
2A   Middle-Range Analysis of Modernization

2B La construcción de caminos de mano de obra y el subempleo rural
3A Ups and Downs
3B Crecimiento del circulante monetario
4A Foundation Treatment
4B Tratamiento de la cimentación
5A Unsuspected Uveal Melanomas
5B Melanoma de coroides

1A   Teleprocessing

Teleprocessing is the processing of data received or sent to remote locations by way of communications facilities.

A teleprocessing network consists of communication lines connecting a central data processing system with remote teleprocessing devices. Such devices can be terminals, control units, or other data processing systems. The elements of the complete network consist of a host processor (central data processing system), communications control devices, modulation/demodulation devices (modems), communications lines, other terminals and programming systems. Three of these, the communications control devices, modems, and communications lines, comprise a *data link*.

Requirements for the host processor include multiprogramming capacity, adequate <u>storage</u> capacity, storage protection, adequate speed and potential for expanding storage capacity and speed. It must be able to handle random and unscheduled input, as well as serialized and scheduled input.

Communications control devices are <u>hardware</u> components that link the host processor to the communications lines. The transfer of data requires non-information transmissions for setting up, controlling, checking and terminating information exchange. These non-information exchanges constitute data link control. Their functions include synchronization of receiver and transmitter, identification of sender and receiver, code translation and error detection and recovery. For data to be sent over communications lines the data must be converted (serialized) to a serial stream of binary digits and reconverted upon reception into machine language for processing. Control devices perform these functions.

After the data has been serialized the binary signals must be converted to audio-frequency signals (modulated) for transmission and reconverted (de-modulated) at the other end. One modem is required at each end of a data link.

The type of terminal used for handling data flow depends on the complexity and capability required for the network.

A programming system is a developed, tested, and documented group of support programs for controlling and scheduling I/O devices, job and data management, and application programs.

from IBM System 370 Summary

I   **Summarize what you understand by the following terms:**
a   host processor   b   input   c   binary   d   I/O

II   **Discuss the advantages and disadvantages of the following different standard translations:**

a   storage
      memoria   almacenamiento
b   hardware
      equipo físico   hardware

c   I/O
      entrada/salida   ingreso/salida

III   **Translate the passage into Spanish.**

1B   Teleproceso

Un sistema de teleproceso permite que el proceso de datos se efectué en un punto alejado de aquél en que se originan los datos. O sea, el teleproceso supone introducción de datos remotos de una computadora o la recepción de datos desde una computadora.

Por ejemplo: la función de proceso de datos coordina las actividades de dos fábricas y controla las existencias en un almacén. Se coordina, digamos, el número de componentes producidos en fábrica B con el número de chasis de automóvil en fábrica A, mientras se mantienen los niveles de existencias en el almacén que requiere la producción.

Un sistema de teleproceso puede desempeñar funciones de transmisión, recolección y comunicación de datos. El sistema actúa como transmisor de datos cuando transmite y procesa a alta velocidad grandes volúmenes de datos remotos. Actúa como recolector de datos cuando dispone de varios puntos de entrada de información (terminales), procesa cantidades limitadas de datos remotos y utiliza para fines de entrada y salida de información dispositivos de I/O lentos. Un sistema de comunicación de datos tiene características tanto de recolección como de transmisión y suele incluir varias terminales y permitir comunicación en ambos sentidos. Las características del sistema se pueden cambiar dándole un enfoque u otro, según convenga. En un banco, por ejemplo, el sistema de teleproceso puede transmitir, durante ciertas horas del día, información respecto a los estados de cuenta y, después, puede recolectar de cada terminal detalles de las transacciones realizadas. Más aún, el sistema puede poseer dispositivos de pregunta y respuesta.

Los sistemas de teleproceso cuentan con tres partes principales: la unidad central de proceso y las terminales se unen mediante líneas de comunicación a través de dispositivos de control.

from Introducción al Sistema 360 IBM

I   Summarize what you understand by the following terms:
a   proceso de datos   b   dispositivo   c   unidad central de proceso

II   Translate the passage into English.

2A   Middle-Range Analysis of Modernization

In this study modernization is viewed as essentially a communication process; modernizing messages must reach the peasant via such communication channels as the mass media, change agents, or trips to the city. These concepts, plus literacy (which facilitates <u>media exposure</u>), are considered the major antecedent variables in our model of modernization. The main consequent variables are innovateness, political knowledge, and aspirations. Empathy, achievement motivation, and fatalism are used as possibly <u>intervening</u> variables between antecedents and consequences.

There are three possible shortcomings of both the model and the method: conceptual oversimplification, arbitrary time-order categorization of concepts (antecedent, intervening and consequent), and the dangers of cross-cultural equivalence.

The methodological approach to theory construction in the present work is *middle-range analysis*, a procedure designed to close the gap between grand theory and raw empiricism. A *theory* is a postulated relationship between two or more concepts, which are defined as dimensions stated in their most basic terms. An *empirical hypothesis* expresses the postulated relationship between two or more operations. An *operation* is an empirical measure of a concept. The correspondence between a concept and its operation is an *epistemic relationship*. In middle-range analysis one may proceed from the theoretical to the empirical level (deduction), or from the empirical to the theoretical (induction).

Data-Gathering

Less developed countries are internally heterogeneous and the wide sub-cultural differences among the village study areas led us to utilize somewhat different sampling procedures in each. However, standard criteria for inclusion of a household in the sample were used within each community. All respondents were both (1) the head of the family and (2) the most influential member in making farm innovation decisions. These criteria excluded family heads who were employed only in nonfarm work or who worked only as farm labourers. Both farm owners and tenant farmers were included. Most respondents were males, but a few widows who satisfied the criteria were included in the sample.

Modernization Among Peasants, Rogers and Svenning

I **Summarize what you understand by the following terms as they are used in the passage:**
a antecedent variable
b innovateness
c empirical
d dimension

II **Select the most appropriate translation of the following expressions.**
a media exposure
  ☐ contactos con los medios masivos de comunicación
  ☐ estar expuesto a los medios mastivos de comunicación
  ☐ estar sujeto a los medios masivos de comunicación
b intervening
  ☐ interpuesto
  ☐ interventor
  ☐ intermedio
c close the gap
  ☐ reducir el espacio
  ☐ reducir la distancia
  ☐ anular la diferencia
d household
  ☐ unidad familiar
  ☐ familia
  ☐ grupo familiar

III **What in your opinion would be the most appropriate translation of:**
the dangers of cross-cultural equivalence
☐ los peligros de establecer equivalencias entre culturas
☐ los peligros de suponer equivalencias en distintas culturas
☐ los peligros de suponer equivalencias culturales

IV   **Discuss the problem of translating** *arbitrary time-order categorization of concepts.*

V   **Translate the passage into Spanish.**

2B   La construcción de caminos de mano de obra y el subempleo rural

Se propone que la hipótesis fundamental del análisis sea que la construcción de <u>caminos de mano de obra</u> actúa sobre la comunidad rural, en cuanto al fenómeno de subempleo, a través de la variable ingreso.

A objetivos de análisis distintos, distintas serían las hipótesis relevantes y la forma de tratar el fenómeno del subempleo rural, es decir, hay una correspondencia entre objetivos de estudio e hipótesis y formas de conceptualización y cuantificación.

Se señala lo anterior puesto que es necesario hacer el siguiente ajuste a la conceptualización en función del salario mínimo regional: dado que la organización de la producción en el campo es colectiva, con transferencia constante de <u>tareas</u> y frutos de trabajo, se cree que una mejor forma de abordar el problema es mediante el concepto de ingreso familiar anual mínimo. <u>El concepto operaría a efectos de cuantificación de la siguiente manera:</u>

a) Determinar la estructura por edades de la familia a efecto de señalar cuales de sus miembros están en edad de incorporarse al proceso de trabajo.

b) Determinar, mediante el señalamiento de ocupaciones e ingresos familiares, el concepto de ingreso familiar real, y

c) Asignar a los miembros incorporados al proceso de trabajo el salario mínimo regional oficial a efecto de arribar a un ingreso familiar mínimo anual que funcione como el <u>dato pivote</u> y actúe como un ingreso mínimo de subsistencia.

La confrontación de los dos conceptos de ingreso, ingreso real y el ingreso mínimo de subsistencia, permitirá determinar si la familia está subempleada o no.

Desde el punto de vista teórico hay dos asuntos que habría que resolver:

a) Determinar la edad mínima para que una persona se incorpore al proceso de trabajo, y

b) Determinar cómo tratar el problema del trabajo femenino en la <u>familia campesina.</u>

Debe enfatizarse que estos problemas rebasan la esfera del análisis económico y que pueden ser resueltos mediante criterios sociológicos.

Caminos y Mano de Obra S.O.P.

I   **Summarize what you understand by the following terms as they are used in the passage:**

a	subempleo	c	cuantificación
b	variable	d	el punto de vista teórico

II **Select the most appropriate translation of the following expressions:**

a caminos de mano de obra
  ☐ labour intensive roads
  ☐ hand built roads
  ☐ manual labour roads

b tareas
  ☐ jobs
  ☐ tasks
  ☐ responsibilities

c dato pivote
  ☐ pivot datum
  ☐ key datum
  ☐ base datum

d familia campesina
  ☐ farm family
  ☐ rural family
  ☐ peasant family

III **What in your opinion would be the most appropriate translation of the following in context?**

El concepto operaría a efectos de cuantificación de la siguiente manera
☐ The concept will operate for purposes of quantification in the following way
☐ This concept would function for purposes of quantification in the following manner
☐ This concept would be applied, for purposes of quantification, in order to

IV **Discuss the difficulty of distinguishing between** *ingresos familiares, ingreso familiar real, ingreso familiar mínimo anual,* **and** *ingreso mínimo de subsistencia.*

V **Translate the passage into English.**

3A Ups and Downs

American monetary growth has been bedevilled by two factors. First, the Federal Reserve has yet to master the techniques of monetary control which it introduced last autumn. Instead of showing modest growth, the money supply figures have been lurching about all over the place. Second, Wall Street is still not sure what the changes mean and, as a result, it is nervous and has feared over-expansion when over-contraction is the real problem.

The Federal Reserve plan, announced in October, was designed to control the money supply through bank reserves (the base for credit creation) rather than by direct manipulation of interest rates. By January and February, however, the money supply had started to bulge as borrowers arranged new credit before the expected credit controls were introduced and interest rates rose higher. In response the Federal Reserve reduced reserves further.

Although the target was for an annual growth of 4–6 1/2% in the money supply, in the six months to the end of April it had grown at an annual rate of only 3% and in March and April it actually fell. Some relaxation is needed if the targets for money aggregates are to be reached.

The growth of bank reserves reached an annual growth of 13.2% in January. By the end of April their growth had fallen by more than half (to 6%) and had steadied. Interest rates are falling not because of intervention by the Federal Reserve to reduce the federal funds rate (which banks charge on loans to each other) but because of the recession and the falling demand for credit. Declining interest rates are therefore not a sign that the Federal Reserve has changed its policy and decided to restimulate the economy.

Economist

I Summarize what you understand by the following terms:

a over-contraction

b relaxation

c recession

d restimulate

II Select the most appropriate translation of the following expressions:

a lurching about

☐ moviéndose irregularmente

☐ tambaleándose

☐ con movimientos erráticos

b target

☐ blanco

☐ objetivo

☐ propósito

c money aggregates

☐ medios de pago en circulación

☐ circulante monetario total

☐ base monetaria

d federal funds rate

☐ intereses sobre fondos federales

☐ la tasa de intereses sobre préstamos interbancarios

☐ crédito federal

III What in your opinion would be the most appropriate translation of the following in context?

a American monetary growth has been bedevilled by two factors.

☐ El aumento en el circulante monetario en los Estados Unidos ha sido influído por dos factores.

☐ Dos factores han complicado el control monetario de la economía de los Estados Unidos.

☐ El control monetario en los Estados Unidos se ha debilitado debido a dos factores.

b it is nervous and has feared over-expansion when over-contraction is the real problem.

☐ está nervioso y teme la sobre-expansión cuando la sobre-contracción es el problema real.

☐ está nervioso, temeroso de tendencias inflacionarias cuando en realidad el peligro es de la contracción de la economía.

☐ se ha mostrado nervioso, temeroso de una sobre-expansión cuando el problema principal es de la contracción excesiva.

IV To translate *the money supply had started to bulge* a translator opted for *se notó un súbito aumento de los medios de pago en circulación*. Can the use of *súbito aumento* for *bulge* be justified?

V Translate the passage into Spanish.

3B Crecimiento del circulante monetario

El mercado financiero se ha caracterizado este año por una considerable expansión de los medios de pago en circulación y avances significativos de la captación y el financiamiento de la banca. Estimamos que el medio circulante aumentó 35% en promedio durante los primeros tres meses del año respecto al mismo período de 1978; creemos muy difícil que la tasa de crecimiento anual de esta variable sea inferior a 26% en 1979, cifra que ha sido calificada como ideal por las autoridades hacendarias en las presentes circunstancias. Por el impulso que llevan y, sobre todo, por la tendencia de las finanzas públicas, lo más probable es que los medios de pago registren una expansión promedio de 31% en todo 1979. Se corre el riesgo de que el exceso de circulante se refleje principalmente en una mayor alza del nivel de precios y en un elevado déficit del intercambio comercial y de servicios del sector no petrolero. El crédito concedido por el Banco de México, determinante principal de la base monetaria sobre todo al sector público, ha sido la principal variable explicativa de los aumentos de los medios de pago. Debe mencionarse que también ha contribuído a la afluencia de fondos del exterior en los últimos meses.

Banco de México, April 1979

I   Summarize what you understand by the following terms in the context of the passage:

a   medios de pago
b   finanzas públicas

c   intercambio comercial y de servicios
d   sector no petrolero

II   Select the translation of the following expressions most appropriate in this context:

a   significativos
☐ meaningful
☐ important
☐ significant

b   expansión
☐ growth
☐ expansion
☐ increase

c   circulante
☐ money in circulation
☐ money supply
☐ money stock

d   afluencia
☐ income
☐ inflow
☐ affluence

III   What in your opinion would be the most appropriate translation of the following in context?

a   Por el impulso que llevan y, sobre todo, por la tendencia de las finanzas públicas
☐ Given the present tendency, above all in the financing of the public sector
☐ Taking into account the rate of expansion and, above all, the tendency in the public sector
☐ After such a beginning and taking into account, above all, the trend in public financing

b   un elevado déficit del intercambio comercial y de servicios del sector no petrolero
☐ a high deficit in the interchange of goods and services of the non-petroleum sector
☐ a considerable deficit in the balance of payments in all other than the petroleum sector
☐ an increased deficit in the balance of trade in goods and services of the non-petroleum sector

c El crédito concedido por el Banco de México, determinante principal de la base monetaria
- ☐ The credit offered by the Bank of Mexico, which largely controls the monetary base
- ☐ The relaxation of credit controls by the Bank of Mexico, which mainly determine monetary growth
- ☐ The credit given by the Bank of Mexico, the principal determinant regarding the growth of the money supply

IV The phrase *la captación y el financiamiento de la banca* has been translated as *bank reserves*. Is this translation too broad to convey the precise sense of the original?

V Translate the passage into English.

4A Foundation Treatment

Treatment of the foundation rock was carried out to impermeabilize, consolidate and drain the rock affected by the dam. Suture grouting of the rock-concrete contact was also undertaken.

The primary curtain consisted of two rows of boreholes, upstream and downstream, each drilled at 5-m centres. This curtain was drilled and grouted from the arch gallery to a depth of 100 m in the central portion of the arch and to a depth of 40 m below the thrust blocks. Permeability tests and grouting were carried out in descending 5-m long sections. Injection pressures per metre depth of the grouted lengths were 0.2 and 0.6 kg/cm^2 for the upstream and downstream rows, respectively. Some 6,900 m of EX-diameter boreholes were drilled, with a mean cement consumption of 225 kg per metre drilled.

Consolidation treatment consisted of three rows of grouted EX-diameter boreholes. The upstream and downstream rows were drilled from the outside at the base of the dam faces, whereas the intermediate row was drilled from the arch gallery. Lengths of the boreholes varied from 15 to 30 m. Some 4,800 m were drilled, with a mean consumption of cement of 75 kg per metre.

The rock-concrete suture curtain comprised three rows of boreholes drilled from the arch gallery to a depth of 10 m into the rock. Approximately 1,800 m of EX-diameter boreholes were drilled, with a mean cement consumption of 40 kg per metre.

The drainage curtain was drilled both from the arch gallery and from the two abutments.

I Summarize what you understand by the following terms:

a grouting
b curtain
c arch gallery
d consolidation treatment

II   Select the most appropriate translation of the following expressions:

a grouted
   ☐ tratada
   ☐ inyectada
   ☐ llenada

b arch
   ☐ cortina
   ☐ presa
   ☐ arco

c lengths of the boreholes
   ☐ tramos perforados
   ☐ la longitud de los barrenos
   ☐ las profundidades perforadas

d abutments
   ☐ márgenes
   ☐ lados
   ☐ empotramientos

III   What in your opinion would be the most appropriate translation of the following in context?

a drilled from the outside at the base of the dam faces
   ☐ se perforaron fuera de la traza de la cortina
   ☐ se perforaron desde las bases exteriores de la cortina
   ☐ se perforaron al pie de la cortina

b from the arch gallery
   ☐ desde el túnel en la cortina
   ☐ desde la galería de la cortina
   ☐ desde la galeríe del arco

c The rock-concrete suture curtain comprised three rows of boreholes drilled from the arch gallery.
   ☐ La pantalla de sutura se perforó a partir de la galeria de la cortina y consistió de tres hileras de barrenos.
   ☐ Se perforó la pantalla de sutura de tres hileras de barrenos desde la galería de la cortina.
   ☐ Tres hileras de barrenos formaron la pantalla de sutura ligando la roca al concreto, perforadas desde la galería de la cortina.

IV   A translator chose to translate *primary curtain* **as** *pantalla de impermeabilización.* **Is the decision justified?**

V   Translate the passage into Spanish.

4B   Tratamiento de la cimentación

El tratamiento tuvo como objeto consolidar e impermeabilizar la roca por medio de inyecciones y aliviar, mediante drenes, las fuertes presiones intersticiales aguas abajo de la presa. Comprendió las siguientes pantallas: impermeabilización, consolidación, sutura y drenaje.
Impermeabilización. Se llevó a cabo desde el sistema de galerías de ambas márgenes y de la cortina. La pantalla se formó con dos hileras de barrenos separados 5 m entre sí. La hilera aguas arriba tuvo una inclinación de 15 grados hacia aguas arriba y la de aguas abajo una inclinación de 12 grados en el mismo sentido. Se perforaron 25,800 m de barrenos con un consumo total de cemento de 635 ton, lo que corresponde a un promedio de 25 kg por metro lineal.
Consolidación. Para mejorar las propiedades mecánicas de la roca en la zona de

cimentación de las pilas y vertedor, así como en la cimentación del espolón y atraques de la cortina, se efectuó un tratamiento de consolidación. Para tal efecto, los barrenos se dispusieron al tresbolillo con separación de dos consecutivos y profundidades alternadas de 5 m y 10 m. La inyección se efectuó en tramos de 5 m. Para ejecutar la pantalla de consolidación del espolón y del vertedor se perforaron 3870 m de barrenos con un consumo total de cemento de 65 ton, lo que corresponde a un promedio de 18 kg por metro lineal.

Sutura. El tratamiento de sutura concreto-roca abarcó toda la cimentación de la cortina y el espolón. Se perforaron tres hileras de barrenos separados 2 m entre sí de manera que penetraron en la roca 10 m. Se perforaron 13600 m de barrenos con un consumo total de cemento de 44.4 ton, lo que corresponde a un promedio de 3 Kg por metro lineal.

Drenaje. En ambas márgenes las pantallas de drenaje se dirigieron hacia aguas abajo de la pantalla de impermeabilización. La perforación se hizo después de terminar la inyección.

I Summarize what you understand by the following terms in the context of the passage:

a inyección b pantalla c sutura d cortina

II Select the translation of the following expressions most appropriate in this context:

a galería
  ☐ gallery
  ☐ tunnel
  ☐ boring
b márgen
  ☐ bank
  ☐ margin
  ☐ abutment

c barreno
  ☐ drill
  ☐ borehole
  ☐ boring
d atraque
  ☐ abutment
  ☐ landing
  ☐ wharf

III What in your opinion would be the most appropriate translation of the following in context?

a La pantalla se formó con dos hileras de barrenos
☐ The curtain comprised two rows of boreholes
☐ The curtain was formed by two rows of boreholes
☐ Two rows of boreholes formed the curtain

b separados 5 m entre sí
☐ 5 m apart
☐ at 5-m centres
☐ with 5 m between each

c para ejecutar la pantalla de consolidación del espolón y del vertedor
☐ to carry out the consolidation curtain beneath the thrust-block and the spillway
☐ to consolidate the thrust block and spillway zones
☐ to effect the thrust block and spillway consolidation curtain.

IV In this passage the term *pantalla* is best translated as *curtain* in every case except one: in this case the original translator selected the word *system*. In which case is this latter term the more appropriate and why?

V Translate the passage into English.

5A Unsuspected Uveal Melanomas

The diagnosis of malignant choroidal melanoma is difficult to establish in some cases, despite advanced diagnostic aids (radioactive tracing, fluorescein angiography, ultrasound). Only the histopathological report reveals the diagnostic error. Unsuspected malignant uveal melanomas (MUM), and especially choroidal melanomas are histopathologically most frequently discovered in eyes with opaque media and raised intraocular pressure. In published statistics, the frequency of unsuspected melanomas ranges from 7 to 11%.

In the course of 20 years, of 2,370 enucleated eyes, there were 300 histo-pathologically diagnosed MUM (iris, 4; ciliary body, 26; and choroid, 270). In 24 cases the diagnosis of MUM was clinically unexpected.

All 24 eyes were blind, 18 had raised intraocular pressure and all had opaque media. Often, the unsuspected MUM was concealed by the clinical diagnosis of secondary (33.3%) or primary absolute glaucoma (25%); three eyes had been unsuccessfully operated on earlier for glaucoma. Besides the main diagnosis, which was the indication for enucleation, there were secondary diagnoses such as cataract. Transillumination gave a negative result in all cases except one, with a diagnosis of hemorrhagic glaucoma and hemophthalmus.

The MUM found in one of the three phthisic eyes is of special interest; histologically, it showed both a malignant choroidal melanoma and sympathetic ophthalmia. The clinical picture was that of bilateral sympathetic ophthalmia, with the onset of visual impairment three years prior to enucleation. The per-forating injury had occurred two months earlier, and vision became impaired in the uninjured eye 15 days before enucleation.

One injured eye, in a 20-year-old man, had a subluxated cataract that had been operated on two years before enucleation. In a 25-year-old man with retinal detachment, the eye was enucleated because it was painful and glaucomatous. In a third patient, a 29-year-old man, there was a clinical picture of endophthalmitis at the time of enucleation, and histologically, the tumour showed a massive invasion of the sclera.

American Journal of Opthalmology,
Olga Litricin

I Summarize what you understand by the following terms:
a histopathological   b intraocular   c indication   d sympathetic

II Select the most appropriate translation in context of the following expressions:

a raised
- ☐ alta
- ☐ aumentada
- ☐ subida

b clinical picture
- ☐ cuadro clínico
- ☐ diagnosis clínico
- ☐ historia clínica

c visual impairment
- ☐ pérdida de visión
- ☐ disminución de visión
- ☐ deterioro visual

III Discuss the word order of *histopathologically most frequently discovered* and rephrase it if necessary.

IV Translate the passage into Spanish.

5B Melanoma de coroides

No obstante que en la actualidad se cuenta con excelentes medios de diagnóstico clinico, que permiten un tratamienta temprano y con procedimientos terapéuticos como son la fotocoagulación, la radioterapia, la quimioterapia y la combinación de éstas, el prognóstica de melanoma uveal dependerá de la correcta evaluación de cada caso en particular. El motivo del presente trabajo es dar a conocer un caso de melanoma uveal en una mujer de 21 años de edad, quien desarrolló la neoplasia durante el embarazo.

La paciente ingresó al hospital por dolor intenso del ojo izquierdo, ardor y enrojecimiento conjuntival Refirió el inicio de su padecimiento en relación con su último parto un año antes, con fosfenos y disminución progresiva de la visión del 0.1. con escatomas nasal y temporal superiores. Se la había diagnosticado desprendimiento de retina inoperable en otro hospital.

La exploración oftalmológica mostró 0.1. con midriasis, ausencia de reflejo fotomotor, dolor intenso, fotofobia, hiperemia conjuntival, rubiosis iridis y tensión ocular aumentada. El estudio radiológico de órbita no mostró alteraciones patológicas. La ecografía reveló la presencia de un tumor coroideo.

Se realizó enucleación del 0.1. con diagnóstico clínico de 'tumor del tejido coroideo por detrás de la retina'.

Se remitió al servicio de Oncología, en donde se dieron 9 sesiones de radioterapia a dosis no especificadas. Actualmente no hay manifestaciones de actividad neoplásica local, ni de metástasis, y está asintomática.

Es interesante señalar la relación con el puerperio. Los melanocitos se estimulan durante el embarazo y una melanoma silenciosa pre-existente cobre mayor actividad. Por otra parte, el desprendimiento de retina puede desenmascarar a una melanoma que sólo se manifiesta en el campo visual por un escotoma que muchas veces pasa inadvertido. Sin embargo, el desprendimiento de retina dio pérdida de los campos superiores en el caso que nos ocupa, en la fase inicial. Este desprendimiento ha sido señalado por Heathy como un signo más en el diagnóstico del melanoma coroideo.

Anales de la Sociedad Mexicana de Oftalmologia,
González Alvarez y Contreras Chalita

I **Summarize what you understand by the following terms:**
a desprendimiento   b alteraciones patológicas   c enucleación
d asintomática

II **Select the most appropriate translation in context of the following terms:**
a medios de diagnóstico clínico   c dio pérdida
    ☐ aids to clinical diagnosis   ☐ resulted in the loss
    ☐ means of clinical diagnosis   ☐ caused the loss
    ☐ diagnostic techniques   ☐ brought about the loss
b disminución progresiva de la visión
    ☐ progressive loss of vision
    ☐ progressive reduction of vision
    ☐ progressive visual impairment

III **What in your opinion would be the most appropriate translation of the following in context?**
Los melanocitos se estimulan durante el embarazo y una melanoma silenciosa pre-existente cobra mayor actividad.
☐ The melanocites are stimulated during pregnancy and a pre-existing silent melanoma is activated.
☐ The melanocites are stimulated during pregnancy and a dormant melanoma becomes more active.
☐ Pregnancy stimulates the melanocites and activates a pre-existing dormant melanoma.

IV **Criticize the composition of the second sentence of the second paragraph** (*Referió el inicio . . .*) **and rewrite it.**

V **Translate the passage into English.**

APPENDIX A Points of Grammar

1 ADJECTIVES

Word order in adjectives will need care as it is not the same in English as in Spanish, for example:

I.1   *automóviles particulares quemados* — private cars burnt
I.1   *ventanas de edificios públicos rotas* — windows broken in public buildings
I.5   *un periódico extranjero* — a foreign newspaper

Often two adjectives qualifying the same noun will be joined by *y* in Spanish, but placed in juxtaposition in English:

I.45   *las viejas y encantadoras casonas pueblerinas* — the charming old village houses
III.16 *his blue, astonished eyes* — sus ojos azules y asombrados
III.17 *a large, fat, clean-shaven, red face* — un rostro enorme, rubicundo y afeitado hasta la raiz
III.22 *an immense, open, treeless plain, geometrically flat, unfenced and uncultivated* — una inmensa llanura calva, abierta y geométricamente plana, sin cercas ni cultivo

Sometimes the English adjective may need modification in Spanish:

I.10   *a large modern building* — un moderno edificio de gran tamaño

The Spanish *mientras más* and *cada vez más* are often translated by the comparative form of the adjective (or adverb, see Appendix A8 below) in English:

III.2   *mientras más se agrandaba ese silencio* — the longer this pause lasted
II.3A *que presidiría cada vez más la vida del hombre* — which was to have a greater and greater effect on the life of man

Special care is needed in the translation of the adjective *mismo*, depending on its use in the sentence:

I.43	*su misma reiteración* — its very repetition
II.5A	*América y Europa se encontraban en el mismo plano* — America and Europe found themselves in the same position
II.5A	*los mismos europeos* — the Europeans themselves
II.8B	*the myth itself* — el mismo mito

2 CONNECTIVES

Care will need to be taken over the choice of connective used to express the idea of the original most closely. Note the following examples:

I.2	*so the police* — por lo que la policía
I.9	*a pesar de que el fuego* — although the fire
I.13	*con lo que el niño* — so that the child
I.35	*a pesar de que lo practicaba* — although he
I.41	*de tal modo que no caigan en* — so that they won't fall
I.49	*por tanto* — for that reason (therefore)
I.50	*whereas Mary has already attained it* — mientras que María . . .

Although *ni . . . ni . . .* can often be translated by *neither . . . nor . . .* , note the following:

III.1	*sin antecedentes ni consiguientes* — without . . . or . . .
III.1	*nada ata a uno ni uno cuenta para nada* — one has no ties and no importance

Note also the word order in the following examples:

II.1A	*desde que por primera vez traté* — since I tried for the first time
II.7A	*ni física ni moralmente podían* — neither physically nor morally could they

3 DETERMINERS

The use and omission of articles in English and Spanish follow different patterns, so care will be required in translating them.
The articles are used in Spanish and omitted in English in general statements:

I.33	*medio millón de personas de todas las clases* — half a million people of all classes
I.37	*las enfermedades cardiovasculares son las que más muertes causan* — cardiovascular diseases are those which cause most deaths

I.41 *no desciendan . . . a la vagancia* — don't fall into vagrancy
I.43 *El mundo en crisis* — World Crisis
I.43 *la economía mundial* — world economy
I.43 *la mayoría de ellas* — most of them

The articles are used in Spanish and omitted in English before titles:

I.16 *television producer . . .* — el productor (realizador) de T.V.
I.25B *. . . el general Aguirre* — General Aguirre

When a particular thing is referred to, the article is used in both languages:

I.3 *la mina La Caridad* — the La Caridad mine

English often supplies the indefinite article in expressions where the reference is general:

I.27A *cierta renuencia al cambio* — a certain resistance to change
I.35 *con acento inglés* — with an English accent
I.45 *casi todas tienen patio, huerta . . .* — nearly all of them have a patio, an orchard . . .
I.49 *sin título* — without a name
I.49 *Martínez Nadal, legatorio fiel* — Martínez Nadal, a faithful inheritor

The Spanish definite article is sometimes translated by the English possessive adjective:

I.11 *con la cabeza cubierta* — their heads covered
I.35 *para los padres* — by his parents
I.35 *el amor al riesgo* — his love of risk

Sometimes the indefinite article is required in English to translate the Spanish definite article:

I.37 *fomentar . . . la conciencia de la importancia* — foster an awareness of the importance

Occasionally the Spanish *un* is more emphatic than English *a*, and this will be translated by the insertion of another word in English:

I.33 *el que en un día* — the fact that on a certain day
II.3A *de un modo milagroso* — in some mysterious way

Watch the translation of *this, that, these, those* and *ese, estos, esos*:

I.37 *ese mal tiene* — this evil
I.49 *en esa novedad* — in this novelty
II.12A *esos antiguos poderes* — these ancient powers

Note also the following:

II.11A *que la establecida entre* — than that established between

4 NOUNS

Note that nouns are often plural in Spanish and singular in English, and vice versa:

I.11   *con la cabeza cubierta por* — their heads covered with
I.25B   *sus influencias* — his influence
I.31   *interiores churriguerescos* — Churrigueresque interior

Note that *noticias* is usually translated by *news*, but *news* is always singular in English, so *noticias alarmantes* (I.43) will be better translated by *alarming reports*.

5 PRONOUNS

The pronoun *lo* is often omitted in English:

I.33   *lo constituye el Derby* — is the Derby
III.3   *mi madre me lo dijo* — my mother told me
III.14 *no lo esperaban todo de este mundo* — didn't expect everything from this world

But notice

I.27   *eso lo suple* — it makes up for this
II.13A *hace llano que* — makes it plain that

Sometimes a noun must be supplied with *lo* + adjective:

II.3A   *que dejaba de lado lo irremisible de los procesos...* — which ignored the inexorable nature of ... processes
II.8A   *lo interesante del caso* — the interesting thing about this

Ello may sometimes be translated by a demonstrative:

I.49   *Marx había insistido en ello* — Marx had insisted on this

Note also the following:

I.41   *es un hecho* — *cuyas causas son complejas* — the causes of which are (or, more idiomatically, — and its causes are)

and

I.29B *quien pierde el empleo* — anyone who loses his job
II.5B   *whatever the truth may be* — sea cual sea la verdad

6 PREPOSITIONS

The translation of prepositions is perhaps one of the greatest difficulties the beginner has to contend with in translation. Each case must be considered separately, according to the context. The examples given below will give some idea of the variety of translations for each preposition which can be found.

a

before a personal object, not translated into English:

I.35   *¿Quién no recuerda a aquel singular torero . . . ?* — Who does not remember that . . .

I.41   *se calificará a estas personas* — these people will be trained

in expressions of time:

I.3   *al cumplirse hoy ocho días* — as . . . ends
I.45   *a los cinco años* — at the age of five

in expressions of place:

I.33   *a él concurre* — meet in it/there
I.33   *trasladarse al campo* — go out into the country
I.45   *muchos que emigraron a la ciudad* — many who . . . to the city

miscellaneous:

I.35   *a lo largo de* — throughout
I.35   *amor al riesgo* — love of risk

ante, antes de

I.15   *ante la justicia argentina* — before the Argentinian Court
II.2A   *ante el derecho* — before/in the eyes of the law
I.15   *antes de morir* — before he died

con

I.1   *chocan estudiantes con* — students clash with/clash between students and . . .
I.11   *con la cabeza cubierta por* — (with) their heads covered with/in
I.15   *con el pretexto de* — on the pretext of
I.15   *la frontera con Chile* — the Chilean border
I.35   *volaba con un cometa delta* — was flying in a Delta comet
II.4A   *se han constituido con* — have been formed by

de

I.1   *ventanas de edificios públicos* — windows of/in public buildings
I.9   *más de doscientas familias* — more than two hundred families
I.9   *en menos de cuatro horas* — in less than four hours
I.27A   *siempre de agente viajero* — still as a travelling salesman
I.27B   *de noche . . . de día* — by night . . . by day
I.32A   *painted . . . in* — pintada de . . .
I.35   *camino del toreo* — the road to the ring

desde

I.41	*desde todos los puntos del país* — from all parts of the country
II.2A	*desde la revolución* — since the revolution
II.4A	*desde este punto de vista* — from this point of view
II.8A	*desde el principio de* — from the beginning of
II.9A	*desde entonces la Humanidad* — since then humanity

en

I.41	*corriente migratoria que converge en ella* — which is converging upon it
I.41	*en que mejor rendimiento puedan tener* — where they . . .
I.44	*the spread of interest in scientific . . .* el aumento en interés
III.1	*en torno al fuego* — round the fire

entre

I.27	*entre la numerosa colonia* — amongst the . . .
I.39	*entre la población activa española* — amongst the . . .
II.6A	*dividida entre los . . . y los . . .* — divided into the. . . and. . .
II.11A	*la separación entre el hombre y la naturaleza* — the separation between man and nature

frente a

II.2A	*un avance muy grande frente a* — a great advance on
II.6A	*frente a ellos* — in contrast to these

para

I.19	*hacer presión con la mano sobre la tapa para que cierre* — press cover shut
I.37	*para detectarla y controlarla* — in order to detect and . . .
I.39	*para dar una salida a* — to find a way out
I.39	*para hacer frente a* — to face
I.45	*para huir* — to escape from

por

I.11	*la cabeza cubierta por* — their heads covered with
I.29B	*por fuertes que sean los impuestos* — however high the taxes
I.33	*por el marco* — because of the setting
I.37	*mortalidad por cardiopatía* — death from heart disease
I.44	*the spread of interest in* — el aumento en interés por
I.45	*por primera vez* — for the first time
I.45	*se venden por relativamente poco* — are sold for relatively little
II.9A	*por un lado* — on the one hand

sobre

II.9A	*el pensamiento asienta sobre* — thought is based on
II.9A	*sobre todo* — above everything/especially
III.2	*uno sobre otro* — one on top of another

7   THE VERB

a TENSE

The translation of verb tenses will require care. Note the following examples.

Spanish Present — may be translated by English Simple Present, Present Progressive, Present Perfect or Present Perfect Progressive, according to the context. For example:

I.3   *en un clima. . . viven los 18,000 habitantes de N.* — the inhabitants of N. are living. . .

I.5   *sin que él lo lea* — unless he has read it

I.13   *regalan primero el álbum y luego venden cromos* — first they give away the scrapbook and then they sell stamps

Unit VI   Further Exercises   *llevo tres días intentando hablarle* — I have been trying to talk to you for three days

I.41   *corriente migratoria que converge en* — migratory current which is converging

II.8A   *que a través de siglos guía a su pueblo* — who for centuries has guided his people

Spanish Imperfect — *trabajaba* may be translated by any one of the following in English: *he worked, he was working, he used to work,* or *he would work*.

When it is used in description it is usually translated by the Simple Past:

I.23   *que conducían a la plaza, me sentía. . .* — which led to the square, I felt. . .

III.9   *andaba muy bien de estatura* — she was a fairly good size

When it refers to an activity which was going on in the past, it is translated by *was* + verb -ing:

I.3   *cuando se pagaban salarios atrasados* — when back wages were being paid

When it refers to a habitual action in the past it is usually translated by *used to* or *would* followed by the verb:

I.27A   *visitaba Puebla con bastante frecuencia* — I used to visit Puebla fairly frequently

I.27B   *de noche soñaba* — by night I would dream

In certain contexts it will be translated by the English Pluperfect or Pluperfect Progressive:

I.27B   *an los años que llevaba de vivir en México* — during the years I had been living in Mexico

Sometimes a difference in tense will be shown by the use of a different verb in the other language. Note for example the following:

        quería — he wanted to   *quiso* — he tried to
        conocía — he knew   *conoció* — he met

Here is an example from one text:

1.25A *cuando don Ulises quiso reaccionar* — when don Ulises tried to . . .

The Spanish use of auxiliary + gerund stresses duration of action:

I.35 *se fue abriendo paso* — he forged a path for himself (here English would use a verb implying that it took some time to do this, but it was done)

Note also the following:

III.1 *Las voces fueron decayendo hasta cesar* — The voices died away to silence

I.44 *the scale and tempo of change were visibly increasing* — . . . fueron en visible aumento

b MOOD AND MODALS

The Spanish subjunctive is often translated by the English infinitive or gerund:

I.25B *logró que nos pusieran en libertad* — he succeeded in getting us set free

I.49 el autor no quiere que os sintáis . . . — the author doesn't want you to feel as if . . .

It may be necessary to use an English modal such as *may, might, can, could*:

I.15 *que hubiesen aprovechado para sus* . . . — which . . . might have used for their . . .

The future and conditional tenses in Spanish are translated by English modals + the verb:

I.15 *nunca podría aclararse* — might never be revealed
I.21 *podría estar levantada* — might be up
I.39 *que se podrian tomar* — which might be taken
I.39 *dicha medida sólo podrá ser eficaz* — this measure can only be effective

Note also the following:

II.3A *que presidiría . . . la vida del hombre* — which was to control . . . the life of man
II.3A *lo que habría de traer* . . . — what . . . was to bring
II.5A *una cultura que fuese menos frágil* — a culture which should be less fragile
II.12B *hubieran podido hacerle* — might have made him
III.8 *no más oía* — I could only hear
III.12 *debía estar* — must have been

c VOICE

The Passive Voice occurs more frequently in English than in Spanish. It is often used to translate the Spanish reflexive:

l.3 *se pagaban salarios* — wages were being paid
l.3 *se informó también* — it was also learnt
l.9 *no se registraron desgracias personales* — no casualties were reported
l.15 *nunca podría aclararse* — might never come to light
l.39 *si se procura a todos* — if all are given
l.45 *identidad que se pierde en...* — identity which is lost in
l.45 *hay casas... que se venden...* — there are houses... which are sold...

d SPANISH REFLEXIVE

Note that the Spanish Reflexive may also be translated by

a simple verb in English:

l.3 *cumplirse* — end
l.3 *reunirse* — meet
l.5 *se hace indispensable... la escucha* — listening... is indispensable
l.11 *la policía se ha lanzado a la búsqueda de...* — the police have launched a search for ...
l.25B *don Nicéforo... se echó a* — don Nicéforo ... set out to
l.43 *se filtran* — leak out

the Imperative, especially in recipes:

l.17A *se sofríe* — fry
l.17A *se le añade el caldo* — add the stock
l.17B *se sirve inmediatamente* — serve immediately

reciprocal pronouns:

III.1 *se comunicaban* — they told each other about

Note examples of the English Passive translated by the Spanish Reflexive:

l.4 *is situated* — se encuentra
l.14 *children were being labelled* — a los niños se les llamaba
l.14 *so that they could be given* — con el fin de que se les pudiera dar

Sometimes the English Passive is translated by a verb other than *ser* followed by the past participle:

l.2 *were injured* — resultaron heridos

e USE OF INFINITIVE OR GERUND

The Spanish infinitive may be translated by the infinitive or the gerund in English. It is important to note in which cases each is used. For example:

l.5 *no tardan menos de cinco días en llegar* — take at least five days to arrive
l.5 *todo lo que se va a publicar sobre el país* — everything to be published concerning

I.15   *fueron detenidos por haber cometido otros delitos* — were arrested for having committed other crimes

Note also the English gerund translated by the Spanish infinitive:

I.4   *for holding demonstrations* — por realizar manifestaciones
I.16   *after attacking* — después de atacar

Note, however, the following example:

I.15   *una placa sin revelar* — un undeveloped plate

8 ADVERBS

Note that the Spanish expressions *cada vez . . . más* and *cuanto más* are usually translated by the comparative form of the adverb in English:

I.45   *cada vez con más fuerza* — more and more strongly
I.45   *cada vez . . . tiene más alicientes que* — appeals more and more strongly than
II.4B   *reformers were becoming increasingly insistent* — los reformadores insistían cada vez más
II.10A *cuanto más se ven . . . cuanto más hacen* — the more they see themselves . . . the more they . . .
III.2   *mientras más se agrandaba el silencio* — the longer the silence lasted
III.7   *iban espaciándose cada vez más* — were getting less and less frequent

APPENDIX B   Hints on Handling, Some Useful Techniques

1   Handling of Titles

It is important to read the whole passage before translating the title. Compare English and Spanish newspaper headlines: usually English headlines will be more concise; there will be fewer articles. Note the following examples:

I.1   *Chocan estudiantes con la Guardia Nacional panameña en Colón* — Students Clash with National Guard in Colón

I.2   *Tear Gas for Anti-government Demonstrators in Iran* — Manifestantes antigubernamentales dispersados con gases lacrimógenos en Irán

I.9   *Acabó el fuego en Monterrey con una* ciudad perdida — Monterrey *Shantytown* Destroyed by Fire

2   Translation of Proper Names

Most names of countries and well-known cities have a standard translation, for example *Inglaterra* — England; *Londres* — London; *España* — Spain. It is better to keep the same form for less well-known towns or cities such as Colón.

3   Rephrasing

Long Spanish sentences should usually be broken up into two or more shorter sentences in English (see for example the first sentence of I.49).
Sometimes a co-ordinate clause in English will become a subordinate clause in Spanish:

I.12   *He was confronted by the masked intruder and ordered to open the safe.*
Se topó con el ladrón . . . quien le ordenó que abriera . . .

Conversely:

I.41   *Es un hecho — cuyas causas son complejas. . .*
It is a fact — and the reasons for it are complex . . .

A useful technique is to divide the sentence into meaningful segments, and then decide the order of those segments in the translation. For example:

I.3	En un clima de tensión que se agrava cada minuto	(2)
	viven los 18,000 habitantes de la población de Nacozari, Sonora	(1)
	al cumplirse hoy ocho días de paro	(3)
	en la mina de cobre La Caridad, segunda de Latinoamérica.	(4)

The answer to the questions Who. . . ? What. . . ? When. . . ? Where. . . ?. How. . . ? will help to decide the English order. Then, each segment may be divided up into smaller units as follows:

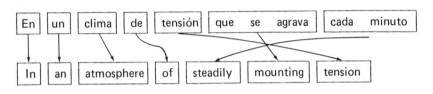

and, further on in the same passage

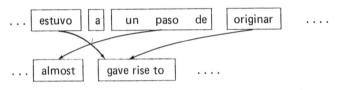

so that the changes in wording may be easily seen, but there must be *no change in meaning*.

4   Omissions and Insertions

Frequently in translating it will be necessary to omit or to insert words or phrases which do not alter the meaning of the original, because of differing constructions and usage in the two languages. It is more usual to omit when translating from Spanish into English, and to insert when translating from English into Spanish, but this is not always the case. Note the following examples carefully:

I.1	*un enfrentamiento* [*ocurrido*] *hoy entre estudiantes y* . . .	
	today's clash between students and . . .	
I.15	*Fue golpeado hasta* [*caerse*] *muerto.*	
	He was beaten to death	
I.43	*la desorganización* . . . [*que padecen*]	
	their . . . lack of organization	
I.43	*proyectos económicos* [*que sirvan*] *para estimular*	
	economic plans to	
I.51	*la* [*deformación*] *caricaturesca*	
	caricature	

II.4A *una primera de transplantación y una segunda de asimilación*
the first, [one] of transplantation and the second, [one] of assimilation

II.10A *la única Europa de total europeidad*
the only completely European [part] of Europe

II.14A *dentro de un barroco y rococó*
in a baroque and rococo [style]

III.9 *de no [andarle] muy lejos*
not far from it

III.12 *manoteaba de tanto en tanto [para despegárselo] de la cara*
brushed away from his face from time to time

III.13 *Necio de mí.*
What a fool [I had been].

Conversely:

I.2 *Tear Gas for . . . Demonstrators*
Manifestantes . . . [dispersados] con gases

I.4 *the security operation against anti-apartheid groups*
la operación de seguridad [que se realizó] en contra de los grupos
[que se oponen] al apartheid

I.10 *confirmed at least eighteen deaths*
confirmaron [que hubo] por lo menos dieciocho muertos

I.18B *Sauté until well browned*
Saltée hasta [que estén] bien dorados.

I.18C *Beat . . . until frothy*
Bata hasta [que haga] espuma

II.3B *new [inventions in] manufactures*
nuevas manufacturas

II.10B *so fundamental . . . [an attachment] as the love of home*
el apego tan fundamental como el del hogar

5 Transposition

Since no two languages have the same grammatical structure, a literal translation
often fails to convey the same idea or the same impression as the original. It is
then necessary to normalize the language of the translation: change word order,
parts of speech, constructions. This process is called Transposition.

Note the variety of changes and the types of changes in the examples below.
The translations given are not by any means the only possibilities.

I.3 *en un clima de tensión que se agrava cada minuto.*
in an atmosphere of steadily mounting tension

I.3 *no pasó a mayores*
didn't get out of control

I.11 *en un automóvil que les esperaba*
in a waiting car

I.15 *una placa sin revelar*
an undeveloped plate

I.15   *la frontera con Chile*
        the Chilean border

I.25B   *alarmado por nuestra ausencia de toda una noche*
        alarmed because we had been gone all night

I.33   *el único atractivo que persiguen*
        the only attraction sought by

I.34   *if you happen to stay in London*
        si por casualidad se encuentra en Londres

I.45   *cada vez con más fuerza*
        more and more strongly

I.47   *todo lo afortunado que*
        quite as successful as

I.48   *the humans on view*
        los seres humanos que vemos

I.50   *the musical makes a plea for positive action*
        en la comedia musical se hace una llamada para la acción positiva

I.50   *much to the chagrin of*
        al gran disgusto de

I.51   *la serie de relatos tiene como denominador común*
        the common denominator of the series of tales is

I.51   *la reputada 'aspera . . . España' por Camile Mauclair*
        the 'harsh . . . Spain' described by Camile Mauclair

II.1A   *en que con frecuencia incurren los traductores*
        that translators frequently make.

II.1B   *would seem on the face of it*
        parecería a la luz de esta afirmación

II.4A   *Para que podamos decir*
        To be able to say

II.5B   *His conclusion is*
        Llega a la conclusión

II.7A   *que era sustituida por el esclavo*
        for which they substituted slaves/ using slaves instead

II.9A   *merced a su propio y voluntario caminar*
        thanks to his following his own wilful way

II.10A *se sienten como necesitados de gritar*
        they feel as if they must shout

II.15A *parece no haber escapatoria a llevar la cabeza*
        we seem to be unable to help looking back

III.4A *A ún faltaba una hora para acudir a*
        There was still an hour before he had to go to

III.6   *Juan. (Saltando regocijadísimo)*
        Juan. (Jumping round in great delight)

III.8   *abrazándome*
        with me in his arms

III.9   *no tenía aspecto de buena salud*
        didn't look healthy

III.9   *tenía la tez cetrina*
        her complexion was sallow

III.9   *blasfemaba las peores cosas*
       uttered the worst blasphemies

III.10   *echa su pregón*
       cries his wares

III.12   *No tenían cara.*
       They were faceless.

III.13   *Necio de mí.*
       What a fool I had been.

III.14   *desarrugar . . . la frente*
       smooth the wrinkles off his brow

III.24   *the torchlit scene*
       la escena iluminada por antorchas

6   Modulation

Sometimes an idea is expressed by a change of conceptual basis, image or metaphor in the other language, for example:

Entiendo — I see; *Te veo bien* — You look well; *¡Salud!* — God Bless you!

This is known as *modulation*. Note the following examples:

I.29B *De Londres a Edimburgo hay seis horas de tren.*
       It takes six hours to go from London to Edinburgh by train.

I.46   *I came to the wreck of a house.*
       Llegué a una casa en ruinas

I.48   *it can't quite do the job for itself*
       no es completamente adecuada en sí

I.48   *whose side we are on*
       con quienes simpatizamos

I.50   *about coming to terms with*
       cómo vivir en

I.50   *it's set in Liverpool*
       la acción se desarrolla en Liverpool

II.8A *seguida al pie de la letra*
       followed literally

II.9A *examinadas por su fría razón*
       seen by the cold light of reason

II.10A *la cuenta llega hasta trece*
       they add up to thirteen

II.10A *han puesto la proa en la punta de flecha del viento turístico*
       they have set their sails to the touristic wind

II.15A *el Pobre Cualquiera que ansia ser algún día don Alguien*
       the poor Nobody who aspires to be Somebody one day

III.2   *Lorenza se metió las manos entre el pelo*
       Lorenza ran her fingers through her hair

III.2   *no hablaba por hablar*
       I wasn't talking for the sake of talking

III.4A *Daban las horas en el reloj*
        the clock was striking
III.5   *Ya entiendo, antigua y nueva, una de cada parte del río.*
        Oh, I see, the old and the new, one on each bank of the river.
III.5   *con hombres hemos de vernos*
        it's with men we have to deal
III.6   *¡Basta ya!*
        That will do!
III.6   *Y yo ¿Qué?*
        And what about me?
III.6   *en el acto*
        right away
III.9   *tenía un humor que se daba a todos los diablos*
        she had the devil's own temper
III.9   *rebuscaba el chaleco del marido*
        went through her husband's pockets
III.13 *buscaba su mirada*
        I looked for his eyes
III.19 *saw eye to eye with in the matter of*
        veían con los mismos ojos respecto a
III.27 *held their court*
        sentaban sus reales

7   Adaptation

Occasionally the literal equivalent of an expression in the original language will convey a completely different idea to the reader of the translation: it may be incomprehensible or even misleading. In this case the translator has to adapt the translation to communicate the message of the writer of the original. Note the following examples:

I.9   Acabó el fuego en Monterrey con una 'ciudad perdida'.

Here *lost city* would give the English reader an idea quite different from that of the original. It will be necessary to use an expression such as *shantytown* or *slum*.

I.35   el torero rubio que hablaba andaluz con acento inglés

To the English reader Andalusian is not a language. To convey the idea we should say *spoke Spanish with an English accent*, or, more exactly, *spoke the Spanish of Andalusia with an English accent*.

I.51   un guadiana literario

A *literary guadiana* has little or no meaning for the English reader. He would need to know that the writer is referring to the River Guadiana in Spain and is thinking here of a literary stream or current. So this might be translated: *a Spanish literary current*.

8   Stock Phrases

I.1   *se informó aquí* — according to information received here
I.9   *informaron que* — it was announced
I.15   *se trata de un caso policial* — this is a police case
II.5A   *tantos europeos como americanos* — Europeans as well as Latin-Americans

SOME USEFUL AIDS TO TRANSLATION

1.   Dictionaries

Spanish—English; English—Spanish

Collins Spanish Dictionary (1971)
Pequeño Larousse, español — inglés, English — Spanish (1976)
Velázquez Spanish Dictionary
Simon and Schuster International Dictionary, English — Spanish, Spanish — English
Beyond the Dictionary in Spanish, A. Bryson Gerrard and José de Heras Heras, Revised Edition, 1972, Cassell.

English — English

The Shorter Oxford English Dictionary, Oxford University Press.
Webster's New International Dictionary
The Advanced Learners' Dictionary, Oxford University Press.
Roget's Thesaurus, Penguin.

Spanish — Spanish

Pequeño Larousse Illustrado
Diccionario de uso del español, María Moliner Ed. Gredos, (Madrid, 1975)
Diccionario ideológico de la lengua española, Julio Casares, Editorial Gustavo Gil, S.A., Barcelona.

2.   Grammar

A Communicative Grammar of English, Leech and Svartvik, Longman.
Esbozo de una nueva gramática de la lengua española, RAE Espasa-Calpe, S.A. (Madrid, 1976)
An Intermediate Course of Modern Spanish, H. Ramsden

3. Reference Books

Introducción a la traductología, Gerardo Vázquez-Ayora, Georgetown School of Language and Linguistics, Georgetown University Press (Washington DC, 1977)
Manual de técnicas de investigación para estudiantes de ciencias sociales, Ario Garza Mercado, El Colegio de México (México, 1972)
The Grammatical Structures of English and Spanish, Stockwell, Bowen and Martin, University of Chicago Press, Chicago.
Ciencia del lenguaje y arte del estilo, Martín Alonso, Aguilar (Madrid, 1975),
Scientific and Technical Translation, Isadore Pinchuk, André Deutsch.
Language Structure and Translation, Essays by Eugene A. Nida, Selected and Introduced by Anwar S. Dil, Stanford University Press (Stanford, 1975)